ESSEX AIRF
IN THE SECOND
WORLD WAR

CW00662994

Graham Smith

COUNTRYSIDE BOOKS

NEWBURY, BERKSHIRE

First published 1996
© Graham Smith 1996

All rights reserved. No reproduction
permitted without the prior permission
of the publisher:

COUNTRYSIDE BOOKS
3 Catherine Road
Newbury, Berkshire

ISBN 1 85306 405 X

The cover painting is by Colin Doggett
and shows Hurricanes of No 56 squadron scrambling
from North Weald airfield in the summer of 1940

Designed by Mon Mohan

Produced through MRM Associates Ltd., Reading
Printed by Woolnough Bookbinding Ltd, Irthlingborough

CONTENTS

ESSEX AIRFIELDS IN THE SECOND WORLD WAR

Little Walden
SAFFRON WALDEN
Debden
Ridgewell
Great Sampford
Wethersfield
Great Dunmow
Andrews Field
Gosfield
Earls Colne
BRAINTREE
Rivenhall
Birch
Wormingford
Boxted
COLCHESTER
HARWICH
CLACTON
Bradwell Bay
Stansted
Matching
Chipping Ongar
Boreham
CHELMSFORD
North Weald
Stapleford Tawney
BRENTWOOD
ROMFORD
Hornchurch
Rochford
SOUTHEND
Canvey Island
Fairlop
RIVER THAMES

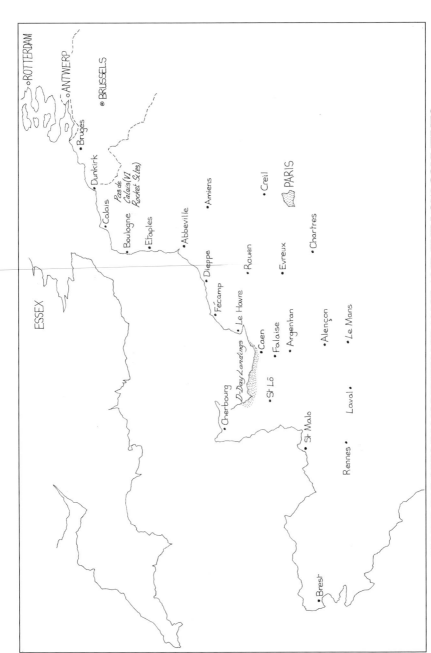

ALLIED TARGETS IN NORTHERN FRANCE AND THE LOW COUNTRIES

I
SETTING
THE SCENE

From that fateful Sunday morning – 3rd September 1939 – when the tired voice of Neville Chamberlain announced to the nation that 'this country is now at war with Germany', the pilots and men at a mere handful of Essex airfields became deeply engaged in the European air war. The three famous pre-war fighter stations, Hornchurch, North Weald and Debden, were immediately placed on a state of readiness. It would, however, be another nine months before their squadrons became heavily committed in the skies over France. And then by July 1940 the pilots and ground crews serving at these and their satellite airfields were stretched to their very limits during the Battle of Britain. In the words of Winston Churchill these stirring times were to prove to be 'their finest hour'.

Then, as Fighter Command took to the offensive, Hurricanes, Spitfires, Typhoons, Mosquitos and Mustangs left Essex airfields for day and night operations over the near Continent and Germany. From 1942 the RAF in Essex were joined by the USAAF, first in the shape of the 'Mighty' Eighth Air Force and later more especially by the various Groups of the Ninth Air Force. All the Allied airmen that served at these Essex airfields added a brave and illustrious chapter to the history of Essex aviation; their massive contribution and the ultimate sacrifice of so many pilots and crews are proudly remembered in the number of airfield memorials that are scattered throughout the county.

Well before these traumatic, thrilling and, ultimately, triumphant

The Roe 1 Triplane nearing completion at Lea Marshes in June 1909. A.V. Roe is the second from the right. (Science & Society Picture Library)

times Essex could lay claim to a long and rich heritage of aviation which can be traced right back to the pioneer days of flying. The first known airfield in Essex was in a most unlikely site – on the marshes to the north of the river Crouch at Fambridge. In 1908 an early flying enthusiast, Noel Pemberton-Billing MP, bought some 2,000 acres of land, built two large hangars and a few workshops and proceeded to establish a flying school there. Pemberton-Billing was really too advanced for his time, his flying school did not prosper, which is probably not too surprising as four years later there were only 382 people holding pilot's licences in the whole of the country! The airfield closed down but Pemberton-Billing went on to establish an aircraft factory near Southampton, which later became the Supermarine Aircraft Company of Spitfire fame.

During 1909 two of the most famous and influential figures of these pioneer days – Alliott Vernon Roe and Frederick Handley Page – were both active in Essex. Vernon Roe had brought his Roe 1 Triplane from Brooklands in Surrey to Lea Marshes, where he rented two railway arches and converted them into workshops. After several minor crashes and a few short flights of 50 feet or so, on 13th July 1909 Roe achieved a flight of 100 feet distance at a height of 10 feet, which was recognised as the first flight by a British airman in an all-British aeroplane, and he later improved on the distance by flying some 900 feet! Encouraged by this success, and along with his brother, he formed an aircraft company in January 1910, which became one of the most successful in the country, producing many of the early commercial aircraft and later some famous RAF aircraft – notably the faithful Anson and the legendary Lancaster bomber.

In June 1909 Frederick Handley Page had, at the age of 23 years, set up his own aircraft company at Barking Creek, and his works there were thought to be the very first buildings in Britain to be erected specially for aircraft manufacture. Several of Page's early aircraft had their first trial flights from Barking to Fairlop (near Ilford), and in 1912 an HP5 – a two-seater monoplane – made the first flight over London. It managed to complete the 30 miles from Barking to Brooklands in just under an hour! Page also used the 'Dagenham Experimental Ground', a small landing field with sheds and buildings, which had opened in February 1909 in Chequers Lane under the auspices of the Aeronautical Society of Great Britain. This airfield was rather short-lived, closing down a year or so later, and now the site is occupied by Ford Motor Company.

It was the outbreak of the First World War that ultimately brought about a mushrooming of Service airfields in Essex. The Royal Flying Corps was formed on 13th April 1912 and its Naval Wing became an independent force on 1st July 1914 as the Royal Naval Air Service. It was this force that was given the task of the home defence of Great Britain as the small nucleus of men and aircraft of the RFC were sent for service in France. From 1915 onwards as the threat of aerial bombardment from the massive German airships, mainly in the shape of the dreaded Zeppelins, began to materialise, it was decided to establish airfields throughout Essex, each about ten to thirty miles apart. Suddenly small landing fields with very basic facilities – a variety of tents, some canvas sheds and workshops and the odd rudimentary building – appeared at Burnham-on-Crouch, Chingford, Fyfield, Goldhanger, Gosfield, Hainault Farm (Fairlop), North Weald Bassett, Orsett, Rochford, Stow Maries and Sutton's Farm (Hornchurch). Far more numerous than at the outbreak of the Second World War!

After several Zeppelin raids in the last months of 1915 it was finally realised that a special Home Defence Force was needed with the result that, during 1916, two night-fighter squadrons – Nos 39 and 37 – were formed and became part of what was called the London Air Defence

The remains of Zeppelin L32 at Great Burstead near Billericay – September 1916. (The Illustrated London News Picture Library)

Area. The squadrons had their headquarters at Woodham Mortimer and Woodford Green respectively with a flight, ultimately eight aircraft, based at each airfield. Most of the aircraft were BE2cs (Blériot Experimental), a two-seater bi-plane which had been designed by Geoffrey de Havilland and was the first British aircraft specially developed for a military role. It had a top speed of 82 mph with an endurance of 3½ hours and was so successful that it remained in service throughout the war. Chingford, although involved in home defence, was also mainly engaged in the training of pilots for the RNAS.

The first success fell to No 39 squadron when on 2nd/3rd September 1916 Lieutenant W. Leefe Robinson shot down Airship SL11, which fell in flames over Cuffley in Hertfordshire. This was the first German airship to be destroyed over Britain and Leefe Robinson was awarded

the Victoria Cross. On the night of 23rd/24th of the same month two of the squadron's pilots – Second Lieutenant Frederick Sowrey and Second Lieutenant A. de B. Brandon – each accounted for a Zeppelin; one crash-landed at Little Wigborough and the other in flames near Billericay. Both crashes created great public interest with special trains being run to view the scenes! About a week later another fell to the Lewis guns of one of the squadron's pilots, Second Lieutenant W. J. Tempest. No 39 had now became known as a 'crack' night-fighter squadron. It was not until June 1917 that the pilots of No 37 squadron made their first kill – Zeppelin L48 was destroyed over Norfolk.

The days of the Zeppelins were fast coming to a close, and in their place came the large and fearsome Gotha V biplane bombers, which first bombed London on 13th June 1917 causing 162 deaths. Two more squadrons – Nos 44 and 78 – were formed to help counter the new threat. New aircraft – Bristol Fighters and Sopwith Camels – were introduced and different tactics were developed to counter the bombers,

The memorial to Captain Henry Clifford Stroud, RFC, at Shotgate – killed in action at midnight on 7th March 1918.

which do bear a striking similarity to those used during the Battle of Britain. The pilots were placed on 'readiness' and on a given signal – a klaxon hooter – the pilots and mechanics would race out of their tents, start up the engines, and the pilots would sit in their cockpits until the patrol signal was given. They would then climb in formation to their allotted patrol areas and would be further directed by signals from the ground. This was a very rudimentary form of fighter control, bearing some similarity to the more sophisticated system employed during 1940.

The squadrons were not quite so successful against the Gotha bombers especially when they changed to night operations. The last Gotha raid on London occurred on the night of 19th/20th May 1918 when the RAF pilots (the RFC and RNAS had amalgamated on 1st April 1918) claimed three Gothas, their best performance of the war. These pioneering night operations over the Essex countryside did bring tragic accidents, as on 7th March 1918, when two pilots, Captains Stroud and Kynoch, flying from Rochford and Goldhanger collided over Shotgate and both were killed. There are two memorials in adjacent fields marking the sites of the crashes.

In 1919 the RAF was the most powerful air force in the world with almost 150,000 officers, men and women, yet within four years it was reduced to just one fifth of that total. In this massive reduction of the Service all the Essex airfields were given up and returned to farming, and only two – North Weald Bassett and Sutton's Farm – would subsequently be developed into permanent Service stations. The first opened in September 1927 and in June of the following year Sutton's Farm became RAF Hornchurch.

Also in 1928 a small private airfield opened at Maylands, set alongside the A12 at Harold Wood. It was initially used for private flying but in 1931 it became Essex's first commercial aerodrome when George Hillman, a local coach operator, established an airline company there operating flights to several places in the country. The first Essex Air Pageant was held at Maylands in 1932 and two years later it became a customs 'approved aerodrome' – the first in the county – which enabled Hillman Airways to operate services to the Continent. One of the company's pilots at the time was Amy Johnson. In June 1934, the airline moved to Stapleford Tawney near Abridge, where it received its first DH86s in June 1935, enabling it to expand its services to Paris, Ostend, Brussels and Antwerp. The following year three small airlines, including Hillman, amalgamated to form British Airways Ltd and operations were moved to Gatwick in May 1936. The first local authority airport in the county was officially opened at Southend (Rochford) on 18th September 1935.

Whilst commercial and private flying was prospering during the inter-war years, the RAF had to fight doggedly to retain its independence and the young Service owes a deep debt of gratitude to its first Chief of Air Staff – Sir Hugh Trenchard. He managed to fight off the other Service chiefs, who had designs on the RAF, and then he built a Service which, although small, was nevertheless very professional, highly motivated and well trained. Trenchard established a Senior Staff College at Andover, an Officer Cadet College at Cranwell as well as an Apprentices' School at Halton. Although Lord Trenchard retired in 1929, the Service that entered the Second World War bore his indelible principles and precepts, and he certainly deserved the title of 'the Father of the RAF'.

It was not until the 1930s that the politicians, when faced with the growing militancy of Nazi Germany and the rapid and frightening growth of the German Air Force, decided that the RAF should be expanded and provided with new and better aircraft. Several expansion schemes were approved, only to be set aside later, but at least these schemes did have some redeeming features in that they resulted in a number of fine aircraft that ultimately saw war service, such as the Wellington, Hampden, Stirling, Defiant, Hurricane and Spitfire. In the five years leading up to the war the Service greatly expanded in size with its operational aircraft increasing fourfold. Such a hurried build-up demanded the provision of new airfields but Debden, which opened in 1937, was the only Essex airfield to emerge from this frantic period of expansion.

The RAF, and Fighter Command especially, was about to face the greatest challenge of its short existence. On 4th September 1939, HM King George VI sent a message to the RAF which stated, '...you will have to shoulder far greater responsibilities than those which your Service had to shoulder in the last war; one of the greatest of them will be the safeguarding of these islands from the menace of the air. I can assure all ranks of the Air Force of my supreme confidence in their skill and courage and their ability to meet whatever calls will be made upon them.' Stirring and confident words indeed but, with such high expectations, a most daunting task lay ahead for the junior Service. To understand how the RAF in Essex faced up to these demands it is necessary to examine how Fighter Command pursued its war aims and objectives and how its operational role changed during the progress of the war.

Air Marshal Sir Hugh C. T. Dowding, KCB, CMG, AOC-in-C, Fighter Command, 1936-40. (Imperial War Museum)

Fighter Command

Fighter Command came into being on 14th July 1936 when the 'Air Defence of Great Britain' was reorganised into four separate and distinct functional Commands – Bomber, Coastal, Training and Fighter. The Command's headquarters were established at Bentley Priory, Stanmore. On that historic day its first Air Officer Commanding-in-Chief, Air Marshal Sir Hugh C. T. Dowding, arrived without any due fuss or ceremony to begin the herculean task of developing the meagre and outdated resources of his Command into a force capable of defending the country against an enemy bombing offensive.

Perhaps it might have been argued that Dowding was a most unlikely person to command the body of rather extrovert, and very young, pilots that manned his fighter squadrons. Although he had served as a pilot during the First World War, he was now aged 54 years and getting close to retirement. An aloof and austere person with a reputation for a difficult and abrasive manner, he acquired the nickname 'Stuffy'! However, Dowding proved to be an ideal choice, being a very able adminstrator who showed complete confidence in his subordinate commanders. He was dedicated in his support and concern for the welfare of his pilots and furthermore he was blessed with considerable foresight. Without doubt, Dowding developed a very fine fighter force and established a sound and effective defensive system, which together ultimately won what was, perhaps, THE most critical battle of the war, against the most powerful air force in the world – the Luftwaffe.

Prior to Dowding's new appointment he had been involved in the Service's various research, supply and development programmes and had been instrumental in the early planning of the Hurricane, Spitfire and Defiant. But more importantly he had actively supported the brand new and revolutionary 'device' of RDF or Radio Direction Finding, later known as Radar. This 'early warning' system could detect the range, bearing and altitude of aircraft approaching the coasts from a distance of about 100 miles, and proved to be an important factor in the Battle of Britain. By July 1940 some 50 of these stations were operating and 30 of them were Chain Home Low, specially designed to seek out low-flying aircraft.

They were just the first line of the Home Defence System, an intricate and very effective communications organisation. Once the enemy aircraft had passed over the coast, it was the responsibility of the

Hurricane IIs of No 87 squadron. This squadron served in France from September 1939 to May 1940.

Observer Corps to track their progress. This information was passed directly to Command headquarters, where it was filtered for errors, and then sent to Group headquarters. Here the enemy forces and their bearings were closely plotted on a large-scale map and the Group Commander decided how many and which of his squadrons he would use to face the threat. The necessary information was relayed to the Sector airfields within the Group. The Sector Controllers would plot the information and 'scramble' their squadrons for interception, and from then onwards they would directly control the fighter pilots in the air. Allied to this fighter control system were the anti-aircraft defences, the barrage balloon force and the searchlight command – all under the control of Dowding and Fighter Command.

On 1st August 1939 Fighter Command comprised 38 squadrons based at the airfields in the four Groups – Nos 10 to 13. Of these squadrons, nine were equipped with Blenheims and Gladiators, not really considered front-line fighters. Dowding had set a target of 53 squadrons as the **minimum** number to form an adequate defence. This situation gave Dowding some 740 front-line aircraft (Hurricanes and Spitfires) against an estimated total Luftwaffe force in excess of 4,500 aircraft, of which perhaps 2,000 could be considered bomber or 'attack' aircraft. Within days of the outbreak of the war, four squadrons of Hurricanes were sent out to France, followed before the end of the year by another two and yet another two were 'lost' in the Norway campaign. This depletion of Dowding's slim resources, which accelerated during the first weeks of May 1940, caused him grave concern as he considered that France was 'a lost cause' and the pure defence of Britain was his primary and major task; he felt so strongly about the situation that he requested to appear before the Cabinet to state his case for the retention of fighters in England. This unique and unconventional action proved successful, as Winston Churchill announced on 19th May that 'no more squadrons will leave this country whatever the need of France.'

It was the battles over France, and especially Dunkirk, that brought Fighter Command its first severe test. From 10th May to 4th June the action was most intensive and during that period the Command lost 450 aircraft (mostly Hurricanes) but with fighter production reaching 400 per month these losses, although heavy, were not too serious; it was the loss of some 140 trained pilots, many of them experienced pre-war officers and men, that proved to be critical. For most of the Battle of Britain it was the supply of trained pilots that caused the greatest concern to Dowding. He ultimately devised a system of moving hard-pressed squadrons out of the front line to enable his experienced pilots to obtain a short respite from almost continual combat.

Contrary to the general belief, there was not much breathing space between Dunkirk and the opening of the Battle of Britain as the Luftwaffe attacked the shipping convoys in the English Channel almost daily. During the brief lull, the depleted squadrons were re-equipped and new pilots were trained, especially those arriving from Europe, the Commonwealth and from America – all of which ultimately made such a vital contribution in the coming conflict.

Despite the hectic air combats of early July the Battle of Britain officially started on 10th July and finished on 31st October 1940, at least those were the dates recognised by the Battle of Britain clasp, which was awarded to all fighter pilots or air gunners flying operational sorties during this period (2,927 in total). The Command had a total front-line strength of 57 squadrons, with six of these being non-operational for various reasons, still short of Dowding's minimum strength. The majority of the squadrons were equipped with Hurricanes and Spitfires with some Defiants. Of the two Fighter Groups that covered London, East Anglia and the south-east, it was No 11, based at Uxbridge, that carried the heaviest burden.

This Group, which controlled the Essex airfields, was commanded by a New Zealander, Air Vice Marshal Keith Park. He had been Dowding's right-hand man since 1936 and took over the vital post early in 1940. Park had served as a fighter pilot in the First World War, and became a highly effective and popular leader, his calm, measured and careful tactics proving to be most decisive during the Battle. His counterpart at No 12 Group, Air Vice Marshal Trafford L. Leigh-Mallory, was a different breed, and had strongly differing views on the conduct of aerial warfare, greatly favouring the use of fighter wings of three or more squadrons rather than operating just single squadrons. Leigh-Mallory, who had been in charge of the Group since 1937, was an energetic and popular commander and bounded with self-confidence. He was vociferous in his criticism of Park and the use of his resources during the Battle. The 'Big Wing' controversy greatly affected the subsequent reputations of both Dowding and Park, whereas Leigh-Mallory became head of the Command in November 1942.

The main German aircraft that 'The Few' would face were the Heinkel 111s, twin-engined bombers capable of carrying 2,000 pounds of bombs, which were the backbone of the Luftwaffe bomber force. The fearsome and infamous 'Stuka' dive-bombers – Junkers 87s – were heavily engaged in the early stages of the Battle, but were later withdrawn because of heavy losses. Another familiar sight to pilots was the very versatile Junkers 88 – a strong, durable and manoeuvrable twin-engined bomber and, at the time, probably the best in the world. There was also the Dornier 17 which, although it was the least effective Luftwaffe bomber with a far lighter bomb load than the Heinkel, could withstand terrific damage and still survive. All these bombers had the advantage of self-sealing fuel tanks, which greatly reduced the risk of fire. The main Luftwaffe fighter was the Messerschmitt 109E, capable of over 350 mph with two 20 mm cannons and two machine guns. On paper it was superior to the Hurricane, and to the Spitfire at higher altitudes, and without doubt it was a formidable opponent. However, its range was somewhat limited and it could just about make London providing it did not get involved in too many aerial combats! The much-vaunted Messerschmitt 110C – the 'Zerstörer' or 'Destroyer' – was a twin-engined, two seater and heavily-armed fighter, with two cannons and five machine guns. It was really a fighter/bomber with a much longer range but it was less nimble and at times proved more of an encumbrance to the Me109s.

Despite being greatly outnumbered, the RAF pilots' one distinct advantage was that they were flying over their own homeland and, although many were shot down, quite a number managed to bale out, survive and return to their squadrons to fly again. The Luftwaffe pilots and crews, however, had the disadvantage of flying over hostile territory as well as crossing the English Channel twice, often returning in badly damaged aircraft. It was said that most suffered from what was called 'Kanalkrank' or Channel sickness, being only too aware of their slim chances should they ditch – an estimated four hours was the maximum time of survival in the Channel without a dinghy. RAF pilots were exhorted not to pursue enemy aircraft over the sea, as the air/sea rescue services were then in their infancy. They were constantly reminded that their main aim was '...the destruction of enemy bombers' and that action against fighters was only a means to an end.

It may be said that the Battle can be divided into several separate phases. The first related to the Luftwaffe's attacks on the Allied shipping in the Channel and on ports, coastal airfields and radar stations, which ended around 24th July. Until the middle of August the Luftwaffe attempted to destroy Fighter Command in the air. On 12th August five radar stations on the south coast were bombed, followed on the next day by heavy raids against southern ports and airfields. For about three weeks the Luftwaffe launched an all-out assault on the fighter airfields and radar stations in the Home Counties. Between 24th August and 7th September there were 33 bombing attacks mostly directed at the airfields in No 11 Group. Air Vice Marshal Park later maintained, 'Had my fighter aerodromes been put out of action, the German Air Force would have won the Battle by 15th September.' But from 7th September the Luftwaffe changed tactics and proceeded to concentrate their forces on daylight raids directed at London, these operations continuing well into the autumn. From then onwards came the night raids against London and other provincial cities.

A pilot at Rochford enjoying a well-earned rest between operations. (Southend Museums Service)

It is quite impossible in such a short summary to detail the intensive air battle, which continued almost unabated for over three months. Two specific days do, however, stand out and both proved to be critical to the outcome of the Battle – 18th August, now known as 'The Hardest Day', and 15th September, which is celebrated as 'Battle of Britain Day'.

On the 15th the onslaught started with heavy lunchtime raids on Kenley, Croydon and Biggin Hill airfields, followed by Stuka attacks, during the early afternoon, on the airfields at Gosport, Thorney Island and Ford as well as the radar station at Poling. Then in late afternoon two strong bomber forces, heavily escorted by fighters, set out to attack Hornchurch and North Weald. Over Kent and Essex these forces were turned back, not necessarily by the strong and fierce fighter opposition they met but because of the cloudy weather, which would effectively preclude accurate bombing. Strange to relate, but at this time the Luftwaffe were under strict and specific orders, from Hitler himself, that they were not to bomb indiscriminately! At the end of the hard and exhausting day of combat, Fighter Command claimed 144 enemy aircraft destroyed with the Stukas losing particularly heavily; they were

1939–45 Star with a replica Battle of Britain clasp. (Spink & Son Ltd)

quickly withdrawn from the Battle on the direct orders of Goering. The Command lost 39 fighters in the air and on the ground, with 21 pilots killed or seriously injured. After the war, it was discovered that the Luftwaffe lost 'only' 69 aircraft on the day (7%). This exaggeration of claims was a feature of air combat throughout the Second World War and it was not done deliberately for propaganda purposes but came about by the speed, confusion and the number of aircraft involved in aerial combats, frequently several pilots very geniunely claimed the destruction of the same aircraft. The day proved critical because the Luftwaffe was convinced that Fighter Command was a spent force, but the strength and ferocity of the opposition encountered on the day made them realise that the battle for air superiority was far from won. Two days later Winston Churchill made his famous speech, '...Never in the field of human conflict was so much owed by so many to so few...'

By 15th September the Luftwaffe had turned its attention to daylight attacks on London. It launched some 1,000 sorties over the capital and in the process lost 56 aircraft, with another three damaged beyond repair (these figures were obtained from Luftwaffe records after the war). Fighter Command lost 29 fighters and 12 pilots were killed. The day was one of almost non-stop aerial combat, with some of the 'dog fights' taking place over the centre of London. The Air Ministry claimed '175 Raiders Shot Down', which was later increased to 185. This was hailed as a historic victory and it gave a massive boost to the public's morale, and was the main reason why the 15th became known as 'Battle of Britain Day'. The fact that this was based on grossly false figures really has little bearing on the matter; from then on the German High Command realised that they could not gain air superiority over the English Channel and the planned invasion of Britain – 'Operation Sealion' – would have to be postponed, as it was just two days later. As Winston Churchill later wrote of the day's fighting, '... It was one of the decisive battles of the war, and like the Battle of Waterloo, it was on a Sunday...'

Nevertheless the raids continued with each side incurring heavy losses and not until the middle of November could it safely be said that the Battle of Britain was really over. The Command had lost over 1,140 aircraft in the air and on the ground and over 900 pilots had been killed or seriously injured, against some 1,730 enemy aircraft destroyed. Although the Command lost many experienced pilots during the Battle, many others survived and emerged as the outstanding fighter leaders and commanders of the war – 'Sailor' Malan, 'Al' Deere, Colin Gray, Peter Townsend, Brian Kingcombe, Donald Kingaby, Douglas Bader, 'Johnnie' Johnson et al. Surprisingly only one Victoria Cross was awarded during the Battle – on 16th August – to a Hurricane pilot, Flight Lieutenant J. B. Nicolson of No 249 squadron. It had been a hard and costly victory for Fighter Command, although by the end of November the two chief architects – Dowding and Park – had been relieved of their posts in favour of Air Marshal W. Sholto Douglas and Air Vice Marshal T. L. Leigh-Mallory. At the time it seemed to be scant gratitude for their gruelling and valiant efforts, but time has righted the balance and their tarnished reputations have been fully restored.

Until about May 1941 the Command had the difficult task of opposing the heavy night incursions of Luftwaffe bombers. The Spitfires and Hurricanes were not really suited to night operations, but the few squadrons of Beaufighters hastily brought into service in September 1940, aided by the Defiants, did provide some opposition to the seemingly endless waves of enemy bombers. The Beaufighter in the hands of experts such as Flight Lieutenant John 'Cat's Eyes' Cunningham and his gunner, Flight Sergeant C. F. Rawnsley, did make some impact despite its AI (Airborne Interception) radar being rather cumbersome and not very refined.

Although the night defence of the country was still the Command's main priority, under their new Chief it began to move onto the offensive. On 20th December 1940 two Spitfires from Biggin Hill were sent out to strafe Le Touquet airfield and in the New Year the Command commenced a new operation, which went under the name of 'Circus', followed later in the year by other offensive operations variously known as 'Rhubarbs', 'Ramrods', 'Jim Crows', 'Rodeos' and 'Roadsteads'. These were a mixture of combined operations with light or medium bombers, individual or squadron fighter sweeps to attack airfields and transportation targets in France and the Low Countries and anti-shipping strikes. With Air Vice Marshal Leigh-Mallory in charge of No 11 Group, his belief in the efficacy of 'Big Wings' resulted in the establishment of Wings at the various Sector airfields, although it was not until 1942 when greater resources were available and the improved marks of Spitfires arrived that these Wings become very effective strike forces, especially under such leaders as Deere, Finucane, Dundas, Rankin, Kingcome, Crowley-Milling and Milne.

The Spitfires and Hurricanes were being refined and improved and with the provision of cannons were becoming quite formidable ground attack aircraft, the Hurricane being especially suited to this role. However, some of the operations were quite costly without showing really tangible results; during June and July 1941 there were 46 'Circus' operations mounted resulting in the loss of 132 pilots, including such famous names as Bader, Mungo-Park and Lock. In September 1941 the Focke-Wulf 190 made its first appearance and its all-round performance proved to be superior to the Spitfire Mark V, which caused Fighter Command considerable problems until the Hawker Typhoons became more reliable and numerous, and superior marks of Spitfires were ultimately developed. By the end of the year the Command had 100 squadrons, of which three-quarters operated by day, and it had also become a most cosmopolitan force with the addition of Polish, Czech, Belgian, French, Norwegian, Canadian, Australian and American squadrons – some 34 in total.

During 1942 Fighter Command suffered several setbacks. In February during the famous, or infamous, 'Channel Dash' of the German battleships the Command launched 398 sorties, losing 17 aircraft without causing any damage to the German vessels. Two months later, with the onset of the so-called 'Baedeker' raids on cathedral towns, the vulnerablility of the home defences to this type of operation was highlighted. From April to July Fighter Command accounted for just 67 enemy aircraft, and of this number the newly arrived de Havilland Mosquito night-fighters claimed almost one third of the victories. The biggest single task for the Command since the Battle of Britain came in August with the ill-fated raid on Dieppe. During the day (19th) the Command mounted almost 2,400 sorties and claimed 91 enemy aircraft destroyed and 200 probably severely damaged. It also lost 91 aircraft in the process so the operation was hailed as a great victory because it was thought that over one third of the Luftwaffe's force on the Western Front had been destroyed. After the war it was disclosed that the 'real' German losses were 48 destroyed and another 24 damaged; effectively a major defeat for Fighter Command, which would have caused deep misgivings if the true figures were known.

In November 1942 a new Commander was appointed – Air Marshal Sir Trafford Leigh-Mallory, who was destined to command the Force during the zenith of its power. By the following June Fighter Command was double its size at the beginning of the war with a massive phalanx of fighters – Hurricanes, Spitfires, Beaufighters, Typhoons, Mosquitos and Mustangs. The new marks of Spitfires, especially, were proving themselves more than a match for the Luftwaffe fighters. Nevertheless, at the time, it gave the appearance of an air force seeking a positive role in the European air war. Intruder raids and large fighter sweeps over France and the Low Countries had become the bread and butter of the squadrons, in addition to pure bomber escort duties, which greatly increased with the entry of the USAAF into Europe.

In November 1943 the Command lost almost two-thirds of its squadrons and its name when the Second Tactical Air Force was formed. This was effectively an amalgam of light bombers, fighters and transport aircraft specially designed to provide close tactical support for the Allied armies in the invasion of Europe. It was heralded as 'the most significant reform by the RAF since the war began.' The name 'Fighter Command' disappeared and in its place returned 'The Air Defence of Great Britain' – echoes of the early 1930s.

During January 1944 the remaining squadrons of the ADGB were faced with a new German night-bombing offensive mainly directed at London. On the 21st of the month the Luftwaffe launched 'Operation Steinbock' in retaliation to Bomber Command's heavy raids on Berlin.

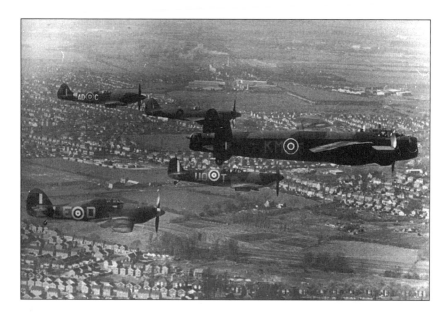

The Battle of Britain memorial flight over East Anglia. (via Gordon Curtis)

However, by now the night defence squadrons were far better prepared and equipped. In the first raid 25 enemy aircraft were destroyed out of a total attacking force of 227. During the 'Little' or 'Baby' blitz, which continued until May, the Luftwaffe suffered very heavily, losing almost 300 aircraft mainly to the Mosquito night-fighters.

With such a crippling defeat of his conventional bombers, Hitler was forced to turn to his 'Vergeltungswaffe' or 'revenge weapons' – the V1 and V2 rockets - for a last desperate bombardment of London, East Anglia and the south-east. Only one week after D-Day (on June 13th) the first V1 rocket fell in Kent and from then until almost the end of the following March a total 9,251 V1s were plotted. Perhaps at long last the fighter pilots had found their true metier – single-handed combat – but this time against unmanned rockets or 'divers' as the pilots knew them. In the whole V1 rocket campaign the RAF managed to destroy 1,979; the most successful fighter at this type of combat was the Hawker Tempest, with their pilots accounting for over 630. In August another new fighter was in action against the 'divers', the Gloster Meteor I, which became the first jet aircraft to see service in the RAF. Then on 8th September the first V2 rocket landed at Chiswick, killing three civilians with another 17 seriously injured. These missiles, which travelled at a speed of more than 3,000 mph, were impossible to intercept, so fighters, especially Spitfire XIVs, were used to attack the launching sites.

On 15th October 1944 the Command once again regained its old and proud designation, with Air Vice Marshal Sir Roderic Hill continuing as its AOC-in-C. The Command was now deeply involved in escorting the massive daylight operations which were becoming such a feature of Bomber Command's operations over Germany. These escorts were mainly conducted by Mustang IIIs. During March 1945 there were some isolated night intruder raids over eastern England with the object of attacking airfields as the bombers returned from operations. The Luftwaffe's last incursion over England occurred on 17th March, which proved to be the final death throes of what was once such a powerful air force. The last operation mounted by the Command during the Second World War was on 9th May when fighter squadrons provided air cover for the forces landing on Guernsey.

The men of Fighter Command could feel very proud of their valuable contribution to the air war. They had been called upon to carry out a multitude of tasks and in the process lost 3,690 airmen with 1,215 wounded or crippled for life and another 601 taken prisoner of war. Many of these brave airmen, who sacrificed their young lives, lie buried in the country churchyards that surround their old wartime airfields, although many more had no known graves and are remembered in the impressive RAF memorial at Runnymede. Without doubt, Fighter Command's greatest hour had been in those few brief months of the summer of 1940 when its young pilots held the fate of the country and the outcome of the war in their hands; for that Battle they will never be forgotten.

The United States Army Air Force

The old adage 'Large streams from little fountains flow, Tall oaks from little acorns grow' could easily have been coined especially for the USAAF during the Second World War. Known as the Army Air Corps since 1926, it was the Cinderella of the US armed forces. Due to America's isolationist foreign policy, it had been consistently starved of funds and resources. But from its redesignation to the Army Air Force on 20th June 1941, it grew from a mere infant organisation into the largest air force in the world in less than three years. When the United States entered the Second World War it had less than 600 combat aircraft, but from then onwards the growth of the USAAF was nothing short of phenomenal, with powerful, separate and self-contained air forces operating in the Pacific, North Africa and Europe. But it is the latter 'theater' of operations that is the concern of this book.

The first American airmen to arrive in Britain served with the Eighth Air Force, which had been formed on 2nd January 1942; originally designated the 'Fifth' it was renumbered just four days later. This new air force was planned to provide air support for the invasion of North Africa, but when this offensive was postponed, it was decided to move the Eighth to Britain to form the nucleus of the USAAF in Europe, and it ended up being the mainstay of American operations there.

The plans for the build-up of the Eighth Air Force were quite staggering in their ambition and immensity – 60 operational Groups (Bombardment, Fighter, Transport and Observation) comprising over 3,500 aircraft, all by April 1943, with all the support units necessary for such a large organisation. Indeed, had these figures been realised by the set date, the Eighth Air Force would then have exceeded in size all the three operational RAF Commands operating from Britain! Largely because of shortages of aircraft and the pressing demands of operations in other 'theaters of war' these grandiose plans became modified along the way. Nevertheless the Eighth still became a massive and powerful air force, well deserving its famed sobriquet – the 'Mighty'.

It was on 24th February 1942 that Brigadier General Ira Eaker, along with six fellow officers, arrived in England, charged with the formidable task of establishing the Eighth Air Force in Britain. Eaker was destined to command the Eighth's bomber forces until the end of 1943. He saw it through its early painful growing pains almost to its pinnacle of strength, and it was mainly due to his foresight, determination and leadership that the Eighth developed into such a powerful, disciplined and destructive strike force. Eaker's role was very similar to his counterpart at RAF Bomber Command – Air Chief Marshal Sir Arthur 'Bomber' Harris – and it was vitally important for the future of the Allied air offensive that the two Commanders should work well together. There were no problems on this score and the men became close personal friends.

The first essential was to identify a sufficient number of sites to house the Eighth; at least 75 would be required, and the majority needed to be in eastern England. RAF Bomber Command airfields usually housed

B-17s of 381st Bomb Group in formation. (Smithsonian Institution)

two squadrons, and since the American Bomb Groups comprised four squadrons, it was anticipated that each Group would need to occupy two airfields. This proposal quickly went by the board and each Group – Bomb or Fighter – ultimately had its own airfield. As far as Essex was concerned, nine airfields – Andrews Field, Boxted, Chipping Ongar, Debden, Earls Colne, Great Dunmow, Little Walden, Ridgewell and Wormingford – housed some of the Eighth's operational Groups for certain periods of time.

The Eighth comprised four separate Commands – Bomber, Fighter, Ground Air Support and Service. The Bomber Command, based at High Wycombe, would ultimately be composed of three Bomb Divisions (later renamed 'Air') and these became almost independent air forces in their own right. The Fighter Command, with its headquarters at Bushey Hall, was first commanded by Brigadier General Frank Hunter. It was planned to have three Wings, but an acute shortage of suitable fighters, along with the dictates and pressures of the North African campaign,

All three American fighters of the Second World War can be seen in this shot: P-51s, P-47s and P-38s from several of the Eighth's Fighter Groups. (Smithsonian Institution)

resulted in a much slower build-up, and the Command had to constantly 'borrow' fighters from the Ninth Air Force to assist on escort duties.

By mid-1944 the Eighth Air Force had no less than 40 Heavy Bomb Groups, just over one third equipped with Consolidated B-24s (Liberators) with the majority flying the famous Boeing B-17s (Flying Fortresses). By this time the Fighter Command was up to its full strength with fifteen Groups operating in three Combat Wings. Of these Groups seven were equipped with the much vaunted North American P-51s (Mustangs), four flew Republic P-47s (Thunderbolts) and the other four had Lockheed P-38s (Lightnings). Ultimately all the Eighth's Fighter Groups, bar one – the 56th at Boxted – would be equipped with P-51s.

The Eighth's avowed objective was to conduct a high-altitude air offensive by means of a 'pin-point strategic bombardment' undertaken by strongly armed and fast bombers, of which the B-17 was considered the epitome. This mode of operations was, of course, at direct variance to RAF Bomber Command, which had, from costly experience, resorted to using its heavy bombers solely by night. The Americans were utterly convinced that their philosophy of operating large formations of self-defending bombers at high altitude during the daylight hours would prove to be more successful. For this policy they felt that they had the right aircraft, equipped with an excellent oxygen system, and the 'wonder and deadly accurate' Norden bomb-sight. Furthermore, it was felt that operating at higher altitudes (above 20,000 feet) would limit the effectiveness of pursuit fighters and place their bomber formations largely above the range of the enemy's flak batteries. Unfortunately the Eighth was soon to find out that this theory of high-altitude bombing became somewhat flawed when put into practice.

The self-defensive system of bombers flying in tight formations proved to be rather illusory once the experienced and determined Luftwaffe pilots had devised special tactics to confront the Eighth's heavies. Despite the high altitude German flak took quite a toll of the B-17s and B-24s, especially once their batteries became accustomed to the American daylight operations after coping for almost three years with the night operations of RAF Bomber Command. Almost the same number of American bombers fell victims to enemy flak as were shot down by Luftwaffe fighters. The famed Norden bomb-sight proved not as effective in European weather conditions as in the clear skies over the training fields of America. Nevertheless Eaker and his subordinate officers held their nerve and grimly retained their belief in daylight strategic bombing in the face of some crippling and appalling losses. The

Eighth's almost blind faith in daylight bombing was finally vindicated when it had sufficient long-range fighter escorts to protect their 'big brothers', supported by the various 'pathfinder' and radar techniques which had been first perfected by the RAF.

The USAAF's initial involvement in the European air war was a low key affair with one American crew joining No 226 squadron (RAF) from Swanton Morley in Norfolk for a mission over northern France on 29th June 1942. Five days later – Independence Day – six crews from the 15th Bomb Squadron (Light) 'borrowed' RAF Bostons to accompany RAF aircraft on a bombing mission of enemy airfields. This was the first Eighth Air Force operation of the war and it resulted in the first fatalities and medal awards – sadly two American crews did not return.

It was not until 17th August that the heavy bombers were ready for action. On this historic mission twelve B-17s of 97th Bomb Group took off from Grafton Underwood and General Eaker went along as a passenger in the appropriately named aircraft *Yankee Doodle*. The target was Rouen and there was an escort of RAF Spitfires; all the aircraft arrived back safely but two had sustained flak damage. Air Chief Marshal Sir Arthur Harris sent a message to Eaker, 'Yankee Doodle went to town, and you can stick another well-earned feather in his cap!' Nevertheless it would be another six months before the Eighth began to make a significant contribution to the Allied bomber offensive. The build-up of the Eighth Air Force was very slow and suffered a severe setback when, in the autumn, seven operational units were lost to the Twelfth Air Force for 'Operation Torch' – the invasion of North Africa. The Eighth was left with just a single Fighter Group – the 4th at Debden – which, had been formed out of the three RAF 'Eagle' squadrons, and the American pilots were still flying their RAF Spitfires, which, despite all their other fine attributes, were not noted for their operational range.

At the beginning of 1943 the major Allied conference at Casablanca came to an agreement on the Allied bombing strategy, which, other than some minor changes of priorities, would prevail until 1945. The directive, known as 'Pointblank', stated, 'the primary aim will be the progressive destruction and dislocation of the German military, industrial and economic system, and the undermining of the morale of the German people to a point where their capacity for armed resistance is fatally weakened.' It also listed the essential targets in an order of priority – U-boat bases and yards, the German Air Force and its aircraft factories, ball-bearing plants, the oil industry and road and rail transportation.

B-26s of 394th Bomb Group. (via Bryan Jones)

On 27th January 1943 the Eighth launched its first operation over Germany – the U-boat pens at Vegasack and the naval port of Wilhelmshaven. Both targets were beyond the range of the Spitfires, so it was matter of some relief that only three aircraft were lost on this mission. By the end of February 1943 the Eighth had lost 22 aircraft out of its effective strength of 84, which Eaker called 'his piddling little force'. At this stage of the war Bomber Command considered a 5% loss rate on any operation just about tolerable, but many traumatic months and countless operations would pass before such a 'low' loss rate was finally achieved by the Eighth Air Force. This was especially noticeable from March when the Luftwaffe was beginning to come to terms with the American bomber formations. On one black day in April (17th) whilst attacking the Focke Wulf factories at Bremen, the Eighth lost 16 aircraft (14%), which was their heaviest loss of the war so far. Little did the Eighth's Bomber chiefs realise that this harsh defeat would pale into insignificance with the losses sustained in some major operations later in the year.

In May the first American medium bombers – the B-26 Marauders – appeared in the Eighth Air Force. Their second mission over Holland, conducted at low-level, proved to be so utterly disastrous that the four

B-26 Groups were retrained for operations at a medium altitude and took no part in the Eighth's air offensive for another two months or so. Neverthless the Eighth was slowly building up its strike force with the arrival of new Groups straight from training in the United States, and all these were based in East Anglia, although the only Heavy Bomb Group to serve permanently in Essex was the 381st at Ridgewell.

In retrospect it can seen that the high losses sustained by the Eighth in the second half of 1943 were largely due to the lack of long-range fighters but they were also brought about by a massive increase in the Luftwaffe's day-fighter force. At first the German High Command had not taken the American daylight offensive too seriously, but as the numbers of heavy bombers slowly and steadily increased over German targets, day-fighters were pulled back from other war fronts to confront the growing threat. In a few short months the Luftwaffe day-fighters almost doubled to 800 and the ensuing battle of attrition between the Luftwaffe fighters and the Eighth Air Force proved to be one of the most fierce contests of the war, and was not really won until the final months.

The first major confrontation came in August 1943, on the anniversary of the Eighth's first full operation in Europe. The names of Schweinfurt and Regensburg have now passed into the annals of American Air Force history. The mission on 17th August was brutal, heroic and bloody in the extreme – 60 aircraft out of the total force of 376 were lost! Far worse was to follow. On 6th September came the very costly operation to Stuttgart, now considered to be the Eighth's most disastrous operation of the war. Then in just seven days during October, the Eighth mounted major raids to Bremen, Anklam, Marienburg, Gdynia and Münster. Over 1,400 sorties were flown, resulting in a loss of 173 aircraft along with 1,500 airmen. On 14th October the Eighth returned to Schweinfurt and the Luftwaffe delivered another savage body blow – 60 aircraft and 600 men failed to return from this raid – and with a loss rate of 21% the day became known in the USAAF as 'Black Thursday'. Of necessity the whole policy of daylight bombing came under very serious consideration, and the whole future of the Eighth was in the balance. But any air force that could sustain such losses and still come back fighting deserves to be called 'Mighty'.

Two days after the Schweinfurt operation, the Eighth was joined in the United Kingdom by another American Air Force – the Ninth, which had previously been operating in the Middle East. Its first operations from Egypt had started in November 1942, and its units had been involved in the battles over the Libyan desert and Tunisia as well as

Major General Samuel E. Anderson, Commander of the Ninth Air Force, Bomb Division, at Chelmsford – May 1945. (USAF)

engaging in the invasions of Sicily and mainland Italy. The Ninth was now to become the Americans' major tactical air force preparing the way for the invasion of Europe, and it corresponded with the RAF's 2nd Tactical Air Force, which was formed in November. The Ninth's main responsibility would be the support of Allied ground forces, with the ability to adapt rapidly to changes in the battlegrounds.

Major General Lewis H. Brereton, its Commanding Officer, set up his headquarters at Sunninghill Park at Ascot, and he saw its objectives as gaining and holding air superiority over the Allied land forces as well as providing close tactical support for those forces. It would also attack enemy troops in the front line, road and rail communications, bridges, enemy airfields and coastal fortifications. Asked to sum up the ethos of his force, General Brereton answered with just one word – 'mobility'. The Ninth had three operational Commands – Bomber, Fighter and Troop Carrier, and for this purpose almost 100 units of the Eighth Air Force were transferred to the Ninth, along with some 30 of its airfields, although during 1944 units of the Ninth used 62 airfields or Advanced Landing Grounds in England.

For the first ten months or so the Ninth Bomber Command operated solely from Essex airfields and its headquarters were at Marks Hall near Colchester. From here Major General Samuel E. Anderson controlled the eight medium and three light Bomb Groups equipped with B-26s and A-20s. The Ninth Fighter Command, under the command of Major General Elwood R. Quesada, ultimately comprising 18 Groups, was planned to operate from Advanced Landing Grounds in southern England, although for a short time four of them operated from airfields in Essex, where they were mainly engaged on escort duties under the control of the Eighth Fighter Command. It was with the Ninth Air Force that the first P-51s began to appear in the USAAF at the beginning of December 1943.

During the early months of 1944 the Eighth Air Force was rapidly building towards a major air offensive against the German aircraft industry and airfields. This was code-named 'Operation Argument' but was also known as 'The Big Week'. In five days of concentrated action, from 20th February, over 3,000 aircraft were involved in bombing targets throughout Germany for the loss of 177 aircraft but with nearly 500 enemy fighters claimed to have been destroyed. In March it was the Eighth's turn to tackle the ultimate target – Berlin – just as RAF Bomber Command's long and costly campaign during the winter of 1943/4 was coming to an end. The Eighth mounted five Berlin operations in the month.

Meanwhile the Ninth's bombers from their Essex airfields were engaged in attacking V1 rocket sites, enemy airfields, marshalling yards and other strategic targets in northern France, Holland and Belgium. These operations were conducted with very light losses, certainly when compared with the losses of the Eighth's heavies and they can be considered as one of the shining successes of the European air war. The B-26s had started the war with a wretched reputation, and few of the USAAF's chiefs would have predicted such a fine operational record for these rather vilified aircraft.

By the beginning of April the overall control of the Allied Air Forces had been devolved to General Eisenhower, the Supreme Allied Commander in Europe, and much of the Allied air power was channelled onto targets in France in preparation for the imminent invasion – the so-called 'softening-up process'. These were coastal batteries, road and rail communications, bridges and enemy airfields, particularly within a 150 mile radius of Caen. The most important targets were the rail and road communications and they were part of what was called 'the Transportation Plan', a large-scale offensive closely debated by the Allied Air Chiefs because of the high risk of heavy civilian casualties. Nevertheless the Plan went ahead, and each Air Force was allocated a certain number of specified targets to attack. From 1st April until the eve of D-Day the Allied Air Forces mounted over 210,000 sorties on 'invasion targets', and of this total the Ninth Air Force completed just over one quarter with again the lightest losses.

In conjunction with these priorities the Eighth managed to launch its assault on the German oil industry, commencing on 12th May and continuing for another nine months. Such names as Merseburg, Leuna, Lutzendorf, Zwickau, Brüx, Bohlen and Zeitz, would figure large on the operational schedules of the Eighth's Groups during this period. By June the USAAF was at the height of its power and strength. The Eighth was a prodigious force of heavy bombers backed by a large number of fighters, and the Ninth Air Force had achieved its full complement of Bomb and Fighter Groups, making their presence fully felt in constant missions over targets in northern and central France. The Ninth also had a small number of Tactical Reconnaisance Groups, which provided up-to-the-minute intelligence on the enemy's movements and positions. The Ninth had now grown into a powerful air force in its own right with 45 Combat Groups and some 200,000 personnel. It also had a number of Engineer Aviation Battalions, many of which landed as soon as the Normandy bridgeheads had been secured, in order to construct the first landing grounds in France.

On D-Day the combined Allied Air Forces launched 13,680 individual sorties – a mammoth air armada. Of this total the Eighth flew over 4,000 sorties, bomber and fighter, with the Ninth completing more than 3,500. The Ninth was also the operator of the most formidable troop-carrying force ever assembled, with no less than 56 squadrons in action, either transporting troops or towing gliders. It is thought that on the day the Eighth lost 20 aircraft compared with the 26 lost by the Ninth. The Allied air superiority over the Normandy beach-heads was total, thus justifying General Eisenhower's assertion to his troops, 'Don't worry about the aircraft above you, they will be ours'! By the end of the month the Eighth was concentrating on strategic targets in Germany, and the Ninth Air Force and the 2nd Tactical Air Force were largely left to give close support to the Allied armies, which they did most notably at Caen, Cherbourg, St Lô, Falaise and Brest.

In August there was a change of Commander for the Ninth Air Force, General Brereton handing over to his deputy, Major General Hoyt S. Vandenburg. Also during the month the Ninth Bomber Command was redesignated the Ninth Bombardment Division, and remained so for the rest of the war. By the autumn all of the Ninth's Bomb Groups had left Essex for advanced airfields in either Hampshire or on the Continent, and thus pass out of the scope of this account. The Ninth's Fighter and Bomb Groups later followed in the wake of the Allied armies as they rapidly advanced across France, into Belgium and Holland and finally crossing into Germany; they moved airfields quite frequently, fully justifying General Brereton's concept of 'mobility'.

The latter months of 1944 presented some problems for the Eighth Air Force, mainly with the appearance of the Luftwaffe's rocket-propelled Me163 and the turbo-jet Me262, which caused deep concern. It was acknowledged that should they arrive in sufficient numbers they would pose a very serious threat. This menace resulted in an intensive bombardment of aircraft factories, airfields and jet development centres. Nevertheless the battle against the German jets continued almost up to the end of the war. In March and April 1945 there were more recorded combats with the 'jet fighters' than in any other months, and the last air battle with the Luftwaffe day-fighters occurred on 19th April.

During 1945 the Eighth Air Force was mounting operations at a rapid rate and on a grand scale. Frequently over 1,000 bombers and 500 fighters were in action on a single mission. On many of these operations the Eighth worked closely with RAF Bomber Command, which had also reached the pinnacle of its power, and several German targets were

One of the stained-glass windows in the porch of Chelmsford Cathedral in memory of the American airmen who served in Essex during the Second World War.

bombed day and night – perhaps the most famous (or infamous?) being Dresden in February 1945. Certainly 'round the clock bombing' had become a grim reality for many German cities. This bombing concept had been envisaged by both Eaker and Harris back in 1942 but was rarely achieved until the latter months of the war.

The Eighth Air Force completed its last bombing mission (No 968) on 25th April. In almost three years the Eighth had fought a bitter, costly and harrowing air battle, losing over 43,000 airmen in the process. The Ninth Air Force, much later onto the European scene, flew over 368,000 sorties, lost nearly 3,000 aircraft and had 3,430 airmen killed or missing in action. Many of these American airmen who flew from these shores, never to return, are now remembered on the Wall of the Missing in the fine American military cemetery and memorial at Madingley near Cambridge. Closer to their 'adopted' homes are the countless memorials to the various Groups of the two American Air Forces, dotted around the East Anglian countryside adjacent to their old wartime airfields. The presence of the Ninth Air Force in Essex is also commemorated with two fine stained-glass windows in the porch of Chelmsford Cathedral.

Thousands upon thousands of ex-US servicemen have made the emotional journey back to visit the scenes of their wartime service. Naturally, with the passing of each year the numbers get fewer and fewer, although in the early summer of 1992 there was a special 'Reunion' to celebrate the 50 years that had elapsed since the Eighth Air Force arrived in East Anglia. At the beginning of May 237 'Marauder men' returned to visit the Essex airfields of their youth and were 'overwhelmed' with the welcome and hospitality they received in the county. Before they left to visit their old airfields and the war cemeteries in France, they were entertained to a civic reception at County Hall in Chelmsford given by Essex County Council. It was quite clear to them that the men of the USAAF had not been, nor indeed ever will be, forgotten in Essex.

The Airfields

It has often been said that during the Second World War Britain resembled 'an unsinkable aircraft carrier anchored off the coast of Europe', and with 600 airfields in use it seemed a most apt description.

With such a long and rich history of aviation in the county, it was perhaps inevitable that the Essex countryside would accommodate a fair number of wartime airfields. The experiences of the previous war would ensure that RAF Fighter Command would maintain a strong presence in the county. With the fall of the Low Countries and France during the summer of 1940 when Britain found itself alone, it was thought that victory could only be acheived through air power, and the Air Ministry concentrated on providing bomber bases. Essex was certainly well placed to house such bomber airfields, from which to strike at targets in those occupied territories. The Air Ministry's plan was to build 15 Class A bomber airfields in the county, which turned out to be very providential when the USAAF entered the European air war in 1942, as all of them were occupied by American Air Force Groups.

During the Second World War there were 23 airfields in Essex and all but one of them – Birch – had operational squadrons or groups using their facilities for most of their wartime existence. And yet in that last peaceful summer of 1939 there were just three Service airfields in the county – Debden, Hornchurch and North Weald – all under the control of RAF Fighter Command. The 'civilian' airfields at Rochford and Stapleford Tawney were quickly made operational, followed later by airfields at Fairlop, Bradwell Bay and finally Great Sampford.

At the end of 1941 there were still only six operational airfields in Essex, but in the next two years another 17 airfields came 'on stream', and almost all of them were occupied by American Groups, with the Ninth Air Force being predominant. Although 23 airfields might seem a large number, it was far less than both Suffolk and Norfolk, who had 32 and 37 airfields respectively. Nevertheless Essex could have contained even more airfields if judged by the number of sites that were selected for development, allocated to the USAAF, the construction being then indefinitely postponed. Cold Norton, Beaumont, Southminster and High Roding all received official USAAF 'station numbers', whereas other sites at Bulphan, Ingatestone, Little Clacton, Maldon and Weeley were considered and surveyed but not progressed any further.

It was said that in September 1939 the Air Ministry's Aerodromes Board had identified some 4,000 possible airfield sites in Britain, and of these just over 10% were ultimately developed into airfields. The method of selection was a close examination of Ordnance Survey maps to identify areas of sufficient flat land which were relatively free of obstructions. The terrain, if possible, had to be close to sea level and at least not above 650 feet because of the incidence of hill fog. The

66102A

Aerial view of Station 167 – Ridgewell. Two of the runways are in use. Note the hard-standings in the foreground. (Smithsonian Institution)

adequacy of road and rail communications was considered, as was the proximity of any built-up areas, which tended to be avoided – hence the reason why many of the wartime airfields were situated in rather obscure places. Once a promising site had been identified and passed these litmus tests, it was then physically inspected field by field with due consideration given to the landing and take-off distances as well as the nature of the subsoil. If then a site appeared to be suitable, steps were taken to requisition the necessary land under the Emergency Powers (Defence) Act 1939, and the planning stage was set in motion.

By August 1942 the Air Ministry had devised a standard specification for what became known as a Class A bomber station. This dictated that there would be three intersecting concrete runways, one at 6,000 feet and two at 4,200 feet, each 150 feet wide, forming the shape of a capital A. The main runway was normally aligned to the prevailing wind depending on the natural and man-made obstructions in the

Working on one of the wartime airfields. (John Laing plc)

surrounding area. The runways were joined by a 50 foot wide perimeter road, which could stretch for up to three miles or so, giving access to at least 50 dispersal points for the aircraft, generally known as hard-standings. Lighting was normally only provided for the main runway though a system of lead-in lights was installed for all the runways. This was the basic layout employed on the majority of airfields built in Essex during 1942/3, though, of course, each site might need certain modifications depending on local conditions.

The RAF had no less than 20 Airfield Construction squadrons, but most of the wartime airfields in Essex were constructed either by 'approved' civil engineering companies, such as W. & C. French Ltd, Bovis Ltd and Richard Costain Ltd, or by the various US Engineer Aviation Battalions. Indeed the Americans built 14 airfields in Britain, of which eight were situated in Essex. All of the construction work was under the general direction of the Air Ministry Directorate General, more generally known as 'Works and Bricks'. During the height of airfield construction between 1942 and the end of 1943 it was estimated that some 60,000 men were engaged on the work, which was given top priority. Each completed airfield cost in the region of £1 million, and considering that 444 were built during the Second World War, it was a mammoth construction programme resulting in a massive investment of materials, labour and finance.

One of the surviving control towers – Matching.

Once the hordes of construction workers had moved in with their earth-movers, concrete mixers, heavy lorries and tractors, and settled into their tented accommodation, the peace and tranquillity of the local countryside had vanished especially as the construction work was often carried on by day and night. Soon the whole area would almost disappear under a sea of mud in the winter months, and clouds of choking dust in the summer. Fields were flattened, trees uprooted – usually with the use of explosives – and any natural obstructions were quickly demolished. Local objections were, however, heard and in a few cases they were taken into consideration and the plans changed. Some 20 miles of drains, six miles of water mains and four miles of sewers were laid. The perimeter road and the hard-standings were usually put down first before work was started on the runways. Provision was made for two underground aviation fuel stores and a bomb and ammunition storage area, which was a series of narrow roadways protected by bankings and usually placed away from the station's main buildings, and if possible sited in woodland to give some added protection from blast. Once the runways had been completed grass seed was sown between them to bind the soil. On these airfields two T2 (transportable)

*'...the ruined remains of the odd hut still stand amongst the ploughed fields –
but now they have become very well camouflaged by nature.' – Ridgewell.*

hangars – 240 feet long and 39 feet high with a span of 120 feet – were 'de
rigueur', usually placed at opposite sides of the airfield. Often one was
erected during the construction work and mainly used for storage
purposes, the other being put up after the airfield was occupied.

Next in the construction programme came the station's buildings, and
the first to appear was the watch-house or 'control tower', as it was
known in American parlance. This building was probably the most
familiar sight on any wartime airfield. By 1942 they had become of a
standard design – a functional two-storied brick building with a
concrete rendering, and provided with a railed balcony on the first floor
as well as railings on the roof. It housed the flying control and the
weather office. Perhaps one of the most evocative and lasting images of
these wartime airfields is that of the balcony crowded with officers
straining to hear or see their returning aircraft. Some of these wartime
control towers have survived in Essex, notably at Boreham, Matching
and Little Walden.

There were a multiplicity of other buildings clustered around the
airfield, from the armoury to the water tower – those gaunt and rather

ugly constructions which, along with the hangars, became the most prominent landmarks in the local countryside. There were the headquarters section, technical workshops, an operations block, a briefing room, a photographic section, a hospital or sick quarters, vehicle repair areas, equipment and parachute stores, a guard-house, a cinema, a communal site, kitchens, messes and so on. Most of these buildings were prefabricated huts, some of timber and plasterboard, while others were of precast concrete slabs, and the 'Orlit' or 'Maycrete' huts seemed to be the most prevalent.

The living quarters, usually to accommodate some 2,800 officers and men, were generally provided by curved corrugated iron Nissen huts, which owed their origin to the First World War and a certain Colonel P. Nissen, although the Americans usually referred to them as 'Quonsets'. One writer has described them like '...wrinkled grey elephants sheltering from the cold East Anglian winds'! These living quarters were normally grouped into separate units often numbering ten or more, and they were spread around the surrounding countryside. Because of their distance from the main airfield site the possession of a bicycle became almost an essential 'item of equipment', if only to get to the nearest village pub! With the passage of years most of these wartime buildings have long disappeared, although the ruined remains of the odd hut still stand amongst the ploughed fields – but now they have become very well camouflaged by nature. The wartime concrete has seemed to survive the test of time with several strips of perimeter roads, runways and hard-standings still to be seen at the edges of fields, and they are often the only links with a wartime past.

Of course not all the Essex airfields were built to this standard design. The three pre-war RAF airfields provided a high standard of permanent accommodation and their buildings tended to be rather elegant in design – almost neo-Georgian. All were constructed of brick and normally supplied with central heating. Both officers and men were, therefore, provided with a fair degree of comfort and good sporting facilities, especially in comparison to the wartime airfields. These original airfields seemed to outwardly confirm the ascription that the RAF was 'the best flying club in the world', as it was considered during the late 1930s.

The pre-war airfields were predominantly grass-surfaced, as indeed were Stapleford Tawney, Rochford and Great Sampford. This was despite the fact that it had been recognised, as far back as 1937, that the new aircraft coming into the Service really required concrete runways.

The main objection to the proposal appeared to be on cost terms, but also the problem of camouflage was cited as a disadvantage, as was the lack of natural braking power of concrete!

Sadly many of Essex's wartime airfields have long since disappeared under the plough almost as if they had never existed. However, some survived and are now used for private flying, such as Andrewsfield, Earls Colne, North Weald and Stapleford Tawney, with one, Wormingford, used by a gliding club. Just two out of the 23 have been developed into successful commercial airports – Stansted Mountfichet and Southend. Only two still remain under the control of the Ministry of Defence – Debden and Wethersfield – but no longer as operational airfields. Nevertheless the number of memorials that are dotted around the Essex countryside and in the various village churches recall the days when these wartime airfields echoed to the sounds of Hurricanes, Spitfires, Mosquitos, Typhoons, Stirlings, Marauders, Havocs, Thunderbolts, Lightnings, Mustangs and Flying Fortresses. These memorials act as a permanent reminder of the huge debt we all owe to these countless RAF and American airmen who flew from the Essex airfields.

It is not the intention of this book to list all the squadrons that served at the RAF stations, but merely to reflect the type of operations that were mounted from them. The Ninth Air Force Bomb Groups all operated very similar missions during their short stay in the county, and these have been reflected under the various airfields, as are the operations mounted by the 'Mighty Eighth', which had a relatively minor presence in the county, at least compared with Suffolk and Norfolk.

2

ANDREWS FIELD

Andrews Field (now called Andrewsfield) was unusual amongst Essex airfields in that its name did not provide a clue as to its situation. It was even more exclusive as the only wartime airfield in the United Kingdom to be named after an individual airman rather than a nearby town or village. The American term 'field' to describe an aircraft landing ground was in universal use in the United States. Although the name has been retained for the small private airfield now operating from the wartime site, it is perpetuated in the large USAF air-base in Maryland, which houses the US Presidential Flight.

In July 1942 an advance party of some 800 officers and men of the 819th US Engineer Aviation Battalion arrived at the small village of Great Saling, four miles to the north-west of Braintree, to start the construction of the first USAAF airfield in the United Kingdom. Because all of the land requisitioned fell within the parish of Great Saling, the airfield was so named. The construction of the Class A bomber airfield quickly gathered pace with the American engineeers working around the clock, and within three months the main runway had been laid down. By the time the airfield had been completed over 1½ million man hours had been expended in just ten months. To achieve the completion date the 819th had been joined, in the spring of 1943, by another Engineer Battalion (the 816th), then at Gosfield, to help with the final work.

On 24th April 1943 the airfield was officially opened with all due ceremony, with six American generals present to mark the historic occasion. Thus Great Saling became the first American-built airfield in the country to be ready for operational use. It was placed under the control of the Eighth Air Force's Bomber Command but in less than a month (21st May) it was decided to rename the airfield 'Andrews Field', in memory of Lieutenant General Frank M. Andrews, who was tragically killed in an aircraft accident in Iceland on 3rd May, whilst en route to the United States. He was one of America's most celebrated airmen and had been appointed the overall Commander of American forces in Europe only a few months earlier.

Six days later the first operational aircraft landed at the airfield. They were B-17Fs (Flying Fortresses) of the 96th Bomb Group, the crews having spent their first few weeks at Grafton Underwood near Kettering in Northants. This was one of the first three Groups to form the 4th Bomb Wing, which later became the 3rd Bomb Division. The crews' first taste of operational flying had been experienced over airfields in northern France, as these were then considered 'easy and gentle' missions for new crews to cut their teeth on. But they had also been blooded over Germany, so they were fully aware of what the European air war was all about; in a handful of missions the 96th had lost five aircraft, three of which were missing in action.

In the Group's very brief stay at Andrews Field just two operations were launched – to the marshalling yards at Rennes and U-boat pens at Wilhelmshaven – with the loss of just a single aircraft. By 12th June the crews had packed their bags and moved to another new base – Snetterton Heath in Norfolk – which became their permanent home. The reason for this move was a general re-alignment of some of the Eighth's Bomb Groups. It had been decided that the four Medium Bomb Groups that made up the 3rd Bomb Wing should be placed under the Eighth Air Support Command and based at Essex airfields, which would locate them closer to their targets on the near Continent. Thus the 322nd Group left Bury St Edmunds for their new base.

The four squadrons of the 322nd arrived at Andrews Field on 12th June under the command of Lieutenant Colonel Glenn C. Nye and the Group would adopt the sobriquet 'Nye's Annihilators' after their ebullient CO! Their aircraft were B-26s (Marauders), which would feature large in many of the county's wartime airfields; their distinctive shapes became very familiar in the Essex skies during 1943/4 and they are still fondly remembered by the county's numerous aviation enthusiasts.

The B-26 was one of the classics of the Second World War. It had sharp clean lines, was very streamlined, with a fuselege that resembled a cigar and when it first appeared, in November 1940, the American press quickly dubbed it 'the flying torpedo'! This twin-engined aircraft had been developed by the Glenn L. Martin Company of Baltimore in direct response to a precise specification that called for a fast and heavily-armed medium bomber. The original design so impressed the American Service chiefs that they ordered a considerable number (1,100) straight off the drawing board. Such confidence in an untried aircraft was very unusual in those days, especially as the Army Air Corps tended to be rather conservative in outlook.

The aircraft's design, performance and armament suggested that the company and the Army Air Corps had a real winner on their hands. The B-26 could carry a bomb load of 3,000 pounds to targets within 500 miles at a speed in excess of 260 mph, and it bristled with twelve 0.5 machine guns. Quite soon into the training programme an alarming number of accidents occurred, it proving to be a rather difficult aircraft to handle and its high landing and take-off speeds presenting problems for inexperienced pilots. As the accident rate rose steadily the aircraft gained a very unfortunate reputation and it became known to its crews as the 'widow maker' or the 'Baltimore whore'. The position became so grave that the US Army Air Corps set up a special Board of Enquiry to thoroughly investigate the design and until it reported its findings, the production of the aircraft was halted. The fate of the B-26 seemed sealed but, having considered the damning statistics set before them, the US Service chiefs retained their basic faith in the aircraft, and with a number of modifications, production of the aircraft was resumed.

The B-26 first saw service with the USAAF in the Pacific and later in the Mediterranean 'theater'. Despite its grim early reputation, which took a long time to dispel, the B-26 proved to be one of the most successful medium bombers of the Second World War, with over 5,150 produced, including 520 for the RAF. This quite outstanding aircraft never really gained the renown that its wartime performance deserved. The B-26 had an amazingly low loss rate, far and away the best of any American wartime bomber, and it served with great distinction in most 'theaters' of war but perhaps most effectively with the Ninth Air Force in Europe.

Nevertheless the 322nd's early experiences with their B-26s at Bury St Edmunds only provided even more fuel for the aircraft's many critics. On 14th May the first B-26 operational mission was mounted from England to make a low-level attack on the power station at Ijmuiden in Holland; nine out of twelve returned badly damaged and another crash-landed near the airfield. To rub salt into the wounds the Group's Commanding Officer, Colonel Stillman, was told that most of the bombs had missed the target and so the Group would have to return to the same target and try again.

Three days later eleven B-26s left for Ijmuiden and Haarlem. One returned early with a fault, but the rest of the attacking force was wiped out; no less than 58 airmen missing, including Colonel Stillman and Lieutenant Colonel Puriton, the Group Executive Officer. After this disastrous mission the aircraft's detractors had a field day, especially as a another B-26 crashed whilst on a low-level training exercise. Rumours spread quickly about the 'lethal' aircraft and it was felt by some crews that 'if the Hun did not get you the B-26 would!' It was assumed that the B-26s would be withdrawn from operations. What this tragic operation had proved was that medium bombers making daylight low-level attacks over heavily defended targets would result in heavy losses, irrespective of how speedy or well-armed the bombers might be. No 2 Group of RAF Bomber Command had learned this harsh lesson from costly experience with their Blenheim squadrons, and now they used their medium bombers – Venturas and Mitchells – at a medium altitude (10-14,000 feet) as well as providing them with fighter escorts.

It was after the Group had arrived at Andrews Field that the Eighth decided to operate their B-26s from about 12,000 feet, and RAF Fighter Command was asked about the availability of fighter escorts. This change involved quite a major retraining programme because all of the crews had only low-level experience right from their early days of training in the United States. It also necessitated certain modifications to the aircraft – a different bomb sight, the provision of strike cameras and changed rear guns. Because of these delays, and some trial missions by another Group, it was not until 31st July that 322nd went out on their first operation from Andrews Field – some ten weeks after that fateful May mission. The 22 aircraft that left for Triqueville airfield all came back safely with just five suffering damage, and one of the gunners claimed an enemy fighter – what a difference!

During August and September the majority of the targets were enemy airfields in northern France with the object of forcing the Luftwaffe to withdraw their fighter units away from the coastal areas and thus ease the pressure on the hard pressed heavy Bomb Groups. Slowly the B-26s, ably escorted by RAF Spitfires, began to fully justify the USAAF's faith in the aircraft, and their operational loss rate was less than 1%. By the end of August the 322nd had lost just one aircraft to enemy action whilst on a mission to Rouen power station.

On 16th October 1943 the 322nd, along with three B-26 Groups, was placed in 99th Bomb Wing (Medium) of the Ninth Bomber Command; the Wing had set up its headquarters at Great Dunmow. Nothing changed greatly for the crews as the type of operations were very similar, with enemy airfields figuring large in their operational schedules. It was on 24th October that the crews faced the strongest Luftwaffe opposition so far, whilst attacking Montdidier airfield to the north of Paris. Over 54 individual attacks were made by some 40 enemy fighters and in the fierce air battle the B-26 gunners claimed three destroyed with another three probables. All crews returned to Andrews Field safely – a splendid performance.

There was some concern that the bombing results of the B-26 Groups had not been that impressive, and also that too many missions had to be aborted because of heavy cloud conditions. In an attempt to improve matters the 1st Pathfinder squadron (Provisional) was formed at Andrews Field with B-26s equipped with the 'Oboe' radar blind-bombing device, and manned by experienced crews drawn from the rest of the B-26 Groups. The squadron's aircraft would act as the lead aircraft for all the Groups in the Ninth. The first 'pathfinder' mission was mounted from the airfield on 21st February, and slowly pathfinder-led missions became almost routine especially after D-Day.

All the B-26 Bomb Groups were demonstrating daily that the B-26 was a very effective medium bomber and the reputation of the aircraft was being thoroughly vindicated; suddenly it had gained a host of dedicated admirers, especially amongst the higher echelons of the USAAF! During May, as proof of this reliability and durability, one of the Group's aircraft, *Mild and Bitter*, became the first B-26 to complete 100 missions operating from Europe, but perhaps more surprisingly another B-26, *Flak Bait*, ultimately completed 202 missions with the 322nd, and its nose section is now proudly preserved in the National Air and Space Museum in Washington DC.

On D-Day 48 of the Group's aircraft attacked gun batteries at Ouistreham and Montfarville, whilst the Pathfinder squadron led six missions against other important targets in Normandy. Later in the month the 322nd attacked railway bridges over the Seine and three B-26s were lost. The crews' toughest challenge yet came when the Group was detailed for a night-bombing mission on the night of 7th/8th July. The target was the V1 rocket headquarters at Chateau de Ribencourt, which was thought to house the key personnel responsible for the

B-26 Flak Bait *of 322nd Bomb Group. This aircraft completed over 200 missions. (Smithsonian Institution)*

Germans' rocket offensive. Of the 35 aircraft taking part in this mission, nine were lost to enemy night-fighters with another two returning as 'write-offs' – an operational loss of 31%! In this mission the Group lost one of its most celebrated pilots – Lieutenant Colonel Robert Fry, DFC, who had flown with the 322nd since May 1943, and was an acknowledged expert in B-26 operations. Fry managed to parachute out but was taken prisoner and although he escaped he was subsequently recaptured. On the same night two famous B-26s failed to return – *Pickled-Dilly* on its 106th mission and *Bag of Bolts* on its 98th operation.

As the Allied armies began their speedy advance across France during September, the 322nd moved to the Continent to be closer to the action. On 25th September 1944 it left Andrews Field for Beauvais/Tille airfield, which only twelve months earlier the crews had been bombing! Just one month after leaving Essex the Group was awarded a Distinguished Unit Citation for its 'outstanding performance of duty' from 14th May 1943 to 24th July 1944. The citation read, '..the outstanding record achieved by the 322nd Group throughout these operations...The perseverance, fortitude and devotion of duty displayed by the members of the

Mustang IIIs of No 309 squadron line up along the runway at Andrews Field. (via John Wilkins)

organisation despite the differences and hazards of untried ways place the 322nd among the ranks of those organisations which have contributed in large measure to the blazing of new trails for the Army Air Forces.' The USAAF reserved this highly prized award for a Group's meritorious achievement or performance on a single mission or a succession of operations. They were, of course, greatly valued by the Group's personnel and were formally presented with full military ceremony.

The airfield was handed over to the RAF on 1st October 1944 and immediately came under the control of No 11 Group of the Air Defence of Great Britain. With its broad concrete runways and hard-standings it was deemed to be an ideal airfield to house two wings of fighters – six squadrons in all. These squadrons would escort the Lancasters and Halifaxes of RAF Bomber Command on the increasing number of daylight operations that were being mounted. The one fighter that was pre-eminently suited for this daylight escort role was the North American P-51, or Mustang as it was known in RAF circles; and for the rest of the war Andrews Field would house the largest number of RAF Mustangs operating from a single airfield.

Without a shadow of doubt the P-51 was the finest of all American wartime fighters and it ranks alongside the Spitfire as a superb pursuit fighter – both were real thoroughbreds of the air. For an aircraft that played such an essential part in the Eighth Air Force's long and bitter battle with the Luftwaffe, it is perhaps a little surprising to discover that it owes its inception to the British Air Purchasing Commission, who had asked the American aviation industry to produce a new fighter capable of long range escort duties and with the ability to operate at high altitudes. The North American Company rose to the challenge and managed to produce a prototype within 120 days, which first flew in October 1940. The new aircraft so impressed the RAF that they immediately placed an order, though at the time the US Army Air Corps showed little interest as they had opted for the Lockheed P-38 (Lightning). The first Mustangs appeared in Britain during October 1941.

It was soon discovered that although the Mustang had a most impressive performance at low level, this tailed off at high altitudes and therefore it was considered unsuitable for bomber escort duties. Fighter Command relegated the aircraft to mainly reconnaissance and Army support duties. During the autumn of 1942, at RAE Farnborough, the Allison engine was replaced by a Rolls Royce Merlin V power unit, which radically improved its performance at high altitude. The RAF suggested that the engines should be changed and Packard produced the Merlin engines in America under licence. The 'new' aircraft was an immediate success and thus was developed one of the outstanding pursuit fighters of the Second World War, according to Air Vice Marshal J. E. 'Johnnie' Johnson, it was 'the best offensive fighter of the war'.

The Mustang III or P-51C was capable of a top speed in excess of 400 mph, which was an improvement on the later marks of Spitfires. The aircraft could also operate above 40,000 feet with a long operational range allied to four .50 cannons (later increased to six), and the facility to carry two 1,000 pound bombs or six 5" rocket projectiles; the Mustang became a most redoubtable and destructive fighter and ultimately over 15,000 were produced in a variety of marks.

The first Mustang squadron to arrive at Andrews Field was No 129, which had been actively involved against the V1 rockets, or 'divers' as they were called in RAF circles, and their pilots had notched up 66 victories. They were quickly followed in by pilots of two Polish squadrons – Nos 315 and 316. The latter squadron had also gained some notable successes (50 in July) against the V1s, known to the Polish pilots as the 'flying witches'. The other Mustang Wing – No 122 – comprised Nos 19, 65 and 122 squadrons. The first was one of the oldest squadrons in the Service, having originally been formed in 1915 and gained fame as part of Douglas Bader's Duxford Wing during the Battle of Britain. Nos 65 and 122 will both figure in later Essex airfields.

The two Wings were mainly engaged in providing escorts for Bomber

Command heavies and more especially the Lancaster G-H force of No 3 Group, most of which operated from airfields in Suffolk and Cambridgeshire. These were exciting times for Andrews Field, with up to 72 Mustangs taking-off in pairs and in rapid succession – quite an exhilarating sight! Out of the many escort missions from Andrews Field, one, on 12th December 1944, resulted in a fierce air battle. The Lancasters were directed against the Ruhrstahl steelworks at Wittan and the Luftwaffe sent up a strong force of Me109s; although eight Lancasters were lost, the Mustangs managed to account for five enemy fighters for the loss of just one aircraft.

The make-up of the two Wings did not remain constant. Early in December No 129 moved to RAF Bentwaters in Suffolk to join another new Mustang Wing that was being established there. Another Polish squadron moved in during the month – No 309 – which went out on its first operation on 23rd December to Trier escorting a large force of Lancasters. The following month No 315 'Deblin' squadron reappeared and it was destined to see out the war at Andrews Field. Perhaps the most famous Polish squadron to serve with Fighter Command arrived in April bringing with it the new Mustang IVs, this was No 303, which had achieved 117 victories during the Battle of Britain. It was commanded by Squadron Leader Boleslaw A. Drobinski DFC, one of the legendary Polish fighter aces of the war. He died in July 1995, aged 76 years.

The only Allied jet fighters to see service during the war – Gloster Meteors – arrived at Andrews Field at the end of February 1945, and they were flown by the pilots of No 616 'South Yorkshire' squadron commanded by Wing Commander Andrew McDowall, DSO, DFC, DFM and bar. The squadron was the first to be equipped with the jet fighters. The Meteor had taken a long time to come to fruition – from May 1941 when the first prototype had flown, until July 1944 when it finally entered the Service. The aircraft was powered by two Rolls Royce Welland engines giving it a top speed of just under 400 mph. The squadron had been greatly involved in 'anti-divers', and during their short stay at the airfield they were engaged in affiliation exercises with the Eighth Air Force, which was experiencing a hard time with the Luftwaffe's turbo-jet fighters – Me262s.

Andrews Field's wartime activities came to an end on 25th April when the Mustangs escorted 375 Lancasters and Mosquitos to Hitler's mountain retreat at Berchtesgaden and a nearby SS barracks. Almost 100 P-51s of the Eighth Air Force accompanied 13 RAF Mustang squadrons,

Meteor I of No 616 squadron. (RAF Museum)

which must have made it one of the largest armadas of Mustangs to operate in the Second World War. Although the large force had to fly over some 250 miles of enemy occupied territory not a single enemy fighter was encountered.

Some of the Polish squadrons remained at the airfield after the cessation of hostilities. In August one of the most famous fighter pilots of the war – Alan 'Al' Deere – came to command the Polish Wing until it was disbanded in October. At the end of 1945 the airfield was virtually deserted. Before the concrete runways finally disappeared many 'L' drivers used the airfield for their first tentative attempts at driving and have not forgotten the experience! Over 25 years later a grass landing strip was laid and Andrewsfield (as it is now known) once more echoed to the sound of aircraft engines. In 1976 the airfield was officially licensed and it is now used by a variety of small civil and private aircraft.

There is a rather unusual brick memorial in the village of Great Saling on the site of the old station sick quarters, which remembers the men who built the first 'airdrome' and is inscribed to 'our comrades who later made the ultimate sacrifice in western Europe.' The airmen of the 322nd

The memorial at Great Saling.

Group have their own discreet memorial, which was dedicated in May 1992; it nestles beside the road leading into Great Saling.

3

BIRCH

The cost of constructing a Class A Standard airfield during the Second World War was in the region of £1 million, a massive financial investment – considering that 15 such airfields were planned for Essex alone. Furthermore a considerable amount of very valuable farmland, vital for the war effort, had to be given up, besides the large labour force that had to be devoted to the construction programme. In the light of this, and with the benefit of hindsight, the airfield at Birch turned out to be a colossal waste of money, time and other valuable resources. No wartime airfield in East Anglia, or perhaps even in the rest of the country, was so under-utilised as Birch; for virtually the whole of its existence its runways lay idle and sadly devoid of aircraft.

Although named after the village of Birch, the airfield was really closer to Messing, which was about a mile to the south-west and south of the main A12 road. The large site was first allocated to the Eighth Air Force in August 1942 with the intention of providing an airfield that would accommodate a Fighter Group. Work did not commence until the summer of 1943 when the 846th US Engineer Aviation Battalion moved in. The Luftwaffe appeared to be well informed of the construction and presumably felt it needed their attention, because on the night of 17th/18th August the site was attacked by a few FW190s, which proved to be more of a nuisance raid rather than causing any serious damage. By December the concrete runways (one at 2,000 yards and two at 1,400 yards) had been laid, only for them to attract another Luftwaffe raid on 10th/11th December when several bombs were dropped, straddling the new runways, with at least one exploding on the runways.

By the spring of 1944 the airfield was considered to be ready for occupation although the facilities at the camp were still rather basic. Nonetheless the two hangars were in place, as well as 50 hard-standings, with the technical and living sites, seven in total, set to the east of the airfield. During the first week of April the first American airmen appeared at Birch and they belonged to 410th Bomb Group of the Ninth Air Force. They had recently arrived in the country after the usual long and exhausting transatlantic crossing, and their aircraft – A-20s (Havocs) – were following them across by sea. The airmen had hardly sufficient time to unpack their bags and settle in before they found themselves on the move once again; within twelve days of their arrival at Birch the Group left for Gosfield airfield, which was just about eight miles further north.

Any empty and deserted airfield in East Anglia during 1944 was often thought as 'heaven sent' by many pilots limping back home in badly damaged aircraft, or maybe caught out in bad flying weather. On 13th May four P-38s (Lightnings) of the 474th Fighter Group found the atrocious weather too bad for them to continue and decided to land at Birch despite the fact that the runways had obstructions placed along their lengths. All four pilots managed to negotiate their landings safely.

The Eighth Air Force had finally reached its planned complement and had no need for Birch so it was offered to the Ninth, but by now most of the Ninth's Groups were scheduled to move away from East Anglia further south to be nearer to the action in northern France. Therefore the Eighth retained the airfield and earmarked it purely as a reserve base for its Third Bomb Division. However, early in September it was planned that the 52nd Troop Carrier Wing would use the airfield for an Allied airborne operation but in the end nothing came of the proposal.

It was not until March 1945 that Birch saw its only operational use. On 17th March troops of 6th Airborne Division began to move into temporary accommodation in the neighbourhood. This was preparatory to them taking part in the last major airborne operation of the war – 'Varsity' – the crossing of the Rhine. Their transport aircraft – 48 Dakotas (C-47s) of Nos 233 and 437 squadrons of No 46 Group (RAF) with another 12 Dakotas of No 48 squadron from two airfields in Gloucestershire – arrived at Birch a couple of days later. They made up half of the Group's force taking part in the operation. The three squadrons had suffered heavily in the last major airborne operation – 'Operation Market Garden' – over Arnhem, when 15 of their aircraft had been shot down.

C-47 (Dakota) of No 233 squadron with 'invasion' stripes. (RAF Museum)

The Douglas C-47 (they were known as 'Syktrains' in the USAAF) was the military version of the very successful DC-3 commercial airliner, which had first flown in December 1935. It proved to be an excellent military transport aircraft, also doubling as a airborne troop-carrier as well as glider tower. Because it was unarmed and lacked self-sealing fuel tanks, it really needed to operate where the Allied air forces commanded complete air superiority. Nevertheless C-47s played major parts in the airborne landings on D-Day, over Holland in September 1944 and now in 'Operation Varsity'. After the war the Dakota was used by most commerical airlines and cargo freight companies throughout the world. Indeed 60 years later the Dakota is still flying commercially. Considering that over 20,000 Dakotas were built, it must be the most remarkable and prolific aircraft ever produced.

The Dakotas brought their Horsa gliders, which were probably the most successful gliders of the Second World War. Designed by Airspeed, the Horsa was wholly constructed of plywood – in 30 separate units – and usually manufactured in a number of furniture factories. The glider had a high wing with a very large span – 88 ft – and a gliding speed of about 100 mph. But its most impressive feature was its massive flaps,

Airspeed Horsa gliders. (RAF Museum)

said to resemble 'barn doors', which enabled the craft to almost stop dead in mid-air and land in a most docile manner. First flown in September 1941 and used on operations from November 1942, it was manned by two pilots, who were normally from the Glider Pilot Regiment, although by this time of the war many RAF pilots were flying gliders. The Horsa was capable of carrying up to 28 fully-equipped troops, or a jeep and a 75 mm gun. Over 5,000 Horsas were ultimately produced and some 440 saw action in 'Operation Varsity'.

On the morning of 24th September the crews were about very early for final briefing and loading checks, then at precisely 6 o'clock in semi-darkness the 60 Dakotas left Birch. It must have been an impressive sight as lifting a full-loaded Horsa needed most of the long runway. When all of the aircraft had cleared the airfield no more operational flying took place from Birch, although there was still a RAF presence with certain ground organisations.

Some residual signs of the airfield can still be discerned in the fields – the odd piece of perimeter road and hard-standing – it is quite surprising how the wartime concrete has managed to survive the test of time! It is somewhat of a shame that Birch is now almost solely remembered as the scene of a particularly vicious murder in early December 1943. A Colchester taxi-driver was brutally murdered by an American serviceman, who was then engaged in the building of the airfield. The GI was court-martialled in Ipswich in January, when he was found guilty and hanged at the American Detention Camp at Shepton Mallet. A rather tragic and macabre incident with which to remember this 'ghost' wartime airfield.

4

BOREHAM

Of all the airfields built in Essex during the Second World War Boreham is, without doubt, the best preserved, that is if the heavily developed airport at Stansted is discounted. Several of the airfield's original facilties are still surviving, and none more so than the control tower, which since 1990 has returned to its original use, under the operation of the Essex Police Air Support Unit. Even the airfield's wartime identification code – 'JM' – is still clearly visible close to the control tower.

Each wartime airfield was given a unique two letter identification code and this was especially necessary in East Anglia where so many of the airfields were crowded close together. These codes can be said to have originated in the pre-war flying days when the location of each airfield was prominently displayed in large white letters that were required to be visible from 2,000 feet. For obvious security reasons this system was changed at the outbreak of the war and the two letter code was introduced. Most of the codes had some relation to the name of the airfield, for instance 'DB' for Debden and 'MC' for Matching. But because Boreham airfield was rather late coming onto the wartime scene most of the 'B' codes were already in use – 'BO' was Bodney in Norfolk and 'BH' recognised Barkston Heath in Lincolnshire – therefore, and for whatever reasons, 'JM' was selected for Boreham. For night identification purposes a mobile beacon unit known as a 'pundit' was used to flash in red the identity letters in morse code, which is why the letters became more generally known as the 'pundit code'.

Boreham was yet another wartime Essex airfield built by American

The control tower at Boreham with the 'pundit code' – 'JM' – in the foreground.
(via Bryan Jones)

Army engineers. In this case the 861st Engineer Aviation Battalion, who
when they arrived at Boreham on 13th May 1943 had stepped ashore at
Greenock just two days earlier, so they were complete 'greenhorns' in
the task they had been set. Before any serious construction work could
start the complete removal of some 86 acres of Dukes Wood, on the
eastern side of the 620 acre site, was needed, which is just another
example of how some of these wartime airfields completely transformed
the local landscape. The project was almost fully completed by the
spring of 1944, but not before the first fatality had occurred. On 10th
October 1943 a badly damaged P-47 (Thunderbolt) from the 56th Fighter
Group, returning from an escort mission over Münster, made an
emergency landing at the airfield, but in the process the aircraft
unfortunately collided with a bulldozer and the driver later died from
his injuries. The airfield or 'Station 161', which was about four miles to
the north-east of Chelmsford, had been first allocated to the Eighth Air
Force as a bomber base, but in October 1943 it was transferred to the
Ninth Air Force for use by a B-26 Group.

It fell to the 394th Bomb Group to occupy Boreham for about five

Lieutenant Colonel Thomas B. Hall, CO of 394th Bomb Group at Boreham. (via Bryan Jones)

months. This Group had been formed in February 1943 and was activated on 5th March with Lieutenant Colonel Thomas B. Hall as its Commanding Officer. Unlike the majority of the Ninth's Group commanders Hall led the 394th for most of the war (until late January 1945). He was a graduate of the West Point Military Academy and in 1941 had been a member of the US Air Commission to Brazil. Colonel Hall proved to be a most popular commander, leading by example and always ensuring that he took part in the Group's most difficult missions. After surviving the Second World War, he was, sadly, killed in action in 1951 whilst serving in the Korean War.

The Group's crews had spent virtually twelve months in preparation, training and final processing in various American states, Michigan, Oklahoma, Indiana, Georgia and Florida, before they were considered ready for service in the 'ETO' or the 'European Theater of Operations' to use its full title. They were required to fly their B-26s to England, which was the normal procedure for both heavy and medium bombers; a southern ferry route was taken during the winter months and a northern crossing in the summer. The crews left left the United States from Morrison Field, West Palm Beach, Florida on 7th February 1944 and it became a long drawn-out, if somewhat leisurely, affair via Puerto Rico, British Guiana, Natal in Brazil, Ascension Island, Liberia, Dakar and Marrakesh before landing at St Mawgan in Cornwall. The whole trip, some 11,000 miles, took 17 days including rest days, quite a formidable test for relatively inexperienced pilots.

It was not until 24th February that the B-26s began to appear at Boreham. The ground personnel undertook a less tiring crossing – they came over from Boston to Glasgow on the troopships *George W. Goethals* and *George Washington* and they did not arrive at Boreham until 10th March. Their new home must have proved quite a shock to them because the airfield was not yet fully completed and it was said to resemble 'a sea of mud', which really could describe most of the wartime airfields in East Anglia, where mud, mud and more mud was the constant bugbear especially during the winter months.

The Group had been placed in the 98th Bomb Wing of the Ninth Bomber Command, alongside two 'veteran' B-26 Groups then operating from Chipping Ongar and Earls Colne. As was the normal practice, a few 'battle-hardened' crews, this time from the 387th at Chipping Ongar, were transferred in to give the tyros of the 394th help and guidance, and the benefit of their experience. On 23rd March, less than a month after the Group's arrival at Boreham, Lieutenant Colonel Hall led 36 crews on

B-26 of 586th Bomb squadron at Boreham – 1944. (via Bryan Jones)

their first operational mission to Beaumont le Roger airfield – a distance of some 190 miles. Unfortunately, heavy cloud cover over the target, allied to the crews' inexperience, resulted in only moderate bombing results – the Group's mission report shows that '... Bombs fell long on the target..'! Nevertheless the CO received a congratulatory telegram from Brigadier General Samuel Anderson, the CO of the Ninth Bomber Command, for its bombing performance. It was a promising start for the 394th and augured well for the future.

Three days later (26th) the Ninth Bomber Command launched its biggest operation to date, which quickly became dubbed the 'revenge mission'. Some 340 B-26s were despatched to the E and R boat pens at Ijmuiden, from where ten months earlier ten B-26s of 322nd Group had failed to return. This 'revenge' operation proved to be anything but successful, the specific targets suffered no real damage and the Ninth Bomber Command were very disappointed with this first major bombing operation. I suppose the only crumb of comfort for the Ninth's chiefs was that only one aircraft was lost in action. However, a B-26 from the 585th squadron crashed near Bishop's Green, Great Dunmow, shortly after taking-off from Boreham for the Ijmuiden mission; this was due to an engine fire, and it was the Group's first loss.

B-26 of 394th Bomb Group taking off from Boreham. (via Bryan Jones)

Like the rest of the B-26 Groups, the 394th was mainly engaged on bombing marshalling yards, gun fortifications and V1 rocket sites during the first weeks of April. Some days the Group mounted two missions, with 36 aircraft being the normal complement, only rarely was a maximum effort called for when 54 crews would be in action. On 22nd April the Group flew a morning mission to 'the construction works' (a euphemism for rocket sites) at Bois Coquerel, with excellent results. Later in the day Lieutenant Colonel Hall led 19 aircraft to targets around Heuringhem. Within minutes of the target area the aircraft came under very intense and accurate anti-aircraft fire during which Hall's B-26 was severely damaged. Despite this, he still led the formation into the bombing run, before turning for home as his co-pilot had been seriously wounded and needed urgent medical attention. When Hall's aircraft was later examined no less than 264 flak holes were counted – another potent demonstration of the B-26's ability to sustain considerable damage and yet still survive. Colonel Hall was awarded the Distinguished Flying Cross (US) for his leadership and bravery on this mission.

By the end of April the Group had completed 25 missions (over 500 sorties) and over 1,500 tons of bombs had been dropped – all in five weeks – which was no mean achievement, especially as there was now a marked improvement in the accuracy of the bombing. Perhaps as an acknowledgement of the Group's contribution to the tactical air war, Air Chief Marshal Sir Trafford Leigh-Mallory, Commander in Chief of the Allied Expeditionary Air Forces, visited Boreham on 7th May. It proved to be a good day to see the Group in action and to witness at first hand the heavy flak opposition the B-26 crews faced daily over northern France. On the second mission of the day 36 aircraft had attacked gun fortifications at Dunkirk (a favourite target for the Ninth) and 23 B-26s returned with battle damage, resulting in one man killed in action and several more wounded.

Besides the Air Chief Marshal's visit the month proved to be a rather auspicious one for the Group. On 10th May Captain Darrell Lindsey led a particularly successful operation against marshalling yards at Creil, which was to the north-east of Paris. It was thought that after this particular raid over 70% of the railway sheds were destroyed. This successful operation brought deserved praise from the Ninth Bomber Command, 'Your bombing at Creil was excellent and the results are a big step forward in the current campaign to impede the movement of enemy troops and equipment. I congratulate you and your Group.' Despite fierce flak opposition only one B-26 was lost; moreover two of its crew managed to evade capture and ultimately arrived back at Boreham to great acclaim. However, they were returned to America and took no further action in the European air war; this was the normal procedure for successful airmen evaders, as it was thought that they might know too much about the French underground system to be risked again in action in case they were shot down and captured. Captain Lindsey was later (August 9th) awarded a posthumous Congressional Medal of Honor for another operation – an attack on a bridge – where he sacrificed his own life in order that his crew could bale out. He was the only B-26 crewman to receive America's highest bravery medal, which was equivalent to the Victoria Cross.

Just three days later the Group had their first tangle with the Luftwaffe when a group of FW190s attacked them, fortunately they survived intact, one gunner claiming one fighter destroyed. From the middle of May the 394th began its operations against railway and road bridges, becoming so expert in this kind of precision bombing that they gained, and thoroughly merited, the name of 'The Bridge Busters'. During their stay at Boreham some 22 bridges were attacked, invariably with impressive results. From 3rd June, whilst attacking a road bridge at Rangiport, the Group began to drop propaganda leaflets as well as bombs, a task that acquired them another name amongst the rest of the B-26 Groups – 'The Paper Boys'!

Like all the other B-26 Groups, the 394th mounted two missions on D-Day. The first left Boreham early in the morning when a maximum effort was called for. The target was gun positions at St Martin-de-Varreville to the north-west of the 'Utah' beach-head. This was the most westerly of the five beach-heads and had been allocated to the Ninth's Bomb. The poor weather and low cloud cover blunted the standard of bombing, and furthermore four aircraft were lost; there was a mid-air collision over Gillingham in Kent, and a second one over Sussex. The evening mission, which was led by Colonel Hall, was directed at the coastal gun batteries at Bénerville to the west of Deauville. It produced far better bombing results and no further casualties. Nevertheless at the end of this momentous day the 394th had suffered the loss of 23 crewmen killed in action, but it had completed 59 missions in just over two and a half months!

Six days after D-Day the Group was back to the business of 'bridge busting', and on 14th June it launched probably its most successful operation from Boreham. Captain Dolan led 35 B-26s in an attack on a railway bridge at Cloyes, which was an important rail link to the west of Orléans. Just a single aircraft was lost on this mission but 23 suffered heavy flak damage. This operation received commendations from the Ninth Air Force's chiefs, which were thoroughly deserved. Brigadier General Anderson wrote that this '...was the finest precision bombing I have seen... This indicates a very high morale, superior training, teamwork and marked agressiveness... I commend the group commander and all personnel of the group for the superior job they are doing...'

Fuel dumps, coastal defences and enemy troop concentrations were attacked throughout June, but come July most of the Group's attentions were directed against bridges. During this period a tail gunner with 584 squadron – Staff Sergeant Paul Mathis – became the first B-26 airman to complete 100 missions in the ETO. Fifty-two of these had been undertaken whilst serving with the Twelfth Air Force in North Africa, where Mathis had claimed two Me109s. This was quite an amazing record of operational service, especially as Mathis was only 23 years old! At the time 50 missions had become 'generally accepted' as completing a tour of operations with B-26s. Well, at least, that was the theory but shortage of aircrews (many new replacements were siphoned off to the Eighth) often resulted in many airmen completing far more than this number. And even later, when the tour was extended to 65 missions, this figure was frequently exceeded by airmen. It should be pointed out that 35 missions completed an operational tour on the heavy bombers of the Eighth Air Force.

The break-out of the Allied land forces from Normandy meant that the Group's days in Essex were rapidly coming to a close. On 17th July a 'reconnaissance' party left for the Group's new home at Holmsley South in Hampshire, followed a week later by an advance party. The Group's last operation from Boreham was flown on 23rd July and it was directed, rather appropriately, at a railway bridge at Mirville; all 32 B-26s arrived back safely. During their time at Boreham the Group had completed 96 missions for the loss of 16 aircraft, with 60 crewmen killed in action and another 24 taken as prisoners of war. This was a fine record by any standard, and the crews had become very experienced and successful in precision bombing. So perhaps it was not surprising that in the following month the 394th was awarded a Distinguished Unit Citation for five separate operations conducted over three days (7th to 9th August), which included four road and rail bridges. This award was a full and just recognition of the Group's excellent bombing performances.

The empty airfield was assigned to the Air Disarmament Command, which had the task of occupying and disarming captured Luftwaffe airfields, but by January 1945 the small party of American personnel had left. Like several others in Essex the airfield briefly came back to life again in March 1945 when some 80 C-47s (Skytrains) of the 315th Troop Carrier Group of the Ninth Air Force moved in from Spanhoe in Leicestershire, and on 24th they carried troops of the British 6th Airborne Division on 'Operation Varsity'. It proved to be the Group's most costly operation of the whole of the war, six aircraft being shot down, and another seven were so badly damaged by flak that they were forced to make crash-landings on the Continent.

It was in the autumn of 1949 that the old airfield echoed once again to the sound of engines, but this time it was high-performance motor vehicles. The West Essex Car Club developed a three-mile race circuit, with names redolent of the wartime days – such as Hangar Bend, Tower Bend and Dukes Straight. The meetings attracted some of the famous racing drivers of the time – Mike Hawthorn, Stirling Moss, Ken Wharton, Peter Collins and Luigi Villoresi. By the end of 1952 the racing circuit was closed. Three years later Ford Motor Company bought the airfield and it was used as a testing facility for the company's new trucks and rally cars. Forty or so years later the company is still in residence and Boreham is now the headquarters of Ford Motorsport in Europe.

The 394th is well remembered in the locality, with two memorials at the old airfield. The first dates back to June 1948 and was erected by the Essex Anglo-American Goodwill Association. The other is more recent, an impressive granite stone which is located near the offices of Ford Motorsport.

5

BOXTED

During the Second World War it was the Air Ministry's general principle to name a new airfield either from the nearest village, or the parish in which it was situated. Boxted was one of the exceptions to this rule because although it was sited close to Langham, it took its name from the village of Boxted, which was further away to the north-west. The reason for this was that there was already a RAF operational airfield named Langham in Norfolk.

Boxted was allocated to the Eighth Air Force in August 1942 and was first occupied by one of the Medium Bomb Groups to operate with the Eighth. The 386th had spent ten days at Snetterton Heath in Norfolk before bringing its B-26s to Boxted on 10th June 1943. The Group was commanded by Colonel Lester Maitland, a famous American aviator, who was one of the two pilots to make the first flight across the Pacific from the USA to Hawaii. Maitland's crews had undertaken training at MacDill Field, Florida, and Lake Charles Airbase, Louisiana, most of which had been almost exclusively devoted to low-level flying.

The necessary retraining programme and the aircraft modifications meant that the crews were not ready for operations until the end of July, which was almost seven weeks after their arrival at Boxted. The first two missions were nothing more than diversionary operations, effectively sham combat missions over the English Channel in an attempt to draw enemy attention from the real offensive operations. But as a direct contrast the operation mounted on 30th July proved to be a vastly different affair. Although 24 B-26s took-off for Woensdrecht airfield, about 15 miles north of Antwerp, only eleven managed to bomb. To add

B-26 of 386th Bomb Group climbs away from Boxted in the summer of 1943. (Imperial War Museum)

insult to injury the Luftwaffe, in the shape of FW190s, attacked the Group despite the presence of a goodly number of RAF Spitfires. One B-26 was shot down and another seven were badly damaged, one of which crash-landed at the airfield on return. The gunners claimed six enemy aircraft destroyed but much to their chagrin they were only allowed three when the combat films had been examined. This was the first time that the Luftwaffe had attacked a B-26 mission and they had to pick the 386th's first live operation!

From now on the B-26 crews found that although they were operating at the higher altitude the German flak batteries at their airfields could prove quite savage and very accurate. Unfortunately, the 386th's crews appeared to suffer more heavily than the other three B-26 groups, although their losses were admittedly slight compared with the Eighth's heavies. On the night of 17th August the 386th found the boot on the other foot when their airfield was bombed, which resulted in two fatal casualties and another 29 men injured. Five days later on a mission to Beaumont le Roger airfield, of the 36 aircraft (two squadrons) a quarter returned to Boxted with quite severe battle damage, and one failed to return. This B-26 was named *Pay Off* and was piloted by Lieutenant W. Caldwell. It came under attack from a couple of FW190s just after completing its bomb-run and was set on fire. Caldwell doggedly remained in control of the burning aircraft to allow his crew to bale out but the B-26 exploded before he could escape. For his supreme sacrifice Caldwell was posthumously awarded the Distinguished Service Cross, which was the second highest American award for valour.

By September the Group's time with the Eighth Air Force was coming to a conclusion; soon the B-26 Groups would be transferred to the Ninth Air Force. Boxted was earmarked for a Fighter Group that was due to come 'on stream' in October. The 386th was to take over another new Essex airfield further west at Great Dunmow, where they moved on 25th September 1943.

The next American unit did not move in until the middle of November and it proved to be another Ninth Air Force Unit – 354th Fighter Group. But perhaps of far more import was the fact that it was equipped with P-51Bs – the first Fighter Group to be supplied with these aircraft – and it later took the name of 'The Pioneer Mustang Group' to acknowledge this proud fact. At this period of the war P-51s were more valuable than gold dust. The Eighth Air Force's chiefs were prepared to move heaven and earth to get their hands on these superb long-range fighters. However, the aircraft was still considered a tactical support fighter and as such the scarce P-51s were first allocated to the 'tactical' Ninth Air Force. Until the Eighth's leaders were able to persuade the powers-that-be in Washington that they had a prior need for P-51s some other solution had to be found. In the end a compromise was agreed; it was decided that for the foreseeable future the Ninth's P-51 Groups would support and escort the heavy bombers but under the control of the Eighth's Fighter Command.

Within days of the Group's arrival at Boxted, Lieutenant Colonel Donald Blakeslee, the Group Executive Officer (Deputy CO) of the 4th Fighter Group at Debden, was seconded to the Group to lead them on their early operations. Blakeslee was probably the Eighth's most experienced fighter pilot, with long service with the RAF 'Eagle' squadrons and over a year's command experience with the 4th. Of course all his operational flying had been completed on Spitfires and P-47s rather than P-51s; although in this respect Blakeslee was in the same position as the Group's pilots, who had not flown P-51s until their arrival at Greenham Common in October. They had trained in the States on P-39s (Airacobras).

Fighter Groups, unlike Bomb Groups, comprised three squadrons each normally commanded by a Major (equivalent to Squadron Leader). The Group quickly settled in at Boxted, taking over some empty farmhouses and establishing their headquarters in Langham Lodge, a large house due south of the airfield. Although the P-51s would ultimately prove to be the salvation of the Eighth's daylight operations, their entry into Europe was not without its troubles; various problems such as coolant leaks, plug failures and jammed guns did reduce the operational efficiency of many of the Groups. Nevertheless on 1st December, 23 P-51s led by Lieutenant Colonel Blakeslee with Colonel Kenneth Martin, the Group's CO, as his wingman, left Boxted for a fighter sweep over the Knocke area of the Belgian coast, and all arrived back safely.

Four days later (5th December) proved to be a momentous day for the Eighth Air Force. It was the first time that P-51s went out on an escort mission – a type of operation that was to be the Group's 'bread and butter' for the next four months. In fact on 11th December, whilst escorting heavies to Emden, the 354th lost its first aircraft in action, and it had to wait another four days until the pilots righted the balance, opening their score with a single victory over Bremen – the first of hundreds of enemy fighters that would lose out to the P-51s. At the end of their first month of operations the Group had recorded six victories but had lost nine aircraft, including two in a tragic collision. Also during the month their aircraft had been fired upon by a squadron of P-47s in the mistaken belief that they were Me109s, which shows just how rare these P-51s were! It was the following month (January) that the Group would make their presence felt in no uncertain manner, and clearly demonstrate the merits of the P-51 as an excellent escort fighter. The Group's pilots had discovered in their first air combats that their P-51s could out-climb and out-turn FW190s, and at an altitude of 28,000 ft they were probably about 50 mph faster than their opponents, a marginal advantage which proved vital in the vicious air battles to come later in the year.

On the 5th January 1944, whilst on a escort mission to Kiel, the pilots claimed 18 enemy aircraft without loss, and six days later (11th January) when the Eighth mounted a large operation against the German aircraft industry at Halberstadt, Oschersleben and Brunswick, the American fighters achieved their best day so far with 28 victories, of which the Group claimed the lion's share with 15. Because of the adverse weather conditions over the target area some of the Bomb Groups were recalled,

Major James H. Howard of 356th Fighter Group at Boxted – January 1944. Major Howard was awarded the Medal of Honor shortly before this photograph was taken. (Smithsonian Institution)

and at one stage the 354th found themselves the only Fighter Group over Brunswick with the result that its pilots became heavily engaged in some fierce air combats.

Major James H. Howard, the CO of the 356th squadron, found himself temporarily alone when he sighted a formation of Luftwaffe fighters attacking B-17s of the 401st Bomb Group. Without waiting for his squadron to regroup around him, Major Howard went into the attack and he single-handedly fought off about 30 Me110s for almost 30 minutes. Howard accounted for three aircraft, probably three more and several others damaged. It was a brilliant and bravura performance, in fact Lieutenant Colonel Allison Brooks, who was leading the beleaguered B-17s said, 'It was a case of one lone American against what seemed to be the entire Luftwaffe.' Howard had previously served in the Pacific and had six-and-a-half Japanese victories to his credit. For his conspicuous bravery Major Howard was awarded the highest American gallantry award – the Congressional Medal of Honor. The citation read '... Colonel Howard continued his agressive action in an attempt to protect the bombers from numerous fighters. His skill, courage and intrepidity on this occasion set an example of heroism, which will be an inspiration to the Armed Forces of the United States.' Despite the view held in the RAF that 'the Americans handed out medals with the rations', there were less Medals of Honor awarded to American airmen in Europe than Victoria Crosses to RAF airmen. Major Howard proved to be the only American fighter pilot to receive this highly coveted award throughout the air war in Europe. By the middle of February he was given command of the Group.

For the next three months the Group was engaged on all the Eighth's major operations as its B-17s ranged deeper and deeper into Germany – Berlin, Tutow, Leipzig, Strasbourg, Schweinfurt, Regensburg, Merseburg and so on. Indeed it was not until 20th February that the Eighth's first assigned P-51 Group joined them on these long-range missions. Without doubt, the 354th pioneered the fighter tactics that were needed whilst escorting large formations of heavy bombers deep over Germany, their contribution to the Eighth's operations had been very influential. On 18th April they had flown their last escort mission for the Eighth. In the four months 55 missions had been completed with 169 enemy aircraft destroyed and 47 P-51s lost. Their leading squadron was the 353rd, who by the end of the war would account for nearly 300 aircraft – a squadron record unsurpassed in the USAAF.

When the P-51s departed for a new airfield at Lasheden in Kent, they were quickly followed into Boxted by one of the most famous Fighter Groups in the Eighth – the 56th or 'The Wolfpack'. This Group, under the inspired and brilliant leadership of Colonel Hubert Zemke, had established a fine reputation during its service at Halesworth in Suffolk. It was the first P-47 Group to enter operations with the Eighth and now had over a year's operational experience with these aircraft. Zemke, who was considered the finest Group leader in the Eighth and a superb fighter tactician, was fully aware of some of the shortcomings of the P-47 but he had developed tactics which ideally suited the assets of this remarkable fighter. The scarlet nosebands of the Group's aircraft had become a familiar sight in the Eighth Air Force. For most of its time at Boxted the 56th vied closely with the 4th Group at Debden for the right to claim the title of 'the most successful Fighter Group in the Eighth'.

So it was the trusty, if somehat ungainly, workhorses of the Eighth

One of the greatest American fighter pilots of the war – Colonel Hubert Zemke of the 56th Fighter Group. (USAF)

P-47s of No 62 squadron of 56th Fighter Group. (Smithsonian Institution)

Fighter Command that replaced the sleek P-51s at Boxted. The Republic P-47 was probably the most famous American single-seater fighter of the Second World War and was built in larger numbers than any other American fighter. It was variously described as the 'Jug' (short for Juggernaut), the 'Flying Milk Bottle' or some other even cruder names! The first prototype had flown in May 1941 and yet it was in service with the USAAF by September 1942. The aircraft was particularly different from contemporary fighters; it was heavy, almost twice the weight of the Spitfire but it was very rugged and proved capable of sustaining and surviving heavy damage. It did, however, suffer from restricted visibility over the nose so that the pilots had to weave to and fro whilst taxiing and they were described 'as moving like crabs'! Despite its bulk the aircraft was very fast, especially at high altitudes, and was probably the heaviest armed fighter of its time with quite devastating fire power. Although restricted by its lack of range the pilots of the 56th demonstrated just how effective and destructive the P-47 could be. The operational range of the aircraft was subsequently improved with the provision of two 150 US gallon jettisonable fuel tanks, which allowed it to fly more than 500 miles from base. By June 1944 there were over 20 P-47 Groups operating in the USAAF.

The change of airfield made little difference to the Group's missions or indeed its performance, except perhaps that the ground strafing of enemy airfields had increased, as did the use of the P-47 as a dive bomber. These operations were code-named as 'Jackpots' for airfield strikes and 'Chattanoogas' for transportation targets, especially railways and locomotives. The Group's pilots continued to add to their grand total with a remorseless efficiency and almost monotonous regularity. On 12th May 18 enemy aircraft were downed for the loss of three pilots with Captain R. Rankin becoming 'an ace in a day' with five Me109s destroyed. Indeed the 56th had more fighter 'aces' than any other Eighth Fighter Group, a situation that was maintained throughout the war.

The term 'ace' was really a relic of the First World War days. The French had first introduced the term and it was quickly taken up by the Germans and British. Both the Germans and the Americans used the term during the Second World War. The Americans required five positive victories in air combat whereas the Germans required double that number. The USAAF was particularly quick to recognise the promotional and propaganda value of its expert fighter pilots. On the other hand the RAF officially refused to acknowledge 'aces' as such, because it was considered 'bad for squadron morale'! Nevertheless DFCs were awarded for five kills and a bar for the next five, and the Air Ministry was quite happy to publicise the exploits of their most successful pilots without actually referring to them as 'aces'!

Several of the Group's top aces were no longer flying operationally, and on 20th July the 56th lost the Eighth's highest scoring ace – Lieutenant Colonel Francis 'Gaby' Gabreski, the 'Mad Pole' – who was shot down whilst strafing an airfield near Coblenz. He managed to evade capture for about five days before being captured. At the time Gabreski had 28 victories to his name – a total unsurpassed by any Eighth fighter pilot throughout the war. Gabreski had flown 13 sorties on Spitfires with No 315 RAF 'Polish' squadron. His nearest rival, with 27, was Major Robert Johnson, who also served in the 56th, but he had left for the States in May and although he returned to England he did not see any further action. Early in May another of the Group's famous 'aces' returned to Boxted to great celebrations. This was Major Walker Mahurin, who had been shot down on 27th March and had managed to evade capture with the help of the Dutch underground. On the night of 6th/7th May Major Mahurin was picked up by a Lysander of No 138 RAF squadron. Mahurin returned to the USA with 20 victories to his credit and he later served in the south-west Pacific.

During August the Group lost its brilliant leader. Zemke had decided to accept a fresh challenge – the command of the Eighth's newest Fighter Group, the 479th, at Wattisham in Suffolk. It had just lost its CO in action and it had not been performing too well with its P-51s. However, the 56th was very fortunate in Zemke's replacement, Lieutenant Colonel David Schilling, who had been the Group's Executive Officer since November 1943. A rather flamboyant and very popular officer, Schilling was a fine pilot himself (he ended with 22½ victories) and he led the Group with some style and verve until the end of January 1945. Schilling stayed in the USAF after the war and he returned to serve in England but sadly was killed in a car accident in Suffolk in 1956.

On 17th September the Eighth's four remaining P-47 Groups were given the difficult and dangerous task of destroying the flak batteries in the path of the Allied airborne forces landing in Holland. This airborne operation, known as 'Market Garden', has passed into military history for the courage and valour of all those taking part in the battles both in the air and on the ground. On the first day the Group survived the ordeal with the loss of just a single aircraft. But on the following day whilst supporting the second wave of airborne forces 16 of the Group's aircraft failed to return to Boxted; they were either shot down or crash-landed, several behind Allied lines with the pilots being rescued. All the aircraft were the victims of flak batteries and it proved to be the hardest day of the war for the Group. For the crews' actions over the two days the 56th was awarded its **second** Distinguished Unit Citation.

Two days before Christmas, as part of the Eighth's operations in support of the Ardennes campaign, the Group managed to notch up its best daily total when 32 Me109s and FW190s were destroyed. On this operation the Group's pilots were helped by MEW (Microwave Early Warning) Control, which was a mobile radar system with a range of more than 150 miles that could detect the direction and altitude of enemy aircraft and had been first introduced in August. Operations on both Christmas and Boxing Day netted another 11 victories with the loss of a single aircraft and by the end of the year the Group had claimed over 800 enemy aircraft destroyed either in the air or on the ground.

Despite the Group's astounding success with its P-47Ds, the aircraft was showing its age at least compared with its Luftwaffe opposition. In January 1945 the 56th was supplied with the improved P-47Ms, which hitherto had been only available to those Fighter Groups operating from airfields on the Continent. This mark had been provided with a more powerful engine and a better turbo-charger, which gave it a top speed of

473 mph at level flight (faster than the P-51D). Unfortunately several problems were experienced with the new models, and they became serious enough for some P-51s to arrive at Boxted in March, with the strong rumour that the Group was about to change its aircraft. The pilots were dismayed at the thought of this as most of them were utterly convinced that their trusty P-47s were far better and much safer fighters. Ultimately the problems with the P-47Ms were resolved and the 56th became the only Group in the Eighth to retain P-47s for the whole of the war.

Since the previous May there had been another P-47 unit operating from the airfield, the Air Sea Rescue squadron, which had been formed to supplement RAF services. Its Commanding Officer, Captain Robert Gerhart, who had previously served as an Air Sea Rescue controller at Saffron Walden, set up his headquarters in a deserted farmhouse with his aircraft parked at the north end of the airfield. They were basically 'war weary' P-47Cs with high operational flying hours. The squadron was made up of pilots and ground personnel from all the Eighth's Fighter Groups. The aircraft flew regular patrols during the whole period of a combat mission, and were armed with four .50 machine guns for their own protection, although on some patrols they were escorted by P-51s. On 30th June Lieutenant Tucker managed to bring down a V1 rocket over the English Channel to claim the squadron's only 'kill' of the war! In the New Year the unit moved to Halesworth in Suffolk, where it was redesignated the 5th Emergency Rescue squadron.

The rivalry between the 56th and the 4th at Debden to become the Eighth's top scoring Group grew in intensity during the final months of the war in Europe. On one amazing day in April (13th) the pilots returned to Boxted with claims of 95 enemy aircraft destroyed on the ground, but even this massive number was not sufficient to tilt the balance in the Group's favour. After the Group had flown their 447th and final mission on 21st April, their tally amounted to 985½ which was 70 short of the 4th's final total, though the 56th stoutly maintained that their rival's total included victories scored when its pilots had served with the RAF 'Eagle' squadrons! Nevertheless the 56th scored 674½ victories in air combat – more than any other Eighth Fighter Group – as well as claiming more 'aces', and furthermore had a very low loss rate considering the number of missions flown – 128 aircraft lost. Whatever the merits and demerits of the argument it was quite clear that both Fighter Groups made an immense contribution to the European air war. Like its close rivals the 56th was activated again after the Second World

War, returning to serve in East Anglia during 1948 with P-80s.

The Group remained at Boxted until October and then moved briefly to Little Walden. The RAF retained the airfield until August 1947 and during that time Spitfires, Mosquitos and Meteors were stationed there. Nowadays probably the best time to visit the old airfield, which is just off the A12 to the north-east of Colchester, is in spring when the large apple orchards, which now cover much of the old site, are in full bloom. Little remains to be seen but there is a rather fine memorial to the American units that served at Boxted, which was unveiled in 1992; it is unusual in that it has three runway lights incorporated into the design.

The memorial at Boxted.

6

BRADWELL BAY

Many visitors are attracted to this rather secluded stretch of the Essex coast, which borders the mouth of the river Blackwater. Depending on their interest or persuasion, most come to visit either the small Saxon church – St Peter's Chapel – which stands alone and forlorn on the edge of the marshes, or the Visitor's Centre of the massive nuclear power station just to the north of the village. Many of these visitors, I suspect, are blissfully unaware that nearby there was also a very active RAF wartime airfield known as Bradwell Bay.

The grey and brooding presence of the nuclear power station, which dates from the late 1950s, now towers over the site of the old airfield, much of which has long since disappeared. However, the long drive to Bradwell is rewarded by the discovery of a very striking and attractive memorial, probably the most impressive in the county. Its centrepiece is a large cast-iron model of a Mosquito and the memorial stone lists the names of 121 Allied airmen 'who in answer to the call to duty left the airfield to fly into the blue forever.'

The Air Ministry had recognised the value of the area before the outbreak of the Second World War when a small landing ground was established solely as a refuelling point for RAF aircraft using the air-firing range over Dengie Flats. During 1940, in the desperate urgency to locate suitable land for airfields, especially in the south-east, the strategic value of the site was acknowledged. The Luftwaffe also realised the importance of the airfield because in the early morning of 4th September 1940, before construction work had really commenced, the field was bombed, but not very successfully. Two concrete and

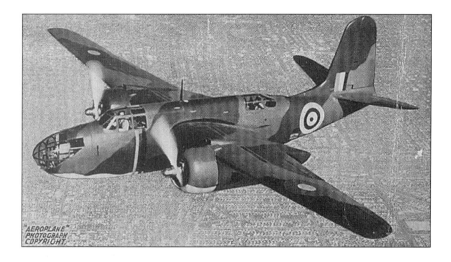

Douglas Boston III: In April 1942 No 418 (Canadian) squadron arrived with these aircraft.

tarmac runways were laid in 1941 and on 28th November the airfield opened. It was allocated to No 11 Group of Fighter Command and placed in the Hornchurch Sector. Although available for operations by January 1942, the severe winter conditions caused a delay in its opening with the result that the first operational squadron did not appear until the middle of April.

It was a Canadian unit that flew in on the 15th from RAF Debden. No 418, probably better known as the 'City of Edmonton', had recently been formed as a night-intruder squadron. It was equipped with American aircraft – Douglas Boston IIIs – on which the Canadian airmen had spent most of their time at Debden working up to operational readiness. Life had not been easy. Shortage of aircraft and the harsh winter had prolonged their training programme and four crews had been killed in training accidents during the period; in fact another three crews would come to grief on training flights from Bradwell Bay before any lives were lost in action.

The twin-engined Boston had originally been designed as a light day-bomber for the French Air Force during 1939, but with the fall of France the RAF took up the order. Because of the dire shortage of night-fighters, the early RAF Bostons were modified into night-fighters and redesignated Havocs. Ultimately the Mark IIIs were used in a bombing role as one of the replacements for the doughty Bristol Blenheims of No 2 Group of Bomber Command. These reliable and versatile light bombers, then designated A-20 Havocs, would later operate with distinction in the Ninth Air Force from three Essex airfields.

The squadron's Bostons were specially adapted for their night intruding role. They were painted black, equipped with flame damping exhausts and fitted with a belly pack of four 20 mm cannons. The crews' main task was to patrol enemy airfields at night, especially during bomber raids to pick off enemy night-fighters on landing or taking-off. Their first success came in May over Gilze airfield in Holland when, attacking from about 5,000 feet, an enemy aircraft was destroyed just as it touched down. They were also involved in 'train busting' – a task well suited to the aircraft as it was designed for low-level attack. Amongst other operations the Canadians went out to drop propaganda leaflets and lost four crews on these rather futile operations; literally billions of leaflets were dropped during the Second World War and it is debatable whether they had any material effect on those who read them – the *Punch* magazine facetiously called them 'bombphlets'! The costs of printing and despatching what was to be equivalent to 30 leaflets for every man, woman and child in Western Europe were colossal and far outweighed the propaganda value.

During the famous '1,000' bomber raid on Cologne in May the squadron was involved in attacks on enemy fighter airfields in advance of the main bomber stream. In the ill-fated Dieppe 'Jubilee' operation two Bostons were detailed to lay a smokescreen. One turned back because of engine trouble and the other was shot down by a Ju88 over the English Channel; all the three crewmen managed to get into a dinghy and were rescued but sadly the pilot died the following day.

The squadron's time at Bradwell Bay was not really a conspicuous success with the crews well aware that they were in the front line. On the night of 13th/14th February the airfield was attacked and a Ju88 was shot down by anti-aircraft fire, crashing near Burnham-on-Crouch. The Luftwaffe returned the next night but all the bombs fell wide of the airfield. Within a month the Canadians had moved further south to Ford in Sussex, where they converted to Mosquitos and from then on the squadron's fortunes changed dramatically for the better. No 418 became a most successful Mosquito fighter squadron and its later exploits have been excellently recounted by one of its members, Dave McIntosh, in his book *Terror in the Starboard Seat*.

The Canadian crews would not have been totally unfamiliar with the

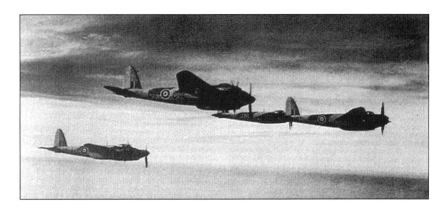

De Havilland Mosquitos; Bradwell Bay became known for its Mosquito squadrons.

sight and sounds of this 'wonder' aircraft because from August to December they had shared the airfield with No 23 squadron, which had recently been re-equipped with Mosquito IIs. The de Havilland Mosquito was, without doubt, the most exciting, versatile and successful aircraft of the Second World War. As is suggested by the memorial, Bradwell Bay became famous for the number of Mosquito squadrons flying various versions of this spectacular aircraft.

The aircraft had been first planned in 1938 and was another example – like the Bristol Blenheim – of development by private enterprise rather than to an Air Ministry specification. The concept of a twin-engined, high speed unarmed wooden aircraft was treated with disdain by the Air Ministry, but despite this lack of official commitment Geoffrey de Havilland, the designer and manufacturer, had enough faith to persevere with the project. The aircraft did have one dedicated and devoted official supporter – Air Marshal Sir William Freeman – who was the Air Member of the Air Council for Development and Production. It was he who ordered the first 50 Mosquitos for the RAF against strong opposition, and in the early days of the project the aircraft became known as 'Freeman's Folly'!

Following the first flight in November 1940 the trials were rushed through in just three months. The first Mosquito arrived in the Service in July 1941 and was used on photographic reconnaissance work. It was powered by two Rolls Royce Merlin engines and claimed speeds in excess of 350 mph, although later marks would exceed 400 mph. It was originally designed as a 'light' bomber, but a fighter version was quickly developed and appeared in the spring of 1942. In its very many versions over 7,700 were produced during the war, not only in Britain but also in Canada and Australia. The Mosquito operated with equal facility as a high or low-level bomber, day or night-fighter, an anti-shipping strike bomber, and perhaps achieved its greatest success with the Pathfinder Force of Bomber Command. However, it was the many brave and thrilling low-level bombing raids undertaken by various Mosquito squadrons that captured the attention and admiration of the British public, and many of these operations have since passed into RAF folklore.

No 23 squadron, under the admirable and forceful command of Wing Commander P. G. Wykeham-Barnes, DSO, DFC and bar, pioneered long-range intruder sorties over the Continent. At the end of the year the squadron was sent to Malta to continue these operations in support of the Allied landings in Sicily and Italy. Some Mosquitos of No 264 squadron used Bradwell Bay during the spring of 1943 before the next permanent Mosquito squadron – No 157 – arrived from Castle Camps in Cambridgeshire. When it departed for Hunsdon in Hertfordshire in May, it was replaced with yet another Mosquito squadron – No 29 – which was in the process of exchanging its Beaufighters for Mosquito XIIs. This was a special night-fighter version which was equipped with Mark 8 airborne radar. Unfortunately the squadron's first victim happened to be a Hurricane shot down in error but within days the pilots had made amends with its first enemy victim – a Ju88. This proved to be the start of a most successful year for the squadron and by November it had amassed a tally of 60 enemy aircraft destroyed.

A change of fighter sector control at the beginning of June – North Weald for Hornchurch – resulted in the first appearance at Bradwell Bay of Typhoon 1Bs with the arrival of No 247 'China' squadron, followed a month or so later by Nos 198 and 56. In the short period they were operating from the airfield the pilots were engaged on a variety of operations; patrolling the coasts to counter any Luftwaffe daylight raids on coastal targets and towns, shipping attacks along the Dutch coast and some bombing missions over northern France and Holland. When these squadrons departed, they were replaced by a New Zealand squadron – No 488 – which, together with No 605 squadron (arriving about a month later) was destined to operate from Bradwell Bay for the next eight months. These two squadron's thus became the longest residents at the airfield.

Hawker Tempest V of No 501 squadron.

It perhaps goes without saying that both squadrons were equipped with Mosquitos. The New Zealanders were largely engaged in night-fighter operations over London and the Thames Estuary and in September claimed a Heinkel 111 and a Dornier 217 in one night. Then on November 8th the squadron shot down its first Me410, a fast twin-engined fighter/bomber the Luftwaffe used for intruder raids over the East Anglian coast. This aircraft was targeted off Clacton and was one of three destroyed on that night. During the winter of 1943/4 No 488's total of enemy aircraft destroyed steadily increased, especially when the Luftwaffe launched 'Operation Steinbock' – a fresh night offensive against London. But perhaps the squadron's most impressive performance was on the night of 21st/22nd March 1944 when a special Luftwaffe bomber force set out to destroy the Marconi works at Chelmsford. This was later thought to be a reprisal raid for the RAF's heavy attacks on the Philips works in Holland. On this night the squadron's pilots claimed five Ju88s, all flying in the leading or 'pathfinder' formation.

No 605 was equipped with FB VIs, a fighter-bomber mark which was capable of carrying two 500 pound bombs. The squadron was commanded by Wing Commander B. R. O'B. Hoare, DSO, DFC and bar, who a year earlier had served at Bradwell in charge of No 23 squadron. One of the squadron's most successful days was on 5th March when its pilots managed to bag two Me109s and a FW190, and by now the 605th was coming close to 100 victories. In May both squadrons left the airfield and were allocated duties with the 2nd Tactical Air Force in the run-up to the invasion of Europe.

One of the most devastating single-seat fighters of the war made its appearance at Bradwell during April 1944 – the Hawker Tempest V, directly developed from the successful and rugged Typhoon. It had a maximum speed in excess of 430 mph, which compared very favourably with all contemporary Spitfire marks. At low-level it had the edge on all fighters, be they Allied or German, and even when the Luftwaffe's dreaded turbo-jet fighter – the Me 262 – began to appear in October 1944, it was found that the Tempests could out-dive them. Certainly the Tempest was a powerful, strong and highly manoeuvrable aircraft that was said to be 'a pleasure to fly'. A Luftwaffe test pilot, on evaluating a captured Tempest, was forced to admit, '... this exceptional aircraft is an improvement on the Typhoon, which in performance and aerodynamics was quite stunning...but there is no doubt about this one; the Tempest is an impressive highly powered aeroplane by any standards.' – praise indeed! It was a ground strike aircraft par excellence but perhaps its true métier was found in countering the V1 rockets; over one third of those shot down by the RAF felt to the Hispano cannons of the Tempests.

The Tempests belonged to the oldest squadron in the RAF – No 3 – which was formed on 13th May 1912, and as its motto recalled 'The Third shall be first'. The squadron made only a fleeting visit to Bradwell Bay before moving on to Newchurch in Kent. However, these aircraft would return in September and would become very familiar to the locals especially during the winter of 1944/5. By then the airfield had the advantage of FIDO, which was short for Fog Investigation Dispersal Operation, or as the RAF later maintained it should more properly be called 'Fog, Intensive, Dispersal Of'! Basically FIDO was a system where large pipelines were laid along each side of the runway. Petrol was injected under pressure and then fired by burners set at certain intervals along the pipeline. The intense heat created caused an up-draught that dispersed the fog near the runway, making it possible to keep the airfield open during adverse weather conditions. At the time Bradwell Bay was the only airfield in Essex to be provided with this excellent facility.

During April the airfield resounded to the distinctive roar of Rolls Royce Merlin engines – the first Spitfires had landed. No 124 squadron had come from Church Fenton in Yorkshire with a flight of a specially developed version of the famous fighter – Mark VIIs. These Spitfires were dedicated high-altitude aircraft, powered by the two-speed, supercharged Merlin 61 engines. The fuseleges had been re-designed and supplied with pressurised cockpits, as well as retractable tail wheels, but the most immediate difference was an increased wing span and the pointed wings. With a maximum speed in excess of 400 mph at 25,000 feet and a service ceiling of 43,000 feet they were particularly suitable for bomber escort duties. The squadron was the first to be equipped with the new mark and only four more would operate with VIIs. During July the squadron reverted to the more familiar and 'normal' IXs, which along with the Mark Vs were built in far greater quantities than any other versions.

The last quarter of 1944 was one of the busiest periods for the airfield. From the last day of August until almost the end of the year a Spitfire IX Wing operated from it and three squadrons – Nos 64, 126 and 611 – were engaged on bomber escorts. Then from from the middle of September the pilots were involved in anti-diver operations. By now the Allied armies had captured all the launching sites in northern France, and the Germans were forced to resort to launching the V1 rockets from specially adapted Heinkel 111s from about 50 miles off the English coast out in the North Sea.

To assist in this task a Tempest squadron, No 501, one of the famous auxiliary squadrons, was drafted in during September. It was also known as the 'County of Gloucester' and under its admirable commander, Squadron Leader Joseph Berry, DFC and bar, had gained a fine reputation against the V1s, claiming over 100 kills. Squadron Leader Berry had the highest individual tally of any RAF pilot – 61½ destroyed. But 501 was no 'one-man band' as there were another seven pilots that could claim to be rocket 'aces'. Sadly, Squadron Leader Berry was killed in action during October 1944 whilst the squadron was operating in support of the Allied armies. The Tempests from Bradwell Bay and Newchurch did particularly well to destroy over 50 V1 rockets during this period. Although No 501 stayed at Bradwell Bay until March 1945, their battle against the V1 had ended when the last air-launched rockets fell on 14th January.

Like others that were situated close to the coast, the airfield became involved in air sea rescue operations with Coastal Command. One of the Command's squadrons – No 278 – was based at Bradwell Bay with a flight of Spitfires out-housed just up the coast at Martlesham Heath. The squadron operated Vickers Warwicks and the amphibian Supermarine Walruses. The Warwicks had originally been designed as heavier contemporary bombers to the successful Wellingtons, but their

The impressive memorial at Bradwell.

performance fell short of what was demanded by Bomber Command, so they were handed over to Coastal Command, who used them mainly on air sea rescue work. Warwicks of 'B' Flight undertook the pioneer work on airborne lifeboats, the first being dropped on five parachutes in early May 1943. Ultimately four air sea rescue Warwick squadrons were specially adapted to take the two models of lifeboats, and they were instrumental in saving many aircrews' lives. The air sea rescue unit remained at Bradwell Bay until January 1945 although the Warwicks left in the autumn.

In the early months of 1945 a Czech Spitfire Wing, comprising three squadrons, Nos 310, 312 and 313, was variously engaged on anti-diver patrols with bomber escorts thrown in for good measure. It must be admitted that the action was not particularly hectic as during January only a handful of operations were mounted, and perhaps that was the reason for the Wing's move further south to Manston in the following month. The Tempests also disappeared and they were replaced, rather appropriately, by a Mosquito night-fighter squadron – No 151 – which was largely engaged on bomber support duties. It was joined about a week later by a flight of Mosquito NF 30s only to be followed later in

March by the whole squadron.

After Canadians and New Zealanders, it seemed appropriate that a Royal Australian Air Force squadron – No 456 – should come and make a home at 'Bradwell-juxta-Mare'. It was commanded by Wing Commander B. Howard, DFC and not too many Australian airmen were now left! This squadron had been formed in June 1941 and it had been equipped with all the major night-fighters, from Defiants and Beaufighters to the superb Mosquito NF 30. The Australian squadron was destined to finish its war at Bradwell Bay and it was formally disbanded on 15th June, although No 151 squadron had already left for Cornwall.

Flying activity had not come to an end at Bradwell; for some weeks during July and August 1945, No 25 Squadron used the airfield flying Mosquito NF 30s. Perhaps no more fitting finale could have been envisaged for this airfield than that one of the most famous aircraft of the Second World War should bring down the curtain on RAF Bradwell Bay, especially as No 25 squadron had operated from another Essex airfield – North Weald – way back in those dark days of the winter of 1940. The Air Ministry decided to close the airfield in 1946 and it rapidly disappeared under farming.

7

CHIPPING ONGAR

The Essex Way, the 81 mile long path which stretches across the county from Epping to Harwich, passes along the edge of the old Second World War airfield officially named Chipping Ongar, although it was, and still is, universally known as Willingale airfield. This name comes from the small village which is a short distance to the north-east of the site of the airfield, but Willingale's main claim to fame is that its two old churches share the same churchyard. The wartime airfield was set in the Roding valley, the heart of some of the finest farmland in the whole of Essex, which until the launching of the Essex Way could be said to be part of '...deepest Essex where few explore...'

The peace and tranquillity of the village was rudely broken in August 1942 when the men of the 831st Engineer Aviation Battalion arrived to carve out a Class A bomber station with the usual runways, perimeter road and hard-standings. Most of the various technical and accommodation sites were dispersed in the surrounding countryside close to Willingale. Much of the hardcore for the construction work came from the blitzed buildings of the East End of London. The airfield had been allocated to the Eighth Air Force, and it was selected to house a heavy Bomb Group of the planned 5th Bomb Wing. This Wing never materialised so the airfield, which was ready for occupation in the early summer of 1943, was appropriated for a Medium Bomb Group then completing its training in the United States.

The 387th Bomb Group had been constituted on November 25th and activated at the beginning of December 1942 at MacDill Field, Florida, where the crews trained on their B-26s. They left for the United

The reviewing stand at the dedication of Station 162 (Chipping Ongar). (via Derek Aspinell)

Kingdom in early June 1943, flying from Godman Field, Kentucky, via the northern ferry route to Prestwick in Scotland. The first B-26s began to arrive at Chipping Ongar on 21st June and by the beginning of July the ground personnel, who had come over on the *Queen Mary*, had also completed their long journey. The four squadrons – 556th to 559th – of B-26s under the command of Colonel Carl R. Storrie would now require some intensive training operating at medium altitudes before the crews would be allowed out on their first operation. The 387th was the last of the four B-26 Groups of the 3rd Bomb Wing to take up residence in Essex.

In line with RAF squadrons, each Eighth Air Force squadron had an identification code and from the autumn of 1942 all USAAF units operating in the United Kingdom were integrated into the British system and issued with letters that had not previously been used by the RAF. For example, the letters FW, KS, KX and TQ marked the 556th to 559th respectively. Later in October 1943 the Group adopted black and yellow diagonal bands on the tails of their aircraft as a further aid to identification. However, the American airmen also devised their own squadrons' badges – for example, the 559th's emblem was a frog leaning on a cloud with a 'comic' bomb hidden behind its back! Missions flown by the aircraft were denoted by yellow or black bomb symbols, and small swastikas indicated enemy aircraft destroyed by the gunners.

From 'time immemorial' airmen had given their aircraft personalised

Sky Queen *of 559 squadron completed 134 missions. (via Derek Aspinell)*

names, which were frequently depicted on the noses of the aircraft. During the Second World War these illustrations on USAAF aircraft became a famous art form – 'nose art'. The most notable and eye-catching examples were those of scantily clothed young ladies in a variety of poses, some of which were sexually quite explicit; just how much so depended on the attitude taken by the Group's Commanding Officer! The quality of the pictures depended greatly on the artistic talent available at each airfield, but many were inspired by the paintings of the famous 'pin-up' artist, Vargas, which appeared regularly in the *Esquire* magazine and on calendars. Some of the aircraft at Chipping Ongar bore such names as *Milk Run Special, Black Magic, Texas Queen, Suzie* and *Sky Queen* – the latter completed 134 missions. Even the CO's personal aircraft had a name – *Bat Outa Hell II*! Of course, the RAF crews and pilots also named their aircraft but generally speaking their illustrations were somewhat more subdued and decorous than those of the USAAF.

The crews went out on their first mission on 31st July, within a month of their arrival, although it was nothing more sinister than a diversionary flight over Dunkirk (which would earn a duck symbol on the side of the aircraft). Nevertheless the B-26s were still escorted by a strong force of RAF Spitfires. Two days later another diversionary mission was made and it was not until 15th August that 36 aircraft left Chipping Ongar to bomb St Omer/Ft Rouge airfield. At least 31 crews managed to bomb the target and 18 returned with flak damage as evidence of the strength of the flak defences around these airfields. For the rest of the month another five bombing missions were directed against various airfields and one power station (at Rouen). On 31st, whilst engaged in attacking Lille/Vendeville airfield, the 387th lost its first B-26 in action, always a sad and very sobering occasion for the rest of the crews.

Early in September the B-26s were actively engaged on 'Operation Starkey' – the Allied Forces' attempt to convince the enemy that a full-scale invasion was imminent on the Pas de Calais coast. It was a concentrated air offensive against communication centres and airfields near the Channel coast by the RAF and the Eighth Air Force. So thorough was the subterfuge that at the first briefings the crews were told that the invasion fleet had already sailed! From 2nd to 9th September the Group attacked airfields, railway centres and coastal defences, and on a few days two missions were launched. The last of the 'Starkey' operations came on 9th when the defences at Boulogne were once again the target. The 387th was the last of the four Essex Groups to take off, and at a quarter to nine in the morning the airfield was shrouded in a heavy ground mist with visibility down to less than 100 yards. Nevertheless the 54 crews (a maximum effort) were ordered to make an instrument take-off and unfortunately one B-26 crashed off the end of the runway; only the tail gunner survived the crash. Over 200 B-26s attacked the target in waves every 15 minutes for a total of two hours with over 330 tons of bombs being dropped. In the whole mission three B-26s were shot down by flak, one coming from the 387th. On return another aircraft crash-landed at the airfield. It had been the hardest day so far for the Group with three B-26s destroyed and eleven airmen killed or missing in action.

It was quite rare for the B-26s to suffer at the hands of the Luftwaffe, as their RAF Spitfire escorts normally managed to hold the enemy fighters at bay. On these B-26 operations the RAF fighters usually outnumbered the B-26s in a ratio of 4:1, which was a far greater proportion than the escorts provided for their 'heavy brothers'. But on 27th September, just after completing their bombing run over Beauvais/Tille airfield a force of FW190s suddenly appeared to make a determined strike at one of the Group's formations. One B-26 was badly hit setting one of the engines on fire. The aircraft *Wuneach* quickly lost height and the four gunners were ordered to bale out, but then with great skill the pilot, Lieutenant George Snyder, managed to coax his badly damaged aircraft back to

Lucky Lou of 559 squadron at Chipping Ongar. (via Derek Aspinell)

Chipping Ongar and make a successful belly-landing. On this mission the Group's gunners entered their first claim of enemy fighters destroyed – two, with another probable. Their first aerial combat with the Luftwaffe had passed tolerably well with just one 'write-off' and another twelve aircraft damaged.

The Group flew only another four missions with the Eighth Air Force, the last coming on 9th October when along with the 323rd (at Earls Colne) they attacked Woensdrecht airfield. In 29 missions for the Eighth, the Group had lost four B-26s in action, and now they were transferred to operate with the Ninth Air Force. Along with the 323rd Group they formed the new 98th Bomb Wing, to provide a core of experience, when the other two Groups (394th and 397th) would become operational. It is very doubtful whether the crews noticed any dramatic change, except from 8th November when a new 'Old Man' – as the Commanding Officers were universally known, irrespective of their ages – arrived at Chipping Ongar; he was Colonel Jack Caldwell, who would remain with the Group for the next five months.

Although the weather during November was not really conducive to operational flying, the Ninth still managed to mount twelve missions. Again airfields came in for special treatment, and on 26th the Group left on a morning mission to Cambrai/Epinoy airfield but the heavy clouds

B-26 flown by Colonel Thomas M. Seymour, CO of 387th Bomb Group, which crashed on 17th July 1944, killing Colonel Seymour. (via Derek Aspinell)

over northern France somewhat frustrated accurate bombing. In the afternoon the crews were briefed for 'construction works' at Audinghem, which, of course they did not know at the time, would prove to be their first strike at V1 rocket sites. Over the next three months or so the sites would figure rather large in their operational schedules. The difficulty in locating these sites was highlighted on 31st December when the Group's crews dropped 23 tons of bombs on an uninhabited wood about 24 miles south of the primary target.

In the New Year operations certainly stepped up a gear with the Ninth launching 1,740 individual sorties and dropping over 1,500 tons of bombs all for the loss of just four B-26s. Once and for all the B-26 crews had demolished the long-held belief that the B-26 was a 'killer' aircraft. Of course, the Ninth's B-26s had been somewhat modified since the days when it had gained its sorry reputation – most notably a six feet increase in the wing span and larger tail surfaces. The B-26 had proved an excellent and safe medium bomber, at least when in the hands of experienced crews, and its operational record made mockery of one of its earlier nicknames – 'the flying coffin'!

During February the USAAF launched its major offensive against the German Air Force and aircraft industry, which became known as 'The Big Week' – 20th to 25th February. Most historical records concentrate on the Eighth Air Force's operations during this week, and almost ignore the contribution made by the Ninth Bomber Command. The unfavourable weather conditions precluded any B-26 operations until 24th when the 387th attacked with some effect the airfield at Leeuwarden, which was then the deepest penetration mission for the Group. Although the heavy cloud formations on the following day were not really suitable, the Group managed to mount another mission when the airfield at Venlo was bombed.

It was during this month that the Ninth conducted an investigation into the bomb-carrying capabilities of its B-26s. The aircraft normally carried a bomb load of six 500 pound GP (General Purpose) bombs or ten 250 pound bombs; but it had been discovered that B-26s operating in the Mediterranean appeared to carry eight 500 pounders. When the Ninth looked into the matter, it was disclosed that a newer type of bomb was being used which was provided with a lug to convert it to naval use; this lug effectively prevented eight being used in B-26s. After conducting some experiments with obsolete bombs, it was confirmed that the capacity of the B-26s could be increased; therefore the lugs were physically removed at the Ninth's depots with the result that the maximum bomb capacity of the aircraft was increased by 1,000 pounds or an extra 36,000 pounds of HE (High Explosives) on a normal Group operation. This partially accounts for the Ninth's biggest total so far – in February over 3,280 tons were dropped.

During March besides airfields, the Group was engaged in attacking rocket sites, as well as marshalling yards for the first time. This was especially so on 20th and 23rd when the 387th attacked the Creil railway yards. Then on 26th the B-26s made their famous return to the E and R boatyards at Ijmuiden. All the Groups took part in this operation, with over 340 aircraft attacking with 1,000 pound Semi-Armour Piercing bombs. These bombs proved to be sadly inadequate for the task and they had little or no effect on the strongly reinforced boat shelters. The crews were not aware that this major operation was not a conspicuous success, although fortunately all survived the mission.

From now on until D-Day the 387th attacked a variety of strategic targets – airfields, bridges and coastal batteries, and like most of the Groups their losses were minimal, though many B-26s returned home with heavy flak damage. On 25th May a B-26, rather inappropriately named *Lucky Lady* experienced a complete instrumental failure shortly after take-off and the pilot was forced to make an emergency landing at the airfield, with the aircraft finally crashing into some trees. Indeed throughout the European air war one in three of the USAAF aircraft 'lost' were due to accidental causes.

On D-Day the 387th bombed along the Normandy coast and for the rest of the month the crews gave air support by attacking railway bridges, road bridges and junctions, fuel dumps, fortified positions and radar stations. It was clear that the operational range of the B-26s was beginning to restrict the choice of targets, therefore the Ninth Bomber Command decided to move the 98th Bomb Wing into airfields in Hampshire as they became available. The 387th was scheduled to move into Stoney Cross once it had been vacated by the 367th Fighter Group and when this Group moved out on 6th July the 387th prepared to bid farewell to Chipping Ongar and Essex.

Before the Group finally left Essex, it suffered a sad and tragic loss when its popular Commanding Officer, Colonel Thomas M. Seymour, who had been in charge since 13th April, was killed in a accident on 17th July, whilst he was attempting to land his B-26 on one engine. The aircraft crashed just short of the airfield; Colonel Seymour was the sole occupant of the aircraft at the time. His successor, Colonel Grover C. Brown, commanded the Group until the end of the war. The following day the Group left on its last mission from Chipping Ongar. Since coming under the aegis of the Ninth Air Force it had completed 204 missions and had lost ten aircraft in action. The 387th became one of the first B-26 Groups to leave Essex, departing on 21st July. It later operated from three airfields in France and Maastricht in Holland, from where the Group was awarded a Distinguished Unit Citation for its operations during the Ardennes campaign.

Chipping Ongar airfield was now allocated to the Air Disarmament Command (as was Boreham) but very little flying took place and by January the Americans gave up the airfield. During the middle of March the airfield once more came to life when 80 C-47s of 61st Troop Carrier Group arrived from their 'new' French airfield at Abbeville. The Group had received a DUC for their operations during D-Day. On 24th March the C-47s loaded up troops of the British 6th Airborne Division and left the airfield on 'Operation Varsity'. The Group lost one aircraft on the operation and the rest of the C-47s returned directly to their home base at Abbeville.

Over the next three years the airfield was under the control of the RAF's Technical Training Command with only a small presence of RAF personnel. Although the RAF departed in October 1948, it was almost eleven years later that the Ministry of Defence relinquished the airfield. During the 1970s the name of Willingale came again to the fore as one of the many possible sites for the proposed third airport for London. There was a very strong and active local opposition to such a proposal, and posters bearing the words 'No to Willingale Airport' and 'Last Wings over Willingale...1945. Keep it that way. NO Airport' began to appear around the area. This campaign proved successful as the International Airport at nearby Stansted testifies! Some vestiges of the old airfield remain – part of the main runway, some hard-standings and a few ruined workshops. Nevertheless the history and exploits of the 387th Bomb Group are excellently recalled and illustrated in the Airscene Museum, which is housed in Blake Hall at nearby Bobbingworth; the museum is open at weekends from Easter to September.

8

DEBDEN

This airfield, about two miles to the south-east of Saffron Walden, owes its existence to the expansion of the RAF during the mid-1930s. Debden was planned to accommodate three fighter squadrons and it opened in April 1937, but it was still being extended during 1940 with the provision of two concrete runways, additional taxiways and further buildings. During the Second World War a greater variety of Allied fighters operated from Debden than any other Essex airfield; but its early wartime fame rested with its Hurricane squadrons, this was well before the airfield became celebrated as 'the Eagles' Nest' – home of one of the finest and most successful USAAF Fighter Groups – the 'Fighting Fourth'.

In September 1939 Debden was a Sector airfield in No 12 Group of Fighter Command, but during the height of the Battle of Britain it would be transferred to No 11 Group. There were three squadrons at the airfield – No 29 with Blenheim 1Fs and Nos 85 and 87 equipped with Hurricane 1s. Like all RAF squadrons their aircraft would be quickly marked on their fuselages with their new identification codes, the pre-war codes having been comprehensively revised. The bold block letters were normally placed to the front of the RAF rondels, thus 'RO', 'VY', 'LK' would distinguish these squadrons respectively throughout the war.

The Hurricane, which became such a feature of the airfield, had been designed by Sidney Camm, Hawker's chief designer, and the first prototype flew in November 1935. The Air Ministry deliberated for about three months before accepting the aircraft and placing an order for

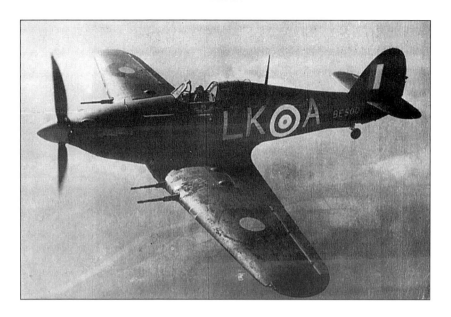

Hurricane of No 87 squadron, stationed at Debden from June 1937. (RAF Museum)

600, although in 1938 this figure was increased to 1,000. Ultimately over 14,000 were produced in the various marks. The first Hurricanes were powered by Rolls Royce Merlin II engines, armed with eight .303 machine guns, and were capable of a top speed of 330 mph. When they entered the Service in December 1937 (with No 111 squadron) they ushered in a new and glorious era for Fighter Command as the first monoplane fighters. Although slower than both the Spitfire and the Luftwaffe's Me109, the Hurricane was a very sturdy and reliable aircraft, highly manoeuvrable, able to withstand considerable damage, and its pilots accounted for more victories in the Battle of Britain than those of its more illustrious rival – the Spitfire. The 'Hurry', as it was fondly called, inspired great loyalty in its pilots, and there was always a keen and heated debate as to which was the better fighter.

Within a week of the outbreak of the war the two Hurricane squadrons were despatched to France as part of the 60th Wing Field Force to provide tactical air support for the British Expeditionary Force. They were replaced by another Hurricane squadron, No 17, from Croydon, followed, a month later, by No 504. During the 'phoney war'

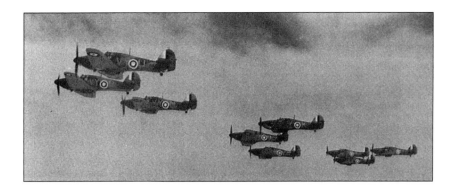

Hurricanes of No 85 squadron – July 1940. (via J. Adams)

the Debden squadrons saw little action and used both Wattisham and Martlesham Heath as forward landing grounds, the latter under the control of Debden's Operations Room. The Hurricanes provided air cover for east coast convoys as well routine patrols to seek out enemy intruders. The German offensive of May 1940 changed all that and both squadrons quickly became engaged in the air war over the Low Countries and France. On 11th May No 17's pilots scored their first victories – a Me109 and a Henschel Hs129 – but lost four aircraft in the process. Both squadrons were sent out to France and after eight days of bitter combat No 504 was left with just four serviceable aircraft! On 20th May the tattered remnants of No 60 Wing returned from France to regroup and of the three squadrons arriving back at Debden, only No 85 remained at the airfield.

The Station Commander at Debden, Wing Commander J. L. F. 'Larry' Fuller-Good maintained '... 85 to my mind will always be the First Fighter Squadron in the RAF...' During the First World War it had been commanded by two VC aces – Majors Bishop and Mannock – and had re-formed at Debden during 1938. Its motto 'We hunt by day and night', would prove to be rather prophetic. Within days of its return from France a new Commanding Officer was appointed, Squadron Leader Peter Townsend, DFC, one of the celebrated pilots of the war, who would lead the squadron until the summer of 1941. Other than a handful of 'veterans' the squadron was manned by inexperienced pilots, mostly with only ten hours flying time on Hurricanes. The squadron would use both Debden and the small satellite airfield at Castle Camps during the Battle of Britain.

Of all the Hurricane squadrons that operated in the Debden Sector during the Battle of Britain, perhaps No 17 had the hardest time as it was not 'rested'. It alternated between Tangmere, Martlesham Heath and Debden; although in the early days of the Battle, Debden was considered a 'quiet' Sector! The squadron had a fair sprinkling of Czech and Polish pilots, but perhaps its most colourful airman was Flying Officer Count Manfred Czernin, DFC. Of Austrian/English parentage he had joined the RAF during the 1930s, and had served with No 85 in France. By the end of October Czernin had twelve victories to his credit. Subsequently he was seconded to the SOE (Special Operations Executive) and was dropped behind enemy lines in northern Italy. He survived the war with a DSO and MC to add to his DFC.

The month of July was relatively quiet, although eight enemy aircraft were destroyed for the loss of two Hurricanes, one of which was piloted by Squadron Leader Townsend, who came down in the sea off Felixstowe on 11th. The following month the action over the Debden Sector became very hectic; this was especially so on 18th when No 85's pilots claimed ten victories for the loss of two aircraft with one pilot missing in action; sadly he was Flying Officer Richard Lee, DSO, DFC, a brilliant young pilot as can be judged from his decorations, who had nine enemy aircraft to his credit. No 257 squadron, which had recently arrived, added another three victories for the loss of one Hurricane. On the following day No 85 left for Croydon and it was replaced by the Hurricanes of No 601 'County of London' squadron, transferred to Debden for a 'rest and re-group'!

During the last week of August the airfield came in for some harsh treatment from the Luftwaffe. The raid on 26th resulted in substantial damage to many buildings and five fatal casualties. Five days later there was a heavier raid with further damage inflicted, including a couple of Hurricanes destroyed on the ground and another three fatalities. This attack temporarily reduced the operational capabilities of the station, with the result that the Sector Operations Room was moved away from the airfield and ultimately housed in the Saffron Walden Grammar School. During the month the Debden squadrons claimed 35 victories for the loss of seven Hurricanes.

The winter of 1940/1 saw the airfield become almost solely devoted to night-flying. The Beaufighter crews of No 25 squadron, which had arrived from North Weald, claimed their first victory on 15th November when a He111 was destroyed near Colchester. After a brief stay they were followed into Debden by the Defiants of No 264 squadron, which was now solely employed on night operations. The pilots of No 85 were also fully engaged on night operations with their Hurricanes. Throughout January they flew almost every night but with scant success, and some even trained on Defiants. It was not until 25th February that the squadron scored its first night victory when Squadron Leader Townsend destroyed a Do17. The Hurricane never really proved itself as a night fighter, so in February the squadron began to convert to Douglas Havocs or DB-7s – the night-fighter variant of this successful twin-engined American medium bomber. Equipped with AI radar and armed with eight machine guns in the nose, the Havoc became a useful 'stop-gap' until the Mosquitos appeared on the scene.

On 13th March a tragic flying accident was a considerable blow to No 85 squadron. A Havoc piloted by Pilot Officer Sammy Allard with Pilot Officers William Hodgson and Francis Walker-Smith as passengers was bound for Ford in Sussex to pick up another aircraft. Shortly after take-off the aircraft developed problems and it crashed not far from Debden, killing the three airmen. Allard had survived France and the Battle of Britain and was the squadron's highest scoring pilot with over 20 victories to his name. The other two pilots had served during the Battle of Britain. In fact, on 31st August 1940, Hodgson, a young New Zealand pilot who was nicknamed 'Ace' for his zeal, was about to bale out of his burning Hurricane when he realised he was over a heavily populated area – Wickford; with great skill and courage he guided the aircraft away to crash-land in a field near Shotgate. Today there is a road in Wickford called Hodgson Way and a memorial to him near the scene of his crash.

The Hurricane IIs of No 258 squadron became regularly engaged on 'Fighter Nights'. This was a system that had been first introduced in November 1940 whereby day fighters made night patrols over a certain height with the strict instructions to shoot down any aircraft with more than one engine! Although the squadron did gain some victories, several pilots were lost in these rather hazardous operations. In November the squadron was taken off operations prior to moving abroad to serve in Singapore.

With the departure of No 258 squadron, Debden became virtually a Spitfire station, except for the Douglas Bostons of another Canadian squadron – No 418 – which had been formed at Debden in November as a night-intruder unit. The Canadians experienced a shortage of aircraft and lost several crews in training whilst working up to operational readiness. They went out on their first mission to Ghent on 26th March, only to move on to Bradwell Bay during the following month.

The Debden Spitfire Wing became fully involved in Fighter Command's offensive war, with another small satellite airfield at Great Sampford becoming operational in April. A famous Battle of Britain pilot arrived in June to command the Wing, he was Wing Commander Raymond M. Duke-Woolley, DFC and bar. He assisted the 4th Fighter Group when it was formed and was later appointed the RAF Fighter Liaison Officer to the Eighth Air Force and became the first non-American airman to be awarded the DFC (US). Debden's days as a wartime RAF station were fast coming to a close. On 7th September 1942 it was allocated to the Eighth Air Force as a fighter station, although it was not officially transferred until May 1943. The three RAF 'Eagle' squadrons, Nos 71, 121 and 133, comprising in the main volunteer American pilots, would be disbanded and transferred to the USAAF to form the 4th Fighter Group.

On 29th September the three squadrons and their Spitfires were formally handed over by the AOC Fighter Command, Air Marshal Sir W. Sholto Douglas, in the presence of Major General Carl Spaatz and Brigadier General Frank Hunter, the Commander of the Eighth Fighter Command. The Air Marshal said '... We, of Fighter Command, deeply regret the parting. In the course of the past eighteen months we have seen the stuff of which you are made. We could not ask for better companions with whom to see this fight through to the finish...We shall watch your future with confidence...' The three squadrons had actually accounted for 71½ enemy aircraft, of which over half fell to No 71 squadron.

The officer selected to command this unique Fighter Group was Colonel Edward W. Anderson, who had been a pilot since 1928 and had come over to England with the first P-38 Groups. He was destined to see the Group through its first difficult ten months of operations before being promoted to Brigadier General in charge of 66th Fighter Wing, which had its headquarters at Saffron Walden. Anderson was fortunate to have some very experienced pilots, none more than Chesley C. 'Pete' Peterson, who had commanded No 71 squadron (now 334 squadron). Peterson was appointed the Group's Executive Officer at the age of 22 years becoming the youngest USAAF airman to attain the rank of Lieutenant Colonel. Another 'veteran' pilot was Donald J. M. Blakeslee, who became one of the highest scoring pilots with 15. Both later commanded the Group.

The Group had about 55 Spitfire VBs on complement and on 2nd

October 21 of them were sent on their first operation on behalf of the Eighth Air Force. It was a diversionary mission over St Omer airfield and the pilots had a most successful day, with four victories and no losses. Wing Commander Duke-Woolley, who was leading the American pilots, shared in the destruction of a FW190; it was certainly a promising entrance into the Eighth Air Force for the Group, which augured well for its future. Other than being far better compensated for their flying (the Americans' air pay was approximately four times that of the RAF pilots!) the 4th's pilots continued similar operations as when serving with the RAF – strafing, Rhubarbs, Circuses, shipping patrols and escorts for RAF Bostons.

Debden was considered the 'show place' of the Eighth's Fighter Command and a number of distinguished people visited the airfield. The first, Eleanor Roosevelt, arrived on 4th November, followed later by the US Ambassador to Britain, J. G. Winart, an experienced pilot himself whose son John would later serve as a bomber pilot with the Eighth Air Force in Suffolk. Many of the USAAF's 'Top Brass' felt that Debden was **the** place to visit. By the end of October 1942 the 4th was left as the only Fighter Group in the Eighth as the others had departed to North Africa to serve with the 12th Air Force.

During January 1943 some of the Group's most experienced pilots were sent to train on P-47s, several of them remaining to act as trainers. The pilots viewed the impending change of aircraft with very mixed feelings; most felt that the Spitfire was the best Allied fighter then in service, and the early reports of the P-47s were anything but complimentary. To their surprise they found that the 'Repulsive Scatterbolts' were 'a lot better than we had been led to believe' and, despite their reputation, the P-47s were able 'to out-turn and out-dive the FW190s but, unlike the Spitfire, could not out-climb them. They were not as pretty as the Spits but more rugged...' The first operation with P-47s took place on 10th March – a fighter sweep over Walcheren in Holland – and their last action with the Spitfires was mounted on 1st April 1943, although a single Spitfire was retained at Debden for sentimental reasons.

Not that the Group's pilots would realise it at the time but 13th April became a rather auspicious day, because on that day just four P-47s of No 56 Fighter Group joined the Eighth's operations from Debden. This Group would become the 4th's closest rival and there was intense competition between the two for the rest of the war. The very success of the 4th, the amount of publicity it received as the oldest Fighter Group in

*P-47s of 4th Fighter Group before taking off on a sweep over the Dutch coast –
May 1943. (Smithsonian Institution)*

the Eighth, and the superior attitude of its elitist pilots, engendered
a certain jealousy amongst other Fighter Groups, who had joined the
air war far later. Indeed the 4th's motto – 'The Fourth but First' – did
not endear them to the pilots of the other Groups, nor did the way that
they studiously fostered their connections with the RAF. The ex-Eagle
pilots wore their RAF wings on the right side of their uniform and the
three squadrons, 334 to 336, had royal crests incorporated into their
badges.

Two days later the 4th achieved its first victories with their P-47s –
three FW190s – with both Chesley Peterson and Don Blakeslee adding to
their score. As the the Eighth Air Force steadily grew, the 4th became
more engaged in escort missions and, on 28th July, it became the first
Fighter Group to penetrate German air space at Emmerich near the
Dutch/German border. This was because their aircraft were equipped
for the first time with jettisonable 100 gallon fuel tanks, which enabled
them to get a valuable extra 30 miles range. On this mission the pilots

111

The presentation of 60 silver medallions to the 'Eagle' pilots by Air Vice Marshal Sir Trafford Leigh-Mallory – Debden, 25th February 1943. (Smithsonian Institution)

claimed nine enemy aircraft for a single loss and two of them were credited to their CO, Colonel Anderson, who at the age of 39 years was considered 'ancient' for combat flying! From now onwards the pilots began to score quite heavily, and their best day so far was on 16th August, when they were supporting a B-17 force to aircraft repair depots in the Paris area and claimed 18 victories (then a record for the Eighth) with just a single loss.

At the end of the year Colonel Chesley Peterson, who had led the Group since August, left Debden and he was replaced by Donald Blakeslee. Under his spirited leadship the Group would achieve some of its greatest successes. A New Year's message went out from General Arnold to all Fighter Groups, which extolled them to 'Destroy the enemy air force wherever you find them, in the air, on the ground, and in the factory.' Certainly the 4th's pilots took this instruction to heart and they managed to deal with more than their fair share of the Luftwaffe's fighters.

P-47s at Debden – May 1943. (Smithsonian Institution)

During January the Group claimed 32 enemy aircraft for the loss of just two pilots. The following month was almost as successful with another 22 being added to the total. During the month the first P-51s appeared at the airfield, first only three – one for each squadron to be used for transition training. Blakeslee was utterly convinced of the worth of the new aircraft and was sure that his pilots would prove even more successful once they were experienced on P-51s. So keen was he to get his hands on these scarce aircraft that he assured General Kepner that he would 'have them on operations within twenty-four hours.' It was said that each pilot had less than one hour's flying on the new aircraft when they took them into action for the first time – on 25th of the month – but nevertheless they returned all intact and with evidence of yet another five enemy aircraft destroyed. Blakeslee was right because from then on the Group proceeded to make their presence felt with a vengeance.

March and April proved to be the most succesful period for the Group. From 4th March to 24th April, 189 enemy aircraft were destroyed in the air, with another 134 on the ground; for this splendid performance the 4th was awarded a DUC, a well-deserved recognition of the continuing excellence of the pilots – both veterans and newcomers. By now the Group had some of the top scoring fighter pilots of the Eighth Air Force – Captain Don Gentile (President Roosevelt called him 'Captain Courageous') was the leading ace, with Major Duane Beeson, Captain James Goodson and Lieutenants John Godfrey and Nicholas Megura. By the end of April the first two had departed, Gentile returning to the States as a test pilot and, sadly, Beeson being shot down by flak on 5th April, although he baled out and ended up as a prisoner. Four months later both Goodson and Godfrey had been shot down with 15 and 18 victories to their credit.

On 4th March the Group notched up another record – first American fighters to engage the Luftwaffe over Berlin. Days later the Group was back over Berlin again and scored heavily, with 14 victories for the loss of 4 pilots. On the next day Berlin was again the target and 16 enemy fighters fell to the 4th's pilots with Lieutenants Godfrey and Megura each claiming two. It was not total success as some missions could be costly, as on 21st March when the Group carried out a ground strafe of the Bordeaux area, losing seven P-51s to heavy and accurate flak. At the end of April the Group had passed a notable milestone – 500 victories – and in the process overtook its close rivals, who had recently moved into an Essex airfield at Boxted.

As with all Fighter Groups the 4th flew an endless number of missions on D-Day and the immediate days after the landings. On D-Day, when using Ashford in Kent as a forward base, they lost the highest number of fighters – ten. The next day although only one aircraft was lost to enemy action, two collided shortly after taking-off, one pilot was killed but the other managed to land his badly damaged aircraft. More losses came on the following days and when the Fighter Groups returned to major German targets once again, the Group lost another three aircraft.

The Group was about to go on its travels. On 21st June its P-51s escorted a force of B-17s of the Third Bomb Division bombing oil targets south of Berlin, whilst en route to the Soviet Union where they would land. This long and physically demanding mission was the first of the 'Frantic' shuttle operations, which had been largely mounted to placate Stalin, but also to enable the Eighth to bomb targets in Poland. The pilots landed at Piryatin airfield in the Ukraine after a flight of some 1,470 miles, which lasted almost 7½ hours. The pilots finally returned to Debden in the first week of July, via Poland and Italy, where they had escorted a force of the 15th Air Force bombing targets in Hungary.

Besides the normal escort operations throughout the length and breadth of Germany, the Group's pilots were engaged in attacking bridges, airfields and transportation targets in France, Belgium and Holland, and some of these missions could be quite costly, as on 18th August when nine aircraft were lost. During August rather unusually, the Group escorted a force of RAF Beaufighters to targets in Norway, losing three aircraft – two ditched in the North Sea. Nevertheless by the end of the month the Group was the top scoring Fighter Group in the Eighth, with over 700 victories.

The appearance of the Luftwaffe's turbo-jet fighter – the Me262 – resulted in a detachment of Meteors of No 616 squadron (then at Manston) being sent to Debden, during October, to practise some affiliation exercises with the Group's pilots. It is debatable how effective such exercises were, as the Me262s continued to take an unhealthy toll of American bombers well into 1945. On 18th November, however, the Group, along with the 353rd, managed to destroy 14 Me262s at Lechfeld airfield, which was the Development Centre for the jet fighters.

During March the Group went on its travels again, this time to Italy to support bombers of the 15th Air Force attacking targets from Italian airfields. The claim of eleven victories on these operations helped the Group in the neck-and-neck race between the 4th and the 56th. The Group had 867 victories compared with 865½ for the 56th! On 16th April the Eighth Fighter Groups launched a massive strafe of enemy airfields, which brought about large-scale claims of enemy aircraft destroyed on the ground, but on the debit side there were losses – the 4th lost eight pilots, missing in action. The Eighth's last major operation took place on 25th April, and the 4th had the dubious distinction of losing the last Eighth Air Force fighter in Europe, its pilot baled out. The Group's final tally of enemy aircraft destroyed stood at 1,052½ with 583½ of this total in air combat, compared with the 56th's figure of 985½ victories. However, the 4th lost 241 aircraft, which was almost double that of the 56th. By July the Group had left for Steeple Morden in Cambridgeshire as the RAF required Debden, although it was not formally handed back to the RAF until 5th September.

Although there is a memorial to the 4th Fighter Group at Debden, there is also a fine obelisk, topped by the national emblem of a bald eagle, situated opposite the American Embassy in Grosvenor Square in London. This commemorates the 244 American and 16 British pilots and other personnel that served with the three RAF 'Eagle' squadrons from 1940 to 1942. Debden now came under the control of Technical Training Command and in June 1975 it finally closed as a RAF station, with the RAF ensign being lowered for the last time; a Hurricane and a Spitfire flew low overhead – a fitting end to this famous fighter station. At the time of writing Debden is an Army base with the 33rd Engineer Regiment in residence.

9

EARLS COLNE

Throughout the county there is no wartime airfield so well used today as Earls Colne. The site houses a small industrial park, a golf and leisure club, an aviation museum and, to revive memories of its wartime use, a busy and flourishing flying club. Earls Colne became the first heavy bomber base to be built in Essex during the Second World War, when it was handed over to the RAF towards the end of August 1942. Although the airfield had already been allocated for the use of the Eighth Air Force, they were in no position to take up their option as the build-up of the Eighth Air Force was far slower than originally planned.

The airfield, which was sited about a mile almost due south of the village of Earls Colne, was virtually inactive until the early summer of 1943. It was not until 27th May that it thundered to the heavy sound of the powerful Wright Cyclone engines of the B-17s of 94th Bomb Group (Heavy) as they landed after a short flight from Bassingbourn in Cambridgeshire. The 94th's crews had been in the United Kingdom for about one month, and this was one of the first Groups to form the new 4th Bomb Wing, which had its headquarters at Marks Hall, an Elizabethan manor house almost on the edge of the airfield. This house later became the headquarters of the Ninth Air Force Bomber Command, but regrettably it was demolished after the war.

Without doubt, these aircraft – the famed Flying Fortresses – will forever epitomise the USAAF in Europe during the Second World War. Perhaps this was due in no small measure to William Wyler's famous wartime documentary film *Memphis Belle* and its fairly recent and successful remake. Personally speaking, however, the Eighth Air Force's

Corporals William Haley and Fox Jackson cleaning the plexiglass nose of a B-26 of 323rd Bomb Group – July 1943. (Smithsonian Institution)

harsh and bitter war seemed to be best captured in that classic war film *Twelve O'Clock High*, which was first shown in 1949.

The first B-17, known as Model 299, had flown as far back as July 1935 and as the first all-metal four-engined monoplane it was most advanced for its time. The slender design was visually attractive but despite that it was its several gun turrets that caught the interest and imagination of the American press, who described it as 'like a flying fortress', and the name seemed highly appropriate so it was adopted. Despite the fact that it was obviously a superior heavy bomber the Army Air Force had only a small number in service at the end of 1939 and yet by September 1943 there were nearly 800 B-17s in England alone. These were mainly B-17Fs, a mark that was more developed and improved than any other. These aircraft had the famous 'Tokyo tanks' – extra fuel cells in the wings – which enabled the Eighth to attack targets the length and breadth of Germany and even further afield. They were so-called in the erroneous belief that the aircraft could bomb Tokyo from mainland America!

Designed to operate at high altitudes with a normal bomb load of 4,000 pounds, and heavily armed with up to twelve .50 machine guns, it was a formidable heavy bomber. The aircraft, in its various models, formed the backbone of the Eighth Air Force and led the American air assault on Germany. Like its RAF counterpart, the Avro Lancaster, it was fondly admired by its crews, who had complete faith in their 'ship' to bring them back home safely despite heavy damage.

The 94th Group had already been 'blooded' with missions over St Omer, Antwerp, Emden, Bordeaux and Flensberg, and was commanded by Colonel John 'Dinty' Moore. Within two days of its arrival at Earls Colne an operation was launched to the marshalling yards at Rennes, which was an important rail centre for supplying the U-boat ports of the French Atlantic coast. On this mission the 94th lost three B-17s, which only extended the Group's unhappy start in the war. Indeed in their early missions the three Groups of the 4th Wing (94th/95th/96th) had all suffered quite heavily at the hands of the Luftwaffe. Almost a week of inclement weather prevented any further missions until 11th June when the main target was Bremen, although heavy cloud cover resulted in a change to a secondary target – Wilhelmshaven. Although the losses were relatively light on this operation – 'just' eight aircraft – the bombing was of a poor quality, largely as a result of the smoke buoys used by the German defences that effectively formed a complete blanket over the port.

The various changes of airfields amongst the Eighth's Bomb Groups has already been noted, and the 94th was due to take over an airfield at Bury St Edmunds. The operation planned for 13th June would require the B-17s to leave from Earls Colne but return to their new base in Suffolk. Just 26 B-17s took off from Earls Colne on their 9th mission, bound for the U-boat yards and pens at Kiel, and once again the 4th Bomb Wing faced severe flak from this heavily defended port. The Group managed to survive intact and were within 30 miles of the Norfolk coast before they were attacked by about a dozen Ju88 night fighters. At the time many of the gunners had rather unwisely stripped their guns and were in the process of cleaning them – a chore which should have been completed once they had landed. In a matter of minutes nine B-17s were shot down. It was a sad lapse of discipline which proved very costly; in under two months the Group had lost no less than 17 aircraft, but ultimately the 94th would became one of the most famous Heavy Bomb Groups in the Eighth Air Force, with a fine war record almost second to none.

Second Lieutenant William R. Hutchens, co-pilot of the B-26 John Bull *of 323rd Bomb Group at Earls Colne – 21st July 1943. (Smithsonian Institution)*

The B-17s were replaced on the same day by the B-26s of the 323rd Bomb Group, which flew in from Horham in Suffolk. The Group was commanded by Colonel Herbert B. Thatcher, who was said to be 'a West Pointer and real regular Army Air Force officer...but a great guy.' After the disastrous low-level mission in May, the B-26s had been grounded from further operations, and it was the 323rd that had been selected to train at medium altitude bombing with its crews acting as 'guinea pigs' in this new mode of operations for the B-26s. Certain modifications were made to their aircraft and the famous Norden bomb-sight replaced the existing D-8 sight, although the Norden sights were in short supply. Colonel Thatcher led the three practice missions over England during the first two weeks of July before he, and Brigadier General Anderson of the Ninth Bomb Command felt the crews were ready to go 'live'.

On 16th July the Colonel led 18 B-26s for their attack on the marshalling yards at Abbeville. He was flying *Bingo Buster*, which later became the Group's first aircraft to survive 100 missions and it was returned to the United States in May 1944 for promotional purposes to sell more War Bonds. Ultimately two of the Group's aircraft – *Jill Flitter* and *Rock Hill Special* – almost made the magical figure of 200 missions! The small force of B-26s (16 because two failed to take off) was escorted by no less than 18 squadrons of RAF Spitfires, which was said to be necessary because around Abbeville were 'the best fighter units in the German Air Force'.

Brigadier General Anderson went along as an observer on this important mission, and all but two crews managed to bomb. Later it was said that the General was not particularly happy with the accuracy of the bombing. Quite heavy flak was encountered, so much so that ten aircraft returned with battle damage. This was the first time that B-26s had been used at a medium altitude in Europe – they made their bombing run at a height of 11,500 feet – and no doubt everybody involved with the operation breathed a deep sigh of relief when all the aircraft landed safely back at Earls Colne. The 'beautiful ladies' – as some crews called their B-26s – were back in business, and there was quite a celebration at the base that evening. The delight spread throughout the Command, Brigadier General Robert C. Candee, the CO of the Eighth Support Command, sent a message 'Well done. In extending my congratulations to the gallant combat crews after their first mission against the Hun, I want to include the ground crews and all others without whose zealous efforts the work of the combat crews cannot produce the maximum results.'

From now until the end of the month the Group launched another nine missions, mainly to airfields, with two coke ovens thrown in for good measure. On their tenth mission (31st July), to Poix/Nord airfield, the Group's aircraft were led by Major Wilson W. Wood and one of the 21 B-26s failed to return to Earls Colne. Two of its crew – Staff Sergeants Hager and Crowe – managed to evade capture and returned to England via Spain, Gibraltar and Morocco. By now the Group had been joined by two other B-26 Groups (322nd and 386th) in these pioneer B-26 missions. They had proved that the aircraft could operate effectively and successfully at medium altitudes, so much so that in August, the Eighth Bomber Command announced rather smugly that 'the much-criticized Maruader medium bomber is now operating on a substantial scale against targets in enemy occupied territory.'

For the next ten weeks, whilst the Group was still under the command of the Eighth Air Force, it was engaged mainly in attacking enemy airfields with railway yards as a secondary priority. The last mission mounted for the Eighth Air Force was conducted on 9th October. The target was Woensdrecht airfield and all 36 B-26s arrived back safely though ten had been damaged by flak. During the 323rd's time with the Eighth only three aircraft were lost in action with another five coming to grief in crash-landings – this was a most impressive record.

Now under the colours of the Ninth Air Force the Group was placed in 98th Bomb Wing and on the 13th of the month Colonel Wilson R. Wood took over as Commanding Officer, as Colonel Thatcher had been promoted to command the 99th Bomb Wing at Great Dunmow. Colonel Wood was only 25 years old and had received very speedy promotion, having entered the Service as a 'buck private' just five years earlier. Such rapid progress was not unknown in the USAAF but nevertheless he was very young to command a Bomb Group. Wood had previously been the Commander of 454th squadron and he proved to be a popular CO known to his men as 'Chico' from his Texan hometown; he remained in charge of the Group until February 1945. The 323rd later became known as 'Wood's Rocket Raiders', largely as a result of a press release on the Group's operations against the V1 rocket sites. Their first such mission took place on 5th November to 'construction works' at Mimoyecques in northern France; it was not thought right to inform the crews of the true nature of their target, only that it was 'the most important target you have been assigned to date'. A 'maximum effort' was called and they were led for the last time by Colonel Thatcher; by the time they had returned to Earls Colne with 23 aircraft damaged, the crews were only too aware of the importance of these targets because they were so heavily defended by flak batteries. Of passing interest, after the war Mimoyecques was opened as a 'tourist attraction'!

By December some 60 or so 'ski-sites', so called because of the shape of the launching apparatus, had been identified by reconnaissance photographs, though it was thought that there could be up to 100 sites, many of which were well concealed in small woods. The V1 rocket site missions were coded 'No Balls' and the massive Allied air offensive directed against the sites was known as 'Operation Crossbow'. Four categories of bomb damage to these sites was introduced from 'A' to 'D'. The first meant that a concentrated burst on the target with one or more direct hits on some of the main buildings had to be seen. At the other end of the scale 'D' applied when there were no hits in the target area. Such a system was considered necessary to prevent wasted effort by the enormous resources devoted by the Eighth and Ninth Air Forces and the RAF to 'Crossbow'.

Nevertheless enemy airfields still demanded the Ninth's attention and on 13th December a large operation involving over 200 B-26s was mounted against Amsterdam/Schipol, which was probably the most heavily defended airfield in the Low Countries. It proved to be a most successful operation with over 60% of the bombs falling in the target area, causing considerable damage. The 323rd lost one aircraft to flak with another 46 damaged, of which three crash-landed. One of these from 453rd squadron returned to make an emergency landing at Halesworth with over 150 flak holes, some of which were said to be 'as large as a dinner plate'! This aircraft was called *Flying Dutchman* and was piloted by Lieutenant Anthony Van Antwerp – there was no reason to doubt his family's origins!

Considering their efforts against the V1 rocket sites during January and February, it was rather appropriate that the Group's 100th mission, on 8th February 1944, was directed against a site at Bois Remprey. This was the first B-26 Group to achieve such an important milestone. But perhaps their most successful raid so far – at least according to the Group's records – came on 25th February when as part of 'The Big Week' the Group led by Major Roy B. Pratt, commander of 453 squadron, attacked Venlo airfield. In this operation at least seven enemy aircraft were destroyed on the ground and the airfield was said to be 'devastated'.

On March 20th the Ninth launched a major mobility exercise, which was a practice for what would happen when the Ninth Air Force would operate from airfields on the Continent. It was anticipated that the Groups would have to move airfields fairly frequently as the battlegrounds dictated. The Ninth's ethos was captured with the slogan 'Keep Mobile'! The exercise involved all the Bomb Groups changing airfields. The 323rd moved to Great Dunmow with the 386th coming to Earls Colne; the latter Group had the misfortune to suffer an air raid whilst they were at Earls Colne, and a Ju88, which had been shot down, happened to crash directly onto one of their B-26s!

In early April a Ninth Air Force report highlighted some of the bombing errors that had crept into the Groups' performances during the spring of 1944. In fact the report pulled no punches and was quite damning with remarks such as '...Lack of aggressiveness...improper tactics and techniques...lack of proper training...' The report also inferred that the 'old' Groups were more guilty and as a result it was decided that these Groups would be taken off operations to receive extra training and reminded of the need for precision bombing with the

B-26s of 454th squadron over France in the summer of 1944. (USAF)

prompt correction of targeting and navigational errors. Because the 323rd had been operational since July 1943 it was the first to undergo such training, the official excuse was 'war weariness'! Thus from 19th to 27th April the Group did not mount any missions.

The crews, suitably refreshed and retrained, returned to operations with a vengeance, and during May some 31 missions were mounted to marshalling yards, coastal defences, airfields and road and rail bridges, with some crews flying two combat missions in a day. From 25th of the month the 323rd launched attacks to nine bridges on consecutive days. Nevertheless it was the port area at Dieppe that proved to be the Group's harshest test. On 19th almost 40 B-26s left to attack this important Channel port, but because of the weather conditions some crews failed to form up correctly and subsequently returned to base. Of those who did attack, 17 returned with heavy damage, which caused two to make emergency landings at other airfields and one was a 'write-off'. The following afternoon Dieppe was again the target and even more severe opposition was encountered, which according to one pilot '...was the heaviest of my career'. On this mission the 323rd lost three aircraft with another 20 badly damaged. Five days later (25th) when the railway bridge at Seraing, just south of Liège, was the target, the Group suffered the loss of another two aircraft.

On D-Day the 323rd was allocated coastal defence targets around the Utah beach-head – Beau Guillot, La Madeleine and St Martin-de-Varreville. The crews were briefed to make their attack between 06.05 and 06.24 as the first American troops were due to land at 06.30; as Colonel Wood succinctly commented '... There is no margin of error'! All the 54 aircraft arrived home intact. The second mission, with 36 B-26s in action, was directed against a road junction at Caen. The crews were briefed to attack between 2,000 and 3,000 feet and they faced a severe and accurate barrage of fire, with the result that one B-26 went down. The aircraft was piloted by Major Paul J. Stach of 455 squadron, who was a most experienced airman. It was later thought that the Major survived the crash but was killed by German troops.

During the rest of the month 21 missions were mounted and on 29th when 36 aircraft attacked gun batteries at Audeville and Digalleville, one B-26 received a direct hit and exploded with no survivors. The pilot, First Lieutenant Oswald Boothe, was on his 81st mission and the aircraft *Classic Lassie* on its 100th! In direct contrast to the previous two months, July proved to be somewhat of an anti-climax. The unseasonal weather, which was said to be the worst for a half a century, severely curtailed operations. Nevertheless the crews were kept active on training flights, especially at night; during August the crews would make their first night mission from Beaulieu. Also during the month the first A-26 (Invader) arrived and soon rumours spread that a change of aircraft was imminent. Also by now the crews were well aware that they would soon be on the move to pastures new in Hampshire. The Group's last mission from Earls Colne was something quite special. On 18th July 36 aircraft left for the heavily defended area at Démouville to the east of Caen, which was holding up the British army's advance on Caen. This area would first suffer a very heavy attack from over 1,000 Lancasters and Halifaxes, followed by over 600 B-24s and B-26s, the total operation being described as 'the greatest bombing concentration of the war so far.' Although no aircraft was lost at least 22 B-26s returned to Earls Colne with heavy damage.

By the 21st of the month the personnel had left Earls Colne for Beaulieu, where in five weeks 28 missions would be mounted without losing a single aircraft. With no less than five further moves in the next nine months the Group would view their 'long' stay at Earls Colne with some fondness and nostalgia. In December the 323rd gained a DUC for

Handley Page Halifax: Nos 296 and 297 squadrons operated Mark IIIs from Earls Colne during 1944/5.

its operations in the Ardennes campaign; this was a belated recognition of the Group's excellent performance since the days of July 1943.

The airfield now entered its third phase as it was passed back to the RAF and it came under the control of No 38 Group. This Group had been formed in the winter of 1943, under the command of Air Vice Marshal L. N. Hollinghurst, really as the air-arm of the British airborne forces. During late September two squadrons – Nos 296 and 297 – arrived from Brize Norton. They were equipped with Armstrong Whitworth Albemarles but were in the process of converting to Handley Page Halifax IIIs.

No 38 Group was now greatly involved in 'Special Operations', which was effectively dropping supplies, instructors and agents to the various resistance forces operating in the enemy occupied territories. During 1944 the Group had been brought in to assist the two squadrons – Nos 138 and 161 – which had been specially formed to undertake these difficult and dangerous missions. Orginally Whitley bombers had been used for the parachuting role by these 'Special Duties' squadrons, but by 1943 the Halifaxes had taken over.

The Handley Page Halifax had made its reputation as a four-engined heavy bomber, which from 1941-5 became, along with the Lancaster, the mainstay of RAF Bomber Command. It had first flown in October 1939, entered the Service in late 1940 and made its first operational mission on

10th/11th March 1941. The early Halifaxes were powered by Rolls Royce Merlin X engines but later marks were supplied with Bristol Hercules powerplants. The later marks were also used for paratroops as well as glider-towers, in fact it was the only RAF aircraft capable of towing the big Hamilcar glider.

Because of the time taken in the conversion programme the two squadrons did not become operational until the end of 1944. January 1945 was dogged with bad weather, and this, allied to the fact that almost all SD (Special Duties) sorties were flown within one week of the full moon, restricted such operations. But on the night of 2nd/3rd January two Halifaxes from Earls Colne attempted drops over Holland, though only one proved successful. In March both squadrons were engaged in 'Operation Varsity' – but soon afterwards the crews were back to SOE work. These operations were not without mishap and on 6th/7th April a Halifax piloted by Squadron Leader Hobb of 296 squadron crashed south of Lille but fortunately all the crew managed to escape without injury.

During the last week of April No 38 Group launched its last Special Duties operation but the two squadrons stayed at Earls Colne until the spring of 1946 when the airfield was placed under Care and Maintenance, and subsequently it was released for agricultural use. The site of the old airfield is well worth a journey if only to pay a visit to the Rebel Air Museum, which houses a good collection of artefacts relating to the USAAF. It is off the B1024 road and well signposted from the A604 at Earls Colne.

10
FAIRLOP

Originally known as Hainault Farm, Fairlop was one of the four airfields in Essex that could trace its origins back to the days of the First World War and the Royal Flying Corps. Not quite as famous or successful as its near neighbour, Suttons's Farm (Hornchurch), all flying had ceased by the end of 1919, and like most World War I airfields the landing ground returned to agricultural use. During the late 1930s the site was purchased by the City of London Corporation with the intention of developing it into a 'major airport' but because of the serious world situation brought about by the Munich crisis of 1938, the project was shelved.

At the beginning of the war the Air Ministry requistioned the site, which now went under the name of Fairlop from the neighbouring village, and on 26th September 1940 it was handed over to the contractors to construct an airfield with three concrete runways (one at 1,600 yards and two at 1,100 yards) and with sufficient accommodation and services for some 1,200 RAF personnel. Although the harsh winter of 1940/1 caused some delay with the construction work, the runways were completed by the following July, and on 1st August 1941 the Air Ministry set an establishment for RAF Fairlop. A month later Group Captain Harry Broadhurst, Hornchurch's CO, flew in and made a trial landing on each runway in turn before pronouncing them up to standard. Ten days later the contractors had completed all the buildings and the telephone services were connected, and on 10th September Fairlop was declared operational, with Squadron Leader H. G. P. Ovendon as the first Commanding Officer of Hornchurch's second satellite airfield.

The first aircraft to use the new runways during November belonged to No 603 'City of Edinburgh' squadron, which had been based at Hornchurch during the latter stages of the Battle of Britain and more recently since the previous May. The squadron was now commanded by Squadron Leader Terence Forshaw, a pre-war officer, who had flown with No 609 squadron during the Battle. In December the pilots met their first FW190s whilst engaged on a fighter sweep over France and in the rather fierce aerial combat three pilots failed to return. On 15th December, three days before the squadron left for Scotland, their commanding officer scrambled to seek out a suspected enemy intruder. Unfortunately Forshaw was badly injured when his aircraft crashed into the sea and he never returned again to the squadron.

During late January and February 1942 Hornchurch's landing field became waterlogged so its three Spitfire squadrons – Nos 64, 81 and 411 – moved into Fairlop for a couple of weeks. It was from this airfield that the squadrons were despatched, on 12th February, to seek out the German battleships *Scharnhorst* and *Gneisenau* – the infamous 'Channel Dash' operation. The pilots left Fairlop at 12.30 hours and after patrolling for almost two hours, they returned without catching sight of the German flotilla; the weather was quite atrocious which certainly aided the escape of the German vessels. It was not until the end of April that a more permanent resident moved in, No 313, commanded by Squadron Leader K. Mrazek, DFC, the third Czech squadron to be formed. During their stay at Fairlop the Czech pilots were mainly engaged on 'Ramrods' – combined bomber and fighter operations directed at specific targets. When they left for the West Country in June they were replaced by No 122 squadron.

This squadron was also known as the 'Bombay' as it was a gift from that City. It had been formed in May 1941 at Turnhouse in Scotland and its early operations were convoy patrols. The pilots' first aerial combat did not come until 24th April 1942 and two pilots were lost without any victories. The squadron's luck changed three days later when a Me109 was downed. No 122 was fairly unusual for this time in that it had previously been commanded by a Czech officer, and now a Belgian airman was in charge. He was Squadron Leader Leon Prevot, who had until recently been a Flight Commander with No 64. Prevot notched up the squadron's first FW190 on 17th May. On 30th July, he was shot down over France, but he baled out and managed to evade capture. The day had proved very costly to the Hornchurch Wing with eight pilots lost, half of which came from No 122. Prevot ultimately escaped via Spain

Spitfire Vs of No 122 squadron taking off from Fairlop in the summer of 1942.

and returned to operational service in November 1942. During early 1944 he went back to Hornchurch in command of No 350 'Belgian' squadron.

Towards the end of 1942 No 122 returned again to Fairlop. This time it was commanded by one of the famous fighter pilots of the war – Squadron Leader Donald Kingaby, DFM, 2 bars (the only airman to be so honoured during the war). As a Sergeant pilot with No 92 squadron he gained the reputation of being a '109 specialist'. Comissioned in November 1941, he later became a Flight Commander with 64 squadron and his total of enemy aircraft destroyed was well into double figures. Kingaby was appointed Acting Wing Commander of the Hornchurch Wing in April 1943. From Sergeant to Wing Commander at the age of 23 years and in less than three years shows the merit of this remarkable airman. He became one of the most highly decorated officers of the war, adding a DSO, DFC(US), AFC, and C de Guerre (Belgian) to his three DFMs! By the time the squadron had left Fairlop at the end of 1942 it had flown 92 operations with nine enemy aircraft destroyed.

During the winter of 1942/3 No 64 squadron occupied the airfield for several months. It had already served there and had been part of the Hornchurch Wing off and on for about two years. It was a fighter squadron with a long and proud history, first in service over France in the First World War and later in the 1930s in Egypt, reflected in its badge – an Egyptian scarab. During its time at Fairlop the squadron was fortunate to have two excellent commanders. The first was a Battle of Britain 'ace', Squadron Leader Colin Gray, DFC and bar. Gray's score had stood at 15½ victories by the end of September 1940. When Gray

130

Several squadrons of Typhoons served at Fairlop from 1943-4.

was posted abroad in December he was replaced by another fine New Zealand pilot – William Crawford-Compton – who was a leader of some style and distinction, especially in command of the Hornchurch Wing from July 1943. Along with Al Deere and Colin Gray they were the leading New Zealand pilots of the war. Much of the 'bread and butter' of the squadron's operations during this period involved acting as escorts for the Eighth Air Force heavy bombers.

On 5th April 1943 Fairlop broke the mould of being a Spitfire station pure and simple, when two Typhoon squadrons – Nos 182 and 247 – arrived. The Hawker Typhoon, known as 'Tiffie' to its pilots, had been designed in 1938 in response to Air Ministry specification F18/1937, really as a faster and more powerful version of the Hurricane. It first flew in February 1940 but with the sudden appearance of the FW190 the Typhoon was rushed into production and came into service in September 1941. Its new Napier Sabre II engines gave it a top speed in excess of 400 mph but certain teething troubles were experienced; this, added to the fact that it was not an easy aircraft to control, resulted in a number of accidents and gave it a doubtful reputation. Ultimately the Typhoon IB developed into an excellent ground attack aircraft armed with four 20 mm cannons and able to carry up to two 1,000 pounds of bombs or eight rocket projectiles under its wings. Without doubt it was a very rugged, powerful and fast aircraft, which found its true métier with the 2nd Tactical Air Force as 'a tank and train buster'. However, the

AOC of the 2nd TAF, Air Marshal Sir Arthur Conningham, maintained 'I suppose that flying one of these aircraft was the most dangerous task the Air Force has ever asked anybody to do'!

No 182 had been formed as a Typhoon/bomber squadron and its pilots were engaged on a number of Army exercises but in April they were involved in dive-bombing enemy airfields in France. The other Typhoon squadron went out on its first operation on 13th of the month, acting as escorts to the Typhoon bombers. Both squadrons later operated with distinction with No 124 Typhoon Wing from Hurn in Hampshire. As the Typhoons left Fairlop several Spitfire squadrons arrived during the summer months. But in September they were replaced by a squadron (No 164) equipped with a rather rare mark of Hurricanes – IVs – used operationally by only eleven squadrons mainly in the Middle and Far East.

This mark had been developed from the so-called 'Hurribomber'. It was powered by either the Merlin 24 or 27 engine and its 'low attack or universal' wings enabled the aircraft to carry either two 1,000 pound bombs or eight rocket projectiles. First introduced into the Service in March 1943, the Mark IV had a top speed of 330 mph, which really made it too slow for action in the war of north-west Europe. Nevertheless the squadron became engaged in bombing operations during November and attacking V1 rocket sites the following month, although during its stay at Fairlop the pilots would convert to Typhoons.

The Hurricane squadron was also known as the 'Argentine-British', with its badge reflecting the close connections between the two countries (then!) – a rising sun (from the Argentine flag) and the lion of Great Britain. On 26th October 1943 HRH the Duke of Gloucester officially presented the badge to the squadron's CO Squadron Leader H. A. B. Russell, DFC. 'Humph' Russell was a pre-war officer, who had been seriously wounded during the Battle of Britain and it was thought that he would not fly again. He was shot down in May 1944 whilst serving at Thorney Island, and he spent the rest of the war as a prisoner.

No 164 shared the airfield with a squadron of Typhoons – No 195 – which had been formed at Duxford in November 1942 and since that time had been commanded by Squadron Leader Donald Taylor, who knew the area quite well as he had served with 64 squadron during the Battle of Britain. The Typhoons conducted a variety of operations – bomber escorts, fighter sweeps and 'Jim Crows', which were patrols along the coastline with the intention of intercepting any enemy intruder raids. On 15th February 1944 the squadron was disbanded at

Fairlop, passing its Typhoons over to No 164 pilots. Fairlop's days as an operational airfield were fast coming to a close. Its final fighter squadron, No 193, arrived in February, equipped with Typhoons. For just a short time the squadron operated from Fairlop, engaged in attacking V1 rocket sites. By the middle of March the squadron had left Fairlop to join No 164 at Thorney Island.

Fairlop, or No 136 airfield as it was now known, was placed under 'Care and Maintenance' until it was decided to install a Balloon Centre there. By the summer of 1944 No 24 Balloon Centre with four squadrons was operating from the airfield, and the balloons were under the control of mainly WAAFs. This centre was just a small part of the massive balloon barrage that surrounded London with the express intention of bringing down the V1 rockets; only 278 fell to the balloons, or about 3% of the total, and it was estimated that just 19 of these were accounted for by the Fairlop balloons. Almost from the time of the Centre's opening the Balloon Command was beginning to be run down, and by February 1945 the Command was disbanded. Fairlop became vacant in September and the station finally closed in August 1946. Already, though, the airfield was being considered as a likely site for the second London Airport but, like the pre-war proposal, this came to nothing and the airfield, situated to the east of Fairlop underground station, quickly returned to farming. The site is now part of Hainault Forest Country Park and all vestiges of its previous use have long since disappeared.

11

GOSFIELD

Nowadays Gosfield is best known for its lake, which is the largest area of fresh water in Essex, and has rightly become a well-known tourist attraction with its splendid facilities for waterskiing and other water sports. Besides the lake the village can also boast a fine Tudor manor hall, which includes amongst its former owners the Marquis of Buckingham and the Courtauld family of textile fame. However, few of the summer visitors to this delightful spot may realise that the village was also the site of a Second World War airfield, where two of the Ninth Air Force Groups were based during the first nine months of 1944.

The village already had a somewhat tenuous aviation heritage because a large field nearby had been used as a landing ground during the First World War. This might have been the reason why the Air Ministry was first alerted to the area and its surveying team decided that the site was suitable for development as a Class A bomber station. Gosfield became the first airfield in England to be constructed by American Army Engineers, though alas not the first to be completed!

The 816th Engineer Aviation Battalion arrived at Liverpool on 17th August 1942, which by coincidence was the very same day that the Eighth Air Force launched its first heavy bomber operation from Grafton Underwood. A day later the Engineers had arrived at Gosfield, set up their tents and were keen to start the construction work. Unfortunately, mainly because of a lack of heavy equipment, work did not really progress as planned, and the winter conditions certainly did not help matters as the site became a morass of mud and clay. Then in early March the 816th were ordered to up sticks and move to another airfield site at Great Saling to assist on its completion; this airfield later became known as Andrews Field.

It was not until the following August – twelve months since they had arrived in England – that the 816th returned to Gosfield to carry on the work. After about another two months of work on Gosfield, the Battalion was moved to yet another site. The 816th later gained fame by completing the first landing ground to be built in Normandy. They landed at Omaha beach-head on 9th June and just eleven days later had almost completed A-3 (Cardonville) airfield, which was the first to be used by aircraft of the Ninth Air Force. It was eventually left to the 833rd Battalion to complete Gosfield, which lies to the north-west of the village and adjacent to Gosfield Hall, which was then occupied by the Army. Virtually all of these Class A airfields had accommodation for some 2,800 personnel, but Gosfield had facilities for more than 3,200, which made it one of the largest airfields in Essex, especially as it covered some four square miles.

During the autumn of 1943 the Luftwaffe made a number of night intruder attacks on East Anglian airfields. In October, before the airfield was officially opened, a couple of high explosive bombs fell harmlessly on the surrounding fields. The next air raid was a quite astonishing affair. On the night of 10th/11th December Gosfield suffered the heaviest bombardment of any East Anglian airfield since Debden's heavy attacks during the summer of 1940. It was thought that about a dozen Do217s and Ju88s were involved in the attack. Flares were dropped and their lights reflected brightly in the lake, which was about a quarter of mile to the south of the airfield. It was estimated that some 65 HE bombs were dropped but surprisingly very little material damage was sustained, although eight US servicemen were killed and another 27 injured. The mysterious reason for such a heavy and sustained raid was later solved when intelligence sources revealed that the intended target that night had been Chelmsford. Fortunately there had been no aircraft at the airfield as it had only been officially opened the previous day.

The airfield had been planned to house a B-17 Group of the Eighth Air Force but, because of all the delay in its construction, it was transferred to the Ninth Air Force in October 1943 for their use as a bomber station. As a temporary measure the Ninth Fighter Group – the 365th – moved in just before Christmas 1943 whilst its Advanced Landing Ground in Hampshire was being made ready. The Group was equipped with P-47s and was commanded by Colonel Lance Call. It was almost two months before the Group was ready for its first operation, and on 22nd February it conducted a short fighter sweep over Holland. Perhaps it would be fair to point out that the Group had to wait a number of weeks before it had received its full complement of aircraft (75), with the result that most of the pilots had only completed five hours of training on the aircraft before they went out on operations. They had, of course, spent a long time in training in the United States, but this was mainly on P-39s (Airacobras).

On 24th February the Group flew two missions, escorting B-17s to and from Schweinfurt, but they were only able to remain with the bomber formations to the limit of their range – which was close to the Belgian/German border. The Group's pilots had to wait until 2nd March to test their mettle against the Luftwaffe in combat, and this came when escorting bombers to Frankfurt. The outcome of their first air battle was one P-47 lost but six enemy aircraft claimed, although only one victory was subsequently credited to the Group. The pilots were involved in the first two Berlin operations mounted by the Eighth in the first week of March; and on the 6th they claimed five victories without a loss. It was on that promising and encouraging note the 365th left for Beaulieu, having completed nine missions with two aircraft missing in action and another two destroyed in training accidents. The Group operated from Beaulieu for four months and during this time its pilots claimed 29 enemy aircraft and the Group's Air Executive Officer, Lieutenant Colonel Robert Coffey Jr, became the Ninth's third fighter ace. Later the 365th became one of the most successful P-47 Groups in the Ninth Air Force, being awarded two DUCs for its operations from airfields in France.

For just a brief period in April Gosfield housed the B-26s of 397th Bomb Group, but by 15th they had departed for Rivenhall, some miles to the south, which would became their permanent base. Already at Birch were the personnel of the 410th Bomb Group (Light) waiting to move into Gosfield, which they did on 16th April, and so became the third Group of the 97th Bomb Wing, which was then controlled from Little Walden; all three Groups were equipped with A-20 Havocs.

It is normally assumed that the differences between 'light', 'medium' and 'heavy' bombers related to their weight. However, one American wartime source suggests that the definitions related to the operational ranges of the aircraft – up to 1,000 miles 'light', then to 2,000 miles 'medium' and above that 'heavy'. Another Washington report maintained that the altitude at which the aircraft operated would prove a more accurate definition for its bombers, for instance low-level meant 'light', medium altitude 'medium' and high altitude 'heavy'. Nevertheless the three A-20 Bomb Groups were shown as 'Light' despite the fact that in Europe they mainly operated at medium altitudes!

The Douglas A-20 was a twin-engined light bomber, which had first been developed back in 1936, and was unique in as much as it was the first twin-engined attack aircraft to be accepted by the US Army Air Corps. With several modifications the Douglas 7B (as it had become designated) made its first flight towards the end of 1938, and one of its most unusual features was the provision of interchangeable nose sections to suit the aircraft for different attack roles. The DB-7 (Douglas Bomber) entered operations with the French Air Force in May 1940, but when France fell the RAF took over the existing aircraft and the outstanding order.

Although it may be said that the aircraft did not have the spectacular success of other American wartime aircraft, it nevertheless served with distinction with the USAAF, RAF and in the USSR in a variety of roles, and perhaps most effectively in the Pacific and North Africa. The A-20G was the most produced model with over 2,800 being built. It was armed with six 0.5 guns in the nose and another two in the dorsal turret, its bomb capacity was 2,000 pounds, which could be doubled with external racks, and it had a maximum speed of just under 340 mph. Without doubt the A-20 was a most effective strike aircraft but really best suited to low-level operations. It is reputed that one of the Group's pilots on hearing the news that the 410th was destined for Europe commented, 'She's [A-20] strictly low level and Pacific theater. Against the Japs she's OK, a really great ship. But at medium altitudes against the Germans? Hell No!' Perhaps a quite natural reaction considering that the crews had spent 3,300 hours in training, all conducted at low-level.

Unlike all other Bomb Groups – Heavy and Medium – the crews, both air and ground, travelled across the Atlantic together. Their aircraft were brought over by sea, normally as deck cargo with their components crated, and they had to be reassembled in England. The Group's personnel left New York on 23rd March on board a rather ancient Italian merchant ship the *Saturnia*, and they arrived at Glasgow on 2nd April. The airmen had spent most of their time training in the wide open spaces of Oklahoma so the confines of their new airfield and the surrounding Essex countryside would be quite a novel experience for them. The four squadrons – 644 to 647 – each had their own identification colours, which was quite rare in the Ninth; this was in addition to a squadron code. The colours, red, white, blue and yellow

A-20G with 'invasion stripes' over the English Channel on D-Day. (USAF)

respectively, were painted on the propellor buds and later the engine cowlings.

Although most references show that the Group went out on its first operation on 1st May, it is clear from the Group's newsletters that the proposed mission to Evreux/Fauville airfield was cancelled, as was the operation for the following day. So it was not until 4th May that the 410th became operational with an attack on gun positions at St Marie au Bosc, the mission led by the Group's CO, Colonel Ralph Rhudy. The subsequent targets during the month included coastal batteries, airfields, V1 rocket sites and marshalling yards. One particularly successful mission during the month was against a marshalling yard at Aerschot, when the excellence of the bombing brought a message of praise from the Ninth's Bomb chiefs. Despite the fact that most of the Bomb Groups felt that their bombing was the best in the Ninth, figures show that during 1944 the 410th was considered to be the most accurate unit. It showed that 40% of the Group's bombs had fallen within 500 feet of the aiming points – the average percentage for the Ninth's Bomb Groups was 30.6%.

On D-Day 45 A-20s left Gosfield at 1 pm and attacked the marshalling yards at Carentan, which were just a few miles inland from the Utah beach-head. All but three aircraft managed to drop 219 bombs (500 pounders) from about 3,000 feet. The Group's records show '...Blew up

Source of Annoyance *completed 101 missions with 410th Bomb Group.* *(USAF)*

string of railroad cars and trucks. Warehouse and fuel oil store also blown up causing terrific fire and "havoc" – excuse the word!...All returned at 16.15 hours.' This was the Group's 33rd mission, not bad going for just over a month in action.

This operation was led by Lieutenant Colonel Robert J. Hughey, who at the age of 27 (his birthday was the following day!) was one of the youngest Lieutenant Colonels in the Ninth Air Force. Hughey's promotion had been rapid because back in April 1940 he was a mere Second Lieutenant. When he was posted to the Group in October 1943 as the Commander of 645 squadron, he had already completed a full combat tour in the Pacific. Hughey, known as 'Jowles' to his crews led the Group on no less than 55 operations and in December 1944 he was appointed the Group's Commanding Officer.

The second D-Day mission was directed at Longpré les Corps Saints marshalling yards near Abbeville. This time 37 aircraft left the airfield at just past eight o'clock in the evening, and they faced severe and accurate flak over the target area, which resulted in 32 returning with flak damage but unfortunately one A-20 was shot down. The last A-20 touched down at Gosfield at 10.30 in the evening, the end of quite a momentous day for the 410th.

The Group's Honorary Historian, Staff Sergeant Tom Traynor, had this to say about its activities after D-Day '...We remember the frags we dropped in support of the ground troops at Caen; frags which burst among the enemy's troops and equipment concentrated in the tiny village of Deauville (sic) [possibly Démouville?] enabling the Allies to push on to Caen, an important communications center which the

Germans had tried stubbornly to hold. And then there was the time the Yanks pressing against Cherbourg fell back 2,000 yards to enable the Group to attack an artillery emplacement which had been pouring shell after shell into the advancing American columns making the Yanks pay for every inch with sweat and blood. The A-20s roared in that day against heavy and accurate flak, but when they peeled off the target, the five hundred pounders had found the mark, and what had been gun emplacements were but a mass of rubble...'

On the afternoon of 22nd June the Ninth Bomber Command suddenly ordered a major strike at marshalling yards and fuel dumps, with all Groups in action. The 410th had a spectacular mission with 33 A-20s dropping 47 tons of bombs with most impressive results. Eleven days later there was a change of command with Colonel Sherman R. Beaty taking over until the end of the year.

During August the Ninth's Bomb Groups had a very busy month with the bridges over river Oise becoming priority targets and from 9th to 15th seven bridges were attacked. In fact during the month over 9,100 sorties were launched and 10,470 tons of bombs dropped with 34 aircraft being lost, besides 1,032 damaged by flak. The following month would show no let-up in this intense bombardment, but the Group's records do report '...Then on 18th September the Group crossed the English Channel and settled into its next location...' Over 120 missions had been mounted from Gosfield for the loss of 20 aircraft, when it became time for the 410th to move across to France. As the Allied armies' advance had gathered pace and momentum, the operational range of the A-20s proved to be critical. On 27th September the Group moved to Coulommiers, east of Alençon, and from there went on to even greater success being awarded a DUC for its bombing excellence over 23rd to 25th December whilst engaged in the Ardennes campaign. The Group subsequently converted to A-26s but only after the war in Europe had finished.

The airfield, which was still under the control of the USAAF, remained rather devoid of aircraft until the New Year, when, in January, a squadron of RAF Stirlings arrived. This was No 299 of No 38 Group, which had been compelled to leave Wethersfield because the concrete runways were breaking-up due to the severe weather. The squadron stayed barely two weeks before passing on to RAF Shepherds Grove in Suffolk. The next aircraft to use the airfield also belonged to No 38 Group. They were the Dakotas (C-47s) of three squadrons – Nos 271, 512 and 575 – and they brought Horsa gliders from their base at Broadwell

The memorial to 410th Bomb Group at Gosfield.

in Oxfordshire. On 24th March the Dakotas and their Horsas left Gosfield as part of 'Operation Varsity'. This operation effectively brought the wartime activities of Gosfield to a close.

Up to the late 1980s the runways and perimeter tracks were still intact, and had been used for a number of years by the Consumers' Association to test the performance and endurance of a variety of cars, with reports ultimately appearing in their magazine *Which*. Today some of the old wartime buildings have survived and are still in use; but the most lasting testimony to the wartime airfield is the rather fine memorial to the 80 airmen who lost their lives whilst serving with the 410th Bomb Group. The memorial was fashioned out of a grey granite boulder in Colorado Springs, USA and brought to England, where it was dedicated in May 1991. It proudly stands in the centre of the village, outside the Maurice Rowson Hall.

12

GREAT DUNMOW

It had been recognised as early as August 1940 that all suitable land should be considered for airfields. Sir Archibald Sinclair, the Secretary of State for War, said, '...There are many large private estates and large parklands, which if trees were taken down, would be suitable as landing grounds, if not aerodromes. We are out to win this war and should not be put off by a desire to maintain intact the stately homes of England...'! Thus the Air Ministry cast its avaricious eyes at the Easton Lodge estate, three miles north-west of Great Dunmow, close to the villages of Great and Little Easton. However, Great Dunmow proved to be the only wartime airfield in Essex to be built on a landed estate.

The estate had been owned by the Maynard family for centuries and had passed to Frances Maynard in 1865. She married the 5th Earl of Warwick and gained fame as a celebrated beauty and a member of the Prince of Wales' circle. The Countess became greatly involved in the world of the theatre and literature, and a convert to socialism, and used her fortune and position to support charitable and social interests. She died in 1938, a few years before the desecration of her beloved estate; over 200 mature trees (mostly oaks) had to be removed from the ancient parkland before construction work could begin.

The site had been allocated to the Eighth Air Force in August 1942 and within a few weeks the 818th US Engineer Aviation Battalion moved in with a scheduled completion date of March 1943. This was quite an ambitious target considering the East Anglian winter weather, one American engineer recalling his time at the site as '...mud, rain, leaky tents, rain and more mud and nightly air raid alerts...'! By the spring of

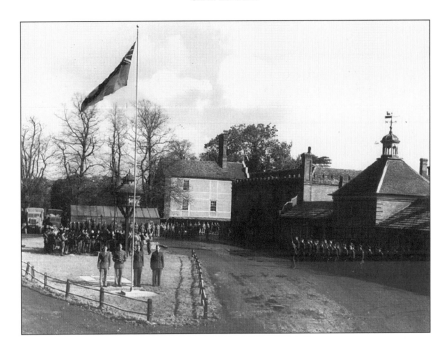

The transfer of Station 164 to the 386th Bomb Group – 20th October 1943. (Smithsonian Institution)

1943 only the runways and perimeter tracks had been laid and it was not until the summer that the airfield was considered ready for occupation, although there was still plenty of construction work to be completed.

It was the 386th Bomb Group from Boxted that moved in on 25th September to take over the new airfield. Their B-26s certainly did not look out of place there because for some months it had been used as a B-26 supply depot. The Group, which had already lost more crews than the other three B-26 Groups, gained or adopted the name 'The Crusaders' – and would achieve a very fine war record with over 400 missions mounted and a high tonnage of bombs dropped with excellent accuracy, but sadly 193 airmen were killed in action.

Their first mission from Great Dunmow (although the Americans tended to use Great Easton as the name for their base) was planned for 26th September but this had to be cancelled because of the weather – which was an all too familar state of affairs. The following day conditions had improved sufficiently for 36 aircraft to be sent to

143

Conches airfield, which was about 80 miles west of Paris; another crew failed to return from this mission. Enemy airfields were again the targets on 3rd October when two separate missions were mounted. In the late afternoon 18 B-26s left for Beauvais/Lille airfield, north of Paris; it turned out to be a rather torrid trip with 17 aircraft receiving battle damage and one crash-landing at the airfield on return. This proved to be the last operation mounted for the Eighth Air Force, because the two scheduled missions for 4th and 8th October were abandoned due to inclement weather.

The transfer of the four B-26 Groups to the Ninth Air Force took place on 16th October and, no doubt, Lieutenant General Ira Eaker, the Commander of the Eighth, breathed a sigh of relief, as he had never really disguised his opinion that the B-26s did not fit easily into his Command, which was solely devoted to high-altitude precision bombing. It was said that he would have preferred to have received four heavy Bomb Groups instead of the B-26 Groups, but nevertheless they had amply redeemed the reputation of the B-26, and in the process had created quite an amazing success story. Over 90 missions (more than 4,000 sorties) had been completed for the Eighth Air Force with a quite remarkable loss rate of 0.3%! This should not have been too surprising because the Twelfth Air Force, operating B-26s in North Africa, had reported, 'We think the B-26 is a good airplane, the best medium for combat that we know of. We like the load it will carry, its manoeuverability and defensive fire power...'

There was a hiatus of nine days before the 386th launched its first mission for the Ninth Bomber Command. Instructions had been received from the Command's headquarters which were unequivocal; the crews were not to bomb any target in occupied Europe unless it could be clearly identified, so that 'the risks would be minimised of inflicting heavy casualties on the friendly peoples near the target.' It was clear that precision bombing was to become the watchword of the Ninth. Furthermore, strict orders were issued to all Groups that 'no airfields in either Holland or Belgium – except Amsterdam/Schipol – are to be attacked unless specific permission granted.'

By coincidence the 386th attacked Schipol airfield on 3rd November and all four Groups taking part faced a murderous barrage of fire, which resembled a huge black cloud, and it was so dense that 'it was amazing only one ship was downed.' By the middle of the month the Group, along with the 'veterans' of the 322nd, was placed in 99th Bomb Wing, which had set up its headquarters at the airfield. There was a change in

Commanding Officer with Colonel Lester J. Maitland bidding a sad farewell. His place was taken by Colonel Richard C. Sanders, who stayed barely two months before Colonel Joe W. Kelly assumed command on 22nd January and led the Group for most of their time at Great Dunmow. Colonel Kelly became a popular figure in the 386th and developed a good relationship with the local community.

November was chequered by gales and poor flying conditions with the result that missions could only be mounted on twelve days. Towards the end of the month the weather did improve and on 26th two operations went out from Great Dunmow. In the morning the airfield at Rosières-en-Santerre was the target, but due to a navigational error a minor landing field further south was bombed. In the afternoon some 'construction works' at Audinghen, near Cap Gris-Nez, were attacked by three B-26 Groups with 'fair' results, although the official reports of the operation state that 'the village of Audinghen was destroyed'. The men who worked on the V1 rocket sites were thought to be quartered in the village, and that was the reason given for such a heavy bombardment of a small French village.

Three days later (29th) Chièvres airfield to the south of Ath in Belgium was attacked and this mission exemplified the bravery of the crews and the durability of their aircraft. They met a ferocious barrage of flak shortly before arriving over the target area, and one aircraft from 553rd squadron was badly hit and so severely damaged that it was forced to drop out of the formation. It was immediately attacked by six enemy fighters; the tail gunner, Staff Sergeant William Norris, managed to account for one fighter. Further damage was inflicted by the fighters and the pilot, Captain LaFramboise, had great difficulty in controlling the aircraft. With great skill and determination LaFramboise managed to coax the aircraft back across the English Channel on just one damaged engine with the expediency of throwing out all unneccesary equipment. The pilot made a successful crash-landing at the airfield despite the landing gear being jammed and the bomb doors open. Staff Sergeant Norris successfully claimed another fighter and both he and the pilot were awarded Silver Stars for their actions.

On 1st December Major General Brereton, the Commander of the Ninth, made a note in his diary '...we are beginning to get evidence that the B-26 is considerably better than its critics admit...' By coincidence on the same day the Group was engaged in its most successful mission against airfields so far. Epinoy and Niergnies, both near Cambrai, were attacked and, unusually, the weather was perfect with clear visibility

General Dwight D. Eisenhower looks on as an armourer loads on a B-26 of 386th Bomb Group at Great Dunmow – 11th April 1944. (Smithsonian Institution)

over the targets and the crews proceeded to demonstrate just how effective B-26s could be in such conditions. The bombing was said to be 'very accurate and excellent', and not a single aircraft was damaged.

Nevertheless during December the V1 rocket sites became familar targets, and often they were very difficult to locate. During the month the Ninth Air Force devoted over 60% of its resources to such targets, but in the following month, when the weather conditions allowed, this figure had risen to 90%! The crews had learnt from bitter experience that these 'No Ball' missions were fraught with dangers. On 14th January the aircraft flown by Lieutenant Burgess of 552nd squadron was almost literally blown out of the sky by a direct hit whilst attacking a rocket site. With great courage he continued his bombing run and then limped back across the English Channel at wave height to achieve a safe crash-landing as soon as he reached the coast.

It was during February that a third 'priority' target was introduced – railway sheds and marshalling yards. The Ninth launched their first attack on the railway system on 6th February. Intelligence sources had revealed that a German Panzer Division was on the move by rail, and the critical rail junction would be Tergnier, which was on the river Oise not far from the ancient battlefield of Crécy. The 99th Wing was given the task of destroying the rail junction, and 54 B-26s struck with quite devastating results, the lines being blocked for almost a week. This type of target would be increasingly attacked by the B-26 Groups in the months leading up to 'Operation Overlord' – the invasion of Europe.

In April (13th) the AEAF (Allied Expeditionary Air Force) issued a directive that a concentrated bombardment should be made on twelve coastal batteries, which extended from Dunkirk to the Normandy peninsula. It stated '...to the end that the harassing effect of our attacks shall prevent the completion by the enemy of the construction now going on at specified targets.' Thus the coastal defences at Dunkirk, Wimereux, Gravelines, Ault, Barfleur, Marck and Mont Fleury to name but some, began to figure large in the Ninth's and the Group's itineraries.

In the run-up to D-Day the Group was involved in variety of tactical targets – airfields, railway yards, beach defences, rail and road bridges and fuel depots. By 24th May seven rail and four road bridges had been identified as 'top priority targets'. They were on the river Seine between Paris and Rouen, and the bridges at Rouen needed five separate attacks before they were considered sufficiently damaged. As is well known, D-Day was originally set for 5th June but weather conditions over the English Channel delayed the invasion for another 24 hours. Along with hundreds of American and RAF bases throughout England, Great Dunmow was a scene of great activity and utmost security. During the day invasion strips – alternative black and white bands, 'zebra stripes' – were painted on the B-26s' fuseleges and wings, ready for the 'Cake Walk', which was so called because that was the name shown on the labels of the paint tins!

The take-off times on 6th June for the B-26 Groups varied between 03.43 and 05.00 hours. The Ninth's bombers were given the task of attacking the enemy fortifications and beach defences at Utah beach-head, on the Cherbourg peninsula, where the American VII Corps would land, although the 101st American Airborne Forces would parachute in first. Because of the cloud conditions over the target areas it proved difficult to discover just how effective the B-26s' bombing had been on the first operations. The Official Histories seem to differ on the point. The Army History suggested, '... on the whole the bombing achieved little in neutralizing the coastal fortifications...', whereas the Ninth Operational History recorded '...it is understood that on the other beaches many of the bombs fell behind the beach and that stiffer resistance was encountered there than on the Utah Beach...' Nevertheless the American Airborne Corps Commander said that the landing had been largely successful 'due to the excellent air force bombing.'

In the weeks after D-Day the Group was engaged in attacking rail and road targets behind the enemy lines, as well as fuel dumps in the Domfront/Alençon areas. Then on the night of 12th/13th June the first V1 rocket landed in England, and thus the Group found itself back attacking rocket sites. During the month the Ninth Air Force was seriously considering replacing both the A-20 and B-26 with a single aircraft – the Douglas A-26 (Invader). As the Ninth was not really aware of the aircraft's full operational capabilities it was decided to undertake a thorough flight test programme; the Group's 553rd squadron was given this task. By 15th August there were seven of these sleek and well-armed aircraft at Great Dunmow.

The A-26 had been designed by Douglas in 1940 to replace the Havoc. It was first flown in July 1942 and was the last American 'attack' aircraft to be developed during the war. It was fast, with a top speed in excess of 350 mph, well-armed with ten .50 inch machine guns, able to carry up to 6,000 pounds of bombs (although 4,000 pounds was its normal bomb load) and needed just a crew of three. With such a performance, armament and bomb load the aircraft had very obvious attractions for the Ninth Air Force. The squadron's early experiences with the aircraft were not that successful; several inherent problems were identified, which needed to be resolved before the aircraft entered the Service. Nevertheless they were used in operations in September and the Group ultimately converted to A-26s in January 1945. It is interesting to note that the Eighth Air Force used some A-26s for dropping agents behind enemy lines. By the end of the Second World War some 1,500 A-26s had been built, and when the B-26 went out of service, the Invader was redesignated B-26 and served with distinction in the Korean War.

Whilst the Allied armies moved steadily east across France and into the Low Countries, a German force was stubbornly resisting in Brittany and especially at the port of Brest. On 1st September General Omar Bradley requested an all-out air offensive against Brest and the surrounding defences. It was decided by Supreme Allied Headquarters that the Ninth should accord these targets a very high priority – if not

A-26 Invader of 553rd squadron at Great Dunmow in the summer of 1944. (USAF)

the highest. This area was known to the crews as 'the Brest Bombing Range' because of the frequency of their attacks and the relatively light flak opposition they encountered. From 1st to 14th September Brest was bombed on five separate occasions by the Ninth, involving over 2,000 bomber sorties. On 6th September 18 A-26s (553rd squadron) operated with 680 B-26s in a massive bombardment of the port. Brest finally fell to the Allied forces on 19th of the month, and the port area and much of the town had been devastated.

Before the Group left Great Dunmow it was awarded a well-merited DUC for all the various operations conducted during the period from 30th July 1943 to 30th July 1944. This was an acknowledgement of their splendid contribution to the USAAF's medium bombing campaign. When they finally left for an airfield in France at Beaumont-sur-Oise, about 20 miles north of Paris, on 2nd October 1944 the 386th was the last B-26 Bomb Group to leave Essex.

Within two weeks the first of the two RAF squadrons – No 190 – arrived with Short Stirling IVs, only to be followed a couple of days later by another Stirling squadron – No 620. Both were in No 38 Group, which during 1944 had been become actively engaged on 'Special Duties'. The arrival of these heavy and rather ponderous aircraft was in direct contrast to the sleek and streamlined B-26s and A-26s that had just left.

The Stirling had been the first four-engined bomber to come into

One of the stained-glass windows in the American memorial chapel at the parish church of Little Easton.

service back in August 1940 and for a short period it was in the forefront of Bomber Command's strike force. Despite having a long operational range, it had a poor ceiling height and as a consequence suffered heavily from flak. Nevertheless the aircraft was very sturdy and able to survive considerable damage. The Stirling proved to be a most versatile aircraft; besides bombing and mine laying, it was used as a troop carrier, glider tower and freight carrier. The Mark IVs had their nose and dorsal turrets removed because by 1944 they had been taken off bombing German targets. However, the squadrons did commence some bombing training and a few straight bombing missions were launched from Great Dunmow.

By the end of the year the airfield was very active, with plenty of Horsa gliders in evidence as there were two Glider Servicing Units based there. Also an Operational Refresher Training Unit used the airfield with Albermarles and Tiger Moths, as well as a Blind Approach Training Unit (No 1526), which was equipped with Airspeed Oxfords, which had become the RAF's first training monoplane with two engines.

Perhaps it was during April 1945 that the two Stirling squadrons had their busiest time, mounting special operations over Denmark, Holland and Norway. On the night of 2nd/3rd No 190 lost one aircraft over Denmark, and twelve days later six Stirlings from No 190 squadron joined a Group force over Norway; one aircraft piloted by Flying Officer Lewis failed to return and the other five Stirlings were forced to make emergency landings at Langham in Norfolk because of poor weather conditions over Essex. Even after VE day the two squadrons were active, ferrying Allied parties into recently occupied territories and also bringing back prisoners-of war. By the end of 1945 both squadrons had left Great Dunmow.

A memorial to the 386th Bomb Group was erected by the Essex Anglo-American Goodwill Association and it stands on the verge of the A120 road to the west of Great Dunmow, adjacent to the high gated entrance to Easton Lodge. In 1987, Colonel Lester Maitland, the Group's first Commander, and the Rector of the Little Easton parish church agreed to establish an American memorial chapel in the delightful church which stands on the edge of the old airfield. In October 1990 the memorial chapel was dedicated to the men of 'The Crusaders'. Two fine stained-glass windows capture the history of the Group and deep bonds of friendship established during the Group's time around the Eastons. This chapel is certainly worth visiting and can be reached from the B184 road out of Great Dunmow.

13

GREAT SAMPFORD

The name of this airfield is somewhat of a misnomer as it could have been more accurately named after Wimbish Green, which was almost a stone's throw to the west of the airfield. Perhaps this name was thought to sound too similar to 'Windrush' – a RAF operational airfield in Gloucestershire – and therefore Great Sampford was preferred. The small landing ground was planned as a satellite for nearby Debden to house one of the fighter squadrons operating in the Debden Spitfire Wing.

The airfield was sited to the north of Tindon End Manor and work commenced in late 1941. Hedges, trees and a small wood quickly vanished as the concrete perimeter road and hard-standings were laid, and temporary accommodation was provided for about 870 personnel. The final work involved erecting four blister hangars and the laying of Sommerfeld tracking (providing two runways, 1,600 and 1,050 yards long). This was 13 gauge, 3″ mesh wire netting secured with metal pickets and strengthened with flat steel bars. It had originated in the First World War, but during 1940 it was developed by an Austrian engineer, Kurt Sommerfeld, for basic landing grounds. The tracking was trialled in 1941 and used successfully in the deserts of North Africa, where it acquired the name of 'tin lino'! Its advantages were that it was easy to transport, lay and repair and it gave a robust and non-skid surface that could be easily camouflaged. The tracking perhaps proved to be most beneficial during the winter months when it provided a reasonably secure and dry landing surface.

The small airfield had a rather brief wartime existence largely because

Spitfire VB: Just three Spitfire squadrons used Great Sampford during the summer of 1942. (via J. Adams)

Focke-Wulf FW190 – the aircraft that caused problems for Fighter Command.

its parent station was assigned to the Eighth Air Force early in September 1942. The first aircraft to use the airfield were Spitfire VBs of No 65 squadron, which had been operating from Debden since the previous December. As will be noted later under Hornchurch, this squadron could really consider itself as 'Essex born' as it had been re-formed at Hornchurch in 1934. It was now commanded by a pre-war officer, Squadron Leader Humphrey T. Gilbert, DFC, who had served with No 601 at Debden during the Battle of Britain. From the middle of April and for the next two months the Spitfires operated from Great Sampford under the direction of the Debden Wing Leader, Wing Commander John Gordon, a Canadian airman, who had commanded No 151 squadron from Martlesham Heath, but was shot down near Rochford in August 1940. After months of treatment for burns he returned to operational flying, but failed to return from a sweep in June 1942. The pilots were fully engaged in a variety of Fighter Command operations – Ramrods, Rhubarbs and pure fighter sweeps.

The pressing problem for the Command at this stage of the war was the Luftwaffe's new fighter – Focke-Wulf 190. This aircraft had first flown in June 1939 and when the first FW190As began to appear in September 1941, it quickly became apparent that they were vastly superior in performance to the Spitfire Vs, then the mainstay of Fighter

Command. More than 20 mph faster at all altitudes and with greater acceleration FW190s could out-climb, out-dive and out-roll the Spitfires, only in their turning circle were they inferior to the British fighters. Rather fortuitously for the RAF a FW190 landed in error (at Pembrey in South Wales) in June 1942 and it was then used to test its performance against various Spitfire marks. Like all Spitfire squadrons operating in No 11 Group, the 65th suffered losses in combats with FW190s, although on 27th April, over St Omer, one of the squadron's pilots – Pilot Officer T. Bark – claimed two FW190s destroyed and Flight Lieutenant Barclay damaged another.

During its stay at Great Sampford the squadron went through a rather difficult period. On 2nd May Squadron Leader Gilbert was tragically killed in a flying accident at Debden, about three weeks later his DFC was gazetted. He was replaced by Flight Lieutenant Anthony Barclay, DFC, another pre-war pilot, who had also been a Spitfire test pilot and had served in the Battle of Britain. Barclay stayed less than two months before being posted away to the Central Gunnery School. After the war he married the film actress Deborah Kerr, and became a test pilot with Vickers Armstrong. During this period the squadron had spells of detachment at both Martlesham Heath and Hawkinge, and in early July it was removed from operations pending a posting abroad. This overseas move was cancelled, and the squadron returned to operational flying but moved away to Gravesend on 21st July.

It was replaced at Great Sampford by one of the most famous Auxiliary squadrons, No 616 or 'South Yorkshire'; already a number of legendary RAF pilots had served with the squadron – 'Johnnie' Johnson, Hugh Dundas, Colin Gray, Howard Burton and Marcus Robinson. Since April the squadron had been equipped with a rare mark of Spitfire – VIs – of which only 100 were produced. This mark had been specially designed to improve the high altitude performance of the Spitfire and to counter the threat of the Junkers 86P – a high flying reconnaissance bomber. The mark VI had a larger wing span (40' 2"), a Merlin 47 engine that provided a better high-altitude performance and it was fitted with a four blade propellor. It was the first British fighter to have a pressurised cockpit, which was said to become 'unbearably hot' when flying below 15,000 feet. According to one pilot it was like 'flying in a Turkish bath', and as the cockpit was secured by clamps it felt like flying in 'a sealed transparent coffin'!

The squadron was engaged in sweeps and Ramrods and after it left Great Sampford towards the end of September greater use was made of its unusual Spitfires as escorts for the Eighth Air Force bomber formations. With Debden in the throes of being transferred to the Eighth Air Force, it was not surprising that No 133 – the third 'Eagle' – squadron arrived at the airfield pending its pilots' transfer to the USAAF; although they did have the option of remaining with the RAF. Since the squadron had been formed at Coltishall in July 1941, the American pilots had served at Duxford, Colly Weston (in Northants), Fowlmere, Eglington, Kirton-in-Lindsey and latterly Biggin Hill, and they must have been pleased to get a permanent base. Their American commander, Squadron Leader Carroll W. McColphin, would later lead the Ninth Air Force's 404th Fighter Group during the summer of 1944 at the rank of Colonel (Group Captain).

On 26th September, just days after arriving at Great Sampford, twelve newly delivered Spitfire IXs of No 133 squadron, under the command of Acting Squadron Leader Gordon Brettell, were despatched on a routine escort mission for American B-17s attacking two enemy airfields at Morlaix and Cherbourg. The weather conditions were quite atrocious and the other fighters, P-38s from No 1 Fighter Group, were recalled. One of the Bomb Groups was also recalled and another Group failed to bomb their target as the crews miscalculated the tail wind. The whole operation was a failure but it proved to be an utter disaster for the Spitfire pilots; four were shot down and killed, and two were seriously injured and taken prisoner, one of whom was the British Squadron Leader Brettell, who was later involved in the 'Great Escape' and was one of the 50 RAF men executed by the Gestapo. Another four pilots crash-landed in France but one managed to evade capture and escaped to Spain with the help of the French underground. Just one pilot made it back to England; but he crash-landed at Kingsbridge because of lack of fuel and survived with minor injuries. The squadron had almost been wiped out; it was a tragic conclusion to the Eagles' final operation with the RAF.

To all intents and purposes the airfield's operational life was at an end. During November Spitfire VBs of USAAF No 335 squadron (previously RAF No 121) used the airfield for some of its missions and in the following February it was used by P-47s of the 4th Fighter Group for practice landings and training. When the Eighth Air Force no longer needed a satellite airfield, it was passed back to the RAF and the RAF Regiment established their Battle School there. The RAF Regiment had been formed on 1st February 1942 mainly from what were known as 'ground gunners'. They dated from the days of May 1940 when the responsibility of the defence of RAF airfields was placed with the station commander. He was expected to organise and train station ground personnel for the task. By the end of 1940 there were some 35,000 ground gunners, who manned the light anti-aircraft guns and machine guns that ringed the airfields. During the Battle of Britain when the fighter airfields came under heavy attacks from the Luftwaffe, these gunners fought very bravely and valiantly.

By 1944 there was a vastly different climate in the country, air attacks on airfields had all but ceased and the threat of enemy invasion was a thing of the past. As a result, in April 1944, Winston Churchill wrote 'I do not think we can afford to continue to maintain a special body of troops purely for the defence of aerodromes. The RAF Regiment was established at a time when the invasion of this country was likely, and when our life depended on the security of our fighter aerodromes...the time has come to consider whether the greater part of it should not be taken to reinforce the field formations of the Army. I consider that at least 25,000 men should be transferred. They will be much better employed there than loafing around overcrowded airfields warding off dangers which have ceased to threaten.' With a sharp reduction in the RAF Regiment as a result of the Prime Minister's edict, the Regiment left Great Sampford. It was mainly used as a practice landing field for glider pilots operating from several Essex airfields, as well as for trial parachute jumps by British airborne troops.

Today it is one of the most difficult Essex airfields to locate so comprehensively has it returned to agricultural use. The wide expanse of farmland to the south-east of Brockholes Farm at Wimbish Green, however, bears all the hallmarks of a flat landing area devoid of trees and hedges, which are such a feature of the surrounding countryside; also nearby is a clutch of old Nissen huts, which could easily date from wartime days.

14

HORNCHURCH

To visit South Hornchurch and not be very aware that it was once the home of one of the most famous fighter stations of the Second World War is almost impossible. Airfield Way and then Squadrons Approach lead to Hornchurch Country Park, which now covers what was the landing and operational area of this celebrated Battle of Britain airfield. Several wartime artefacts have been fittingly retained, blending well into the surroundings. For certain the town has not forgotten its long and historic connections with the RAF because the myriad of roads adjacent to the Country Park are all aptly named; some remember other RAF fighter airfields, such as Debden Walk, Bradwell Close and Tangmere Crescent, but many proudly recall some of the famous airmen that flew from Hornchurch during its heyday – Bader Way, Deere Avenue, Malan Square, Leathart Close, Tuck Road, Kingaby and Finucane Gardens. Hornchurch is a wonderful memorial of those exciting but traumatic wartime days when the airfield echoed to the sounds of countless Spifire squadrons that were based there.

Although the discreet memorial in the grounds of the Mitchell School commemorates 34 years of Service history (1928-62) , the airfield can, in fact, trace its origins back to 1915 when the small and rather primitive landing ground was known as Sutton's Farm. By the summer of 1917 Sutton's Farm had become an important airfield in the London Air Defence Area, and by the end of the year there were no less than 15 young women serving in the 'Women's Legion' – the forerunner of the WAAF.

After the First World War the airfield returned to its previous owner but by the end of 1922, when it was decided that 15 new squadrons were to be raised for the Home Defence, new airfields were required. Air Marshal Sir Hugh Trenchard declared, 'It is decided that Sutton's Farm or an aerodrome in the vicinity is a necessity for the defensive measures of England.' As no other suitable site could be found, a further area of land adjacent to Sutton's Farm was purchased and construction started on a new permanent RAF 'aerodrome'. The new airfield – still retaining its original name – opened on 1st April 1928 when No 111 squadron landed their Armstrong Whitworth Siskin IIIs. Their commander was a celebrated First World War pilot, Squadron Leader Keith Park, who was to gain lasting fame for his command of No 11 Group during the Battle of Britain. In January 1929 the airfield became officially known as RAF Hornchurch, and for the next ten years the latest fighters, from Bristol Bulldogs to Gloster Gladiators, used the airfield. Like most pre-war RAF stations Hornchurch was open to the public from 1935 during Empire Air Days. But perhaps the airfield's finest hour came in February 1939 when the first Spitfires arrived to re-equip No 74 'Tiger' squadron, and in May of that year it was said that almost 60,000 people attended its last peacetime open day, all eager to view this new and exciting fighter. During the Second World War Hornchurch would become the most renowned Spitfire station in Fighter Command.

The Supermarine Spitfire was, undoubtedly, the most famous RAF fighter of the Second World War. It owed its origin to Air Ministry specification F7/30 to which R. J. Mitchell, the chief designer of Supermarine Aviation, responded with his first design of a quite revolutionary monoplane. The company had gained its reputation with seaplanes and the Spitfire was a direct derivative of their famous S6B seaplane, which won the Schneider Trophy in 1931. But it was the successful marriage of Mitchell's airframe with a Rolls Royce PV12 engine, later named Merlin, that ensured the aircraft's ultimate astounding success.

The first prototype (K 5054) flew on 6th March 1936. Jeffrey Quill, the famous Vickers test pilot known as 'Mr Spitfire', who was so involved in all the early trials and the later development of the aircraft, served with No 65 squadron at Hornchurch for a brief period during the Battle of Britain, and died in February 1996, aged 83 years, only weeks before the 60th anniversary. In June the Air Ministry called for at least 310 Spitfires to be supplied by March 1939. Sadly, Mitchell never lived to see the success of his aircraft as he died in June 1937, but his name is perpetuated in the school at Hornchurch. The first Spitfire entered the

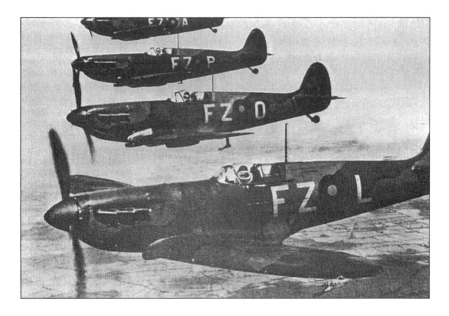

Spitfires of No 65 squadron with their pre-war code 'FZ' – this was changed to 'YT' in September 1939.

Service with No 19 squadron at Duxford during August 1938. With a top speed of close to 360 mph, it was considered then to be the fastest fighter in the world, and armed with eight .303 machine guns, it became a most formidable fighting machine. Ultimately over 20,000 Spitfires were produced in a bewildering number of marks. Adolph 'Sailor' Malan, who was serving with No 74 squadron at Hornchurch, was very impressed with his Spitfire, '...The Spitfire had style and was an obvious killer ... moreover she was a perfect lady. She had no vices. She was beautifully positive...' Another Spitfire pilot maintained '...[it] was the most beautiful flying machine ever invented...'!

At the outbreak of the war Hornchurch was a Sector station in No 11 Group of Fighter Command, covering the important south eastern approaches to London. Like most RAF stations it had no runways, but the large, grassed landing field allowed for three 'runs' of some 1,200, 850 and 830 yards. There was a perimeter track about six yards wide surrounding the field and three large C type hangers. Considering that there were only twelve Spitfire squadrons in Fighter Command, uniquely Hornchuch had three of them – Nos 54, 65 and 74. All three could be considered 'local'; the first two had been re-formed at Hornchurch in 1930 and 1934 respectively, and No 74 had been based at the airfield since its return from Malta in 1936. For a brief period there was also a squadron of Bristol Blenheim IFs (No 600). Hornchurch soon gained a satellite airfield at Rochford and, in November, another at Manston; both airfields were controlled from Hornchurch and were frequently used as advanced landing grounds by the various Hornchurch squadrons.

During the first days of the war when the RAF, and the country, were expecting an all-out Luftwaffe assault almost hourly, all the squadrons were kept on stand-by (take off within five minutes) from first light and were engaged on regular daily patrols. The aircraft were widely dispersed around the airfield, Fighter Command being well aware of how the Polish Air Force had virtually being destroyed on the ground by the Luftwaffe. Only a month earlier a new broadcasting system had been installed at Hornchurch to enable the Controller's instructions to reach the dispersal areas and huts, and it proved such a success that it was introduced at other RAF stations. The company's name was 'Tannoy' and this became the universal name used throughout the Service for radio systems!

The first wartime patrol took place in the early hours of the morning of 4th September, when six Spitfires of No 74 squadron were scrambled to investigate some unidentified aircraft making for Harwich. The pilots patrolled for about an hour or so before the suspect aircraft were declared to be 'friendly'. In such a high state of nervousness and tension some errors were bound to occur, and two days later tragedy struck. Early in the morning an incorrect sighting of what was thought to be an enemy formation resulted in Hurricanes of No 56 squadron at North Weald being scrambled to counter the apparent 'enemy' force. These were followed a little later by Spitfires of 74 squadron. The anti-aircraft defences had also been alerted and unfortunately the Hurricanes were mistaken for hostile fighters and the batteries opened fire on them. So when the pilots of 74 squadron saw shells bursting round the formation they too mistakenly identified the Hurricanes as Me109s, and three Spitfires of 'A' Flight dived to attack the two Hurricanes that were flying slightly behind and below the rest of the squadron, with the unfortunate result that both Hurricanes were shot down. One of the pilots, Pilot Officer Rose, managed, though injured, to crash-land near Ipswich but the other unfortunate pilot, Pilot Officer Hulton-Harrop, was killed. Sadly, he became the first Fighter Command pilot to be killed in the war.

The two pilots from No 74 squadron who were responsible for the tragic incident, were court-martialled but were acquitted and returned to their squadron. This sad and disturbing episode has, for some unaccountable reason, entered RAF folklore as the 'Battle of Barking Creek'.

The station's first 'real' success came on 20th November when pilots from No 74 squadron shot down a Do17 into the sea about 15 miles off Southend. The hard winter of 1939/40, thought to be the most severe in Essex for over 60 years, greatly curtailed operations. The situation drastically changed with the German invasion of France and the Low Countries on 10th May, when the station suddenly erupted into action. Sir Hugh Dowding decided to use some of his precious Spitfire squadrons in the hard and desperate air battle that was taking place over France. Because of the Spitfire's operational range this task fell heavily on the squadrons of No 11 Group. However, it did mean that they could spend only about an hour over the area before having to return for refuelling.

The first 'foreign' patrol by No 11 Group's Spitfires was undertaken by No 54 squadron from Hornchurch on 16th May. The following day No 65's pilots were active over Ostend and a Ju88 was destroyed. From then on the Hornchurch squadrons were in constant action over France and, more especially, Dunkirk. A feature of the campaign was the number of squadrons that used Hornchurch during this period; they arrived to relieve the hard-pressed squadrons, who were then rested. Four new squadrons came to Hornchurch in less than three weeks – Nos 19, 41, 92 and 222. It was the latter squadron that brought Flight Lieutenant Douglas Bader to Hornchurch, and within a day he had claimed his first enemy aircraft of the war – a Me109. During the 19 days of 'Operation Dynamo' – the evacuation of the British Expeditionary Force – the Hornchurch squadrons flew over 1,000 sorties and claimed 83 enemy aircraft destroyed but lost 27 pilots in the process, which was almost a third of the total losses of No 11 Group.

One pilot who managed to survive was Squadron Leader Francis White of No 74 squadron, who was shot down on 23rd May but made a forced landing at Calais-Marck airfield, which was still in Allied hands. The following day Flight Lieutenant James 'Prof' Leathart of 54 squadron persuaded the powers-that-be that White should be rescued. He flew an unarmed two-seater Miles Master escorted by two Spitfires piloted by Al Deere and John Allen. Despite being attacked by twelve Me109s, of which three were destroyed and another three damaged, the daring rescue attempt was successful. Later Deere and Allen were shot

Three cheers for His Majesty! – Hornchurch, 27th June 1940. Pilot Officer J. R. Allen; Flight Lieutenant R. R. S. Tuck; Flight Lieutenant A. C. Deere; Flight Lieutenant A. G. Malan and Squadron Leader J. A. Leathart. (Imperial War Museum)

down over Dunkirk but both made it back to England by boat. Leathart claimed 4½ victories with another two probables over Dunkirk. Squadron Leader White was later moved to Fighter Command headquarters, because at the age of 35 years he was considered too old to lead a fighter squadron! He was succeeded by a 'mere' 29 year old – Flight Lieutenant A. G. 'Sailor' Malan. Malan, a South African, had joined No 74 in late 1936 and he became probably the finest RAF fighter pilot of the war, with 34 victories (including shared victories) to his credit by the end of July 1941. He later commanded Biggin Hill and two Fighter Wings, retiring at the rank of Group Captain with the DSO, DFC and 2 bars. Malan died in 1963 aged 52 years

On 27th June, the station played host to Sir Hugh Dowding and HM King George VI, who came to present the DSO to Leathart and DFCs to Malan, Deere, Allen and Stanford Tuck. The latter, one of the most celebrated fighter pilots of the war, had joined 65 squadron at Hornchurch in August 1936, but by this time he was serving as a flight commander with No 92 squadron at Croydon. Since May he had scored 6½ victories. It was a memorable day for Hornchurch. However, it was back to business very quickly, and although 10th July is officially recognised as the start of the Battle of Britain, the Hornchurch squadrons were in the thick of the fighting during the first week of July. On 7th three Spitfires from No 65 were lost, and on the following day the squadron's CO, Squadron Leader D. Cooke, was shot down and killed. Two days later the squadron lost another three aircraft, and Flight Lieutenant Al Deere had one of his many amazing escapes when he survived a mid-air collision with a Me109.

During those momentous summer months Hornchurch played a crucial role in the Battle of Britain. It could be considered the most important of the seven Sector airfields in No 11 Group, not solely for its position commanding a vital Sector, but also because it was equipped exclusively with Spitfires, it held four out of six of the Group's squadrons of these valuable fighters. For the first month of the Battle just four squadrons took the brunt of the fighting – Nos 41, 54, 65 and 74. Then, in August, when the hard-pressed squadrons and their battle-weary pilots were rested, Nos 222, 266, 603 and 264 squadrons came to replace the 'local' squadrons. Within a week No 222 had destroyed ten enemy aircraft, but had lost several pilots and even more aircraft; by the end of August it had only three serviceable Spitfires. The crews of 264 squadron, which was equipped with Boulton Paul Defiants, operated from both Hornchurch and Rochford, and experienced a most torrid time, losing 15 aircraft and ten pilots in seven days. On 28th August the Defiants were taken out of the Battle.

Like other Sector airfields Hornchurch came under attack from the Luftwaffe. The first raid came in the afternoon of 24th August, which cut the telephone lines and left 85 craters in the vicinity. By the end of 1940 the airfield had sustained another 13 bombing raids, the most severe being the two separate attacks on 31st August. In the first raid (around lunchtime) three Spitfires of 54 squadron were caught taking off and were destroyed. Flight Lieutenant Al Deere was one of the pilots and he had another remarkable escape – his subsequent autobiography *Nine Lives* was aptly named. Although six Spitfires were destroyed, with another five damaged on the ground, the hangars suffered some damage and the landing field was pitted with bomb craters, the airfield was fully operational the following morning. The raiders did not get away scot-free as No 603 'City of Edinburgh' squadron, that had arrived at Hornchurch a few days earlier, claimed 14 enemy aircraft for the loss of two aircraft and one pilot – the highest claim by a squadron in a single day. No 603, under the command of Squadron Leader George Denholm, was destined to remain at Hornchurch almost to the end of the year. Perhaps their most celebrated pilot was Flying Officer Richard Hillary, who in four days had accounted for five Me109s. But on 3rd September he was shot down in flames and suffered quite horrendous burns. After three months of treatment at East Grinstead as a 'guinea pig' under Archie McIndoe, he ultimately returned to flying and was killed in 1943 whilst piloting a Blenheim. Hillary's book *The Last Enemy*, which was published in June 1942, is fully acknowledged as a classic account of air warfare.

By the end of September 1940 the various squadrons that had operated in the Hornchurch Sector during the Battle had claimed 411 enemy aircraft destroyed with another 235 as probable victories – a massive contribution. On the penultimate day of the Battle (30th October) the two squadrons at Hornchurch (Nos 41 and 222) lost five Spitfires with three pilots killed in action. The following day Fighter Command were able to report that not a single fighter had been lost in combat. It was now certain that the Battle was over and the victory was sweet.

Just before Christmas 1940 the station's most famous Commanding Officer, Group Captain Harry Broadhurst, DSO, DFC, AFC, arrived. He had previously commanded Coltishall and Wittering, and during the Battle had flown operational sorties with No 1 squadron. Broadhurst was destined to take his Hornchurch squadrons onto the offensive; he frequently led them by example, perhaps most notably in the Dieppe operation when he claimed four aircraft shot down. When he left Hornchurch in May 1942 he had twelve enemy aircraft to his name. Sir Harry became AOC-in-C Bomber Command in 1956, and retired from the RAF in 1961 at the rank of Air Chief Marshal. He died in August 1995, aged 89 years.

On 10th January 1941 the three Spitfire squadrons (41, 64 and 611), along with three Hurricane squadrons, escorted just six Blenheim bombers from No 2 Group to attack ammunition and supply dumps in the Forêt de Guines, south of Calais. This was the first 'Circus' operation to be mounted by Fighter Command; it was effectively a bombing operation by a squadron of light or medium bombers escorted by a strong force of fighters, with the intention of bringing the Luftwaffe fighters into action. They, along with 'Rhubarbs', 'Ramrods' and 'Roadsteads' would become the staple diet of the Hornchurch

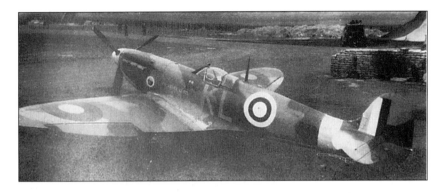

Spitfire II of No 54 squadron at Hornchurch, February 1941.

squadrons. 'Circuses', in particular, did prove rather costly, and as such the last one was mounted in November.

For this new offensive and aggressive role Fighter Command decided to operate its squadrons in 'Wings'. Each of these was commanded by a Wing Commander (Flying), who would lead his three or four squadrons into combat. These officers became the next senior officers to the stations' COs. On 15th March 1941 the Hornchurch Wing was formally established with Nos 54, 64 and 611 squadrons and Wing Commander Andrew Farquhar, DFC, as its commander. He was an experienced fighter pilot, who had seen action with No 275 squadron at Martlesham Heath. This post was filled, at various times, by some of the famous fighter pilots of the Second World War, such as Petrus Hugo, Eric Thomas, William Crawford-Compton and, the last incumbent, Peter Simpson.

Perhaps the most celebrated Wing Commander (Flying) at Hornchurch was Brendan 'Paddy' Finucane, DSO, DFC, 2 bars, who arrived in June 1942. Finucane had previously served with No 65 squadron at Hornchurch during the Battle and had risen from Pilot Officer to Wing Commander in two years. He was a unique fighter pilot who had become a legend in his lifetime. On 15th July he led the Wing in a large sweep over northern France. Finucane's Spitfire was hit by ground fire and he crashed into the English Channel but the rescue launches found no trace of him. It was a tragedy, as the station diary records: 'The loss of Wing Commander Finucane will be deeply felt; quite apart from his personal prowess as a fighter pilot, he was becoming an inspiring leader and an admired example to all the pilots

166

Spitfire VB of No 313 squadron at Hornchurch, December 1941 to June 1942. (Southend Museums Service)

he led. It would be difficult to find a more simple, direct and likeable personality.' At his death he had 32 enemy aircraft destroyed – which proved to be the fourth highest RAF total of the war.

When No 54 squadron finally left Hornchurch in November 1941, it had served at the airfield longer than any other fighter squadron (it had re-formed there in 1930). This famous fighter squadron, which dated back to 1916, and had 'Boldness endures everything' as its motto, had notched its 100th victory in April 1941. The squadron was ultimately re-formed in March 1974 and became part of RAF Strike Command, flying Jaguars. During August 1941 the first Commonwealth squadron – No 403 (Canadian) – arrived at Hornchurch with its Spitfire VBs. This new mark of Spitfire had a more powerful engine (Merlin 45) and was armed with a mixture of two 20 mm Hispano cannons and four machine guns; another version was adopted as a fighter/bomber. It was designed to match the much improved Me109F. The Mark Vs (A, B and C variants) became the mainstay of Fighter Command for most of 1941/2 and some 6,500 were produced; but as previously noted it was seriously outclassed by the FW190.

The Canadian pilots went out on their first Circus on 7th August but in the brief time they served at Hornchurch four pilots were lost, including their commander – Squadron Leader Morris. Before the year was out another Canadian squadron – No 411 – arrived and stayed for over three months. The increasingly cosmopolitan nature of the airfield became apparent when No 313 squadron flew in during December; this was the third Czech fighter squadron to be formed in Fighter Command. During the next two years a Free French (No 340) squadron, a Belgian (No 350), an Australian (No 453) and a New Zealand (No 485) squadron all became part of the Hornchurch Wing, alongside a variety of British squadrons, of which No 129 'Mysore' was the longest serving at Hornchurch.

The shock that Fighter Command received with the advent of the FW190 and its superior performance, really called for a swift riposte. A new Spitfire version was being developed, which would ultimately become the Mark VIII, but an interim and improved variant was desperately needed by Fighter Command. The new mark that was speedily developed and put into production proved to be a more powerful Mark V, with a Merlin 61 engine which was provided with a two-stage, two speed supercharger giving it a speed just in excess of 400 mph. This new Spitfire was designated IX and was vastly superior in performance to the Vs. The new mark made its first appearance in late July 1942 with No 64 squadron at Hornchurch, and Flight Lieutenant Donald Kingaby claimed the aircraft's first FW190 on the 30th, which was his 16th victory. Later on the same day the squadron went into action again and destroyed a further three FW190s. This was to be a significant turning-point for Fighter Command, and it marked the beginning of the Command's superiority in the air. Although the aircraft's performance only just about matched the FW190, over 5,600 IXs were produced and it was still flying operationally in 1945.

During the latter months of 1942 the Hornchurch Wing became greatly involved in escorting the heavy bombers of the USAAF's Eighth Air Force, and later the medium bombers of the Ninth Air Force, which were based in the east of the country. A most celebrated operation conducted by the Eighth Air Force was the Schweinfurt/Regensburg mission on 17th August 1943. Nos 129 and 222 squadrons flew 48 sorties on two escort operations, and they managed to account for four FW190s without a single loss.

When the Second Tactical Air Force was formed and Fighter Command disappeared to become the Air Defence of Great Britain,

Hornchurch remained in No 11 Group but became known as 'Station 136'. However, little changed as the station record for November 1943 states, 'The past month has seen a continuation of the offensive sweeps and escorts which are becoming increasingly uneventful. It is now unusual for enemy opposition to be encountered.'

Nevertheless soon there would be great changes. On January 21st 1944 the airfield was bombed for the first time for over three years. Almost a month later, on the night of 23rd/24th February, a solitary intruder dropped just three HE bombs, which destroyed eight of No 504's Spitfires with another five damaged, and yet the squadron still managed to be operational on the following day. The squadron, under the command of Squadron Leader H. J. L. Hallowes, DFC, DFM and bar, had only arrived at Hornchurch about a month earlier. 'Bert' Hallowes was another 'Halton brat', and as a Sergeant pilot with No 43 squadron had shared in the destruction of an He111 – the first enemy aircraft to come down in England, on 3rd February 1940. Commissioned in September 1940, he became a Flight Commander with No 65 squadron, and had commanded No 122 at North Weald during June 1942.

The station was now under North Weald's fighter control as the Sector Operations Room had been closed down. The writing was on the wall for Hornchurch as an operational airfield. Gradually the Spitfire squadrons left; No 222 at the beginning of April. Except for a brief period in May when three Spitfire squadrons arrived from Italy for re-equipping, the airfield was ominously quiet. A very unusual state of affairs for an airfield that for almost five years had been a most active fighter station with its Spitfire squadrons always in the thick of the action. From November until June 1945 the airfield housed an Air Sea Rescue squadron, a Radar Calibration squadron, and, most unlikely, a Fleet Air Arm squadron equipped with the doughty and trundling Vickers Wellingtons. It must have been strange to see these rather outdated bombers using the airfield, which hitherto had been the sole preserve of the sleek and speedy Spitfires.

By mid-June 1945 all the flying units had left Hornchurch and the airfield passed out of Fighter Command and into Technical Training Command. During the Second World War the station's tally of enemy aircraft destroyed amounted to 907 with another 444 as probable victories, at a cost of 481 pilots killed. A massive and valuable contribution to the European air war but with a heavy sacrifice of young airmen; without doubt throughout the war Hornchurch was a Spitfire station par excellence.

The old airfield is now a Country Park.

For ten years from 1952 thousands upon thousands of young and aspiring airmen passed through the impressive and ornate entrance gates to attend the Aircrew Selection Centre in the hope of being selected for a flying career in the Service. Most of them, this writer included, felt that Hornchurch epitomised the wartime RAF, redolent of memories of all the famous fighter squadrons and their pilots that had served there. It was a sad day – 27th February 1963 – when the Air Ministry put up the 'Sale By Auction' notice, 47 years of Service history had ended but they have certainly not been forgotten, which is much to the credit of the Borough of Havering.

15

LITTLE WALDEN

This airfield was tucked away in the top north-west corner of the county, close to the boundary with Cambridgeshire. It was first called Hadstock, gaining this name from the ancient village, which was a short distance away to the north-east. Despite having a relatively short wartime existence the airfield was used by three famous American wartime aircraft – A-20s, P-51s and B-17s. It is also blessed with one of the best preserved control towers in Essex, which has been splendidly restored by Roger Lynn Associates and is now used by them for offices. The building still retains a fine collection of memorablia relating to its wartime days.

Work started on the site at Hadstock Common in the summer of 1942 with planned completion by the following spring. The proposed Class A bomber airfield was allocated to the Eighth Air Force, and it was assumed that in the fullness of time a Heavy Bomb Group would occupy the airfield. However, the winter of 1942/3 greatly delayed the construction work, and the programme did not really continue with any urgency until May 1943; by then, for some unaccountable reason the official name was changed to Little Walden – from the village that lay about 1½ miles due south of the airfield.

When the airfield was finally ready for occupation in March 1944, it had long since been passed over over to the Ninth Air Force, and on 7th March, the day after the official opening, A-20s of the 409th Bomb Group (Light) arrived at Little Walden, to become the second Havoc Group in the Ninth Bomber Command and the 97th Combat Bomb Wing which established its headquarters at the airfield. The Group had a mixture of

Mural of A-20s in the old control tower at Little Walden. (by kind permission of Roger Lynn Associates)

A-20Gs and Js, and the essential difference between the two marks was that the 'J's were equipped with a 'bombardier' nose section as opposed to the 'solid' noses of the earlier mark. The Ninth had introduced the tactic of 'bombing on the leader' with at least one A-20J aircraft per squadron taking the lead in order to establish and calculate the precise target positions for the following aircraft to bomb on a given signal from the lead aircraft. These tactics required an extra fourth crewman – bombardier/navigator – which further strained the acute shortage of trained crews that faced the Ninth Air Force during the spring of 1944. Of necessity a number of extra bombardiers were drafted into the 409th, and these mainly came from the existing B-26 Groups.

Colonel Preston J. Pender, the Commanding Officer, quickly set up a retraining programme for his crews, and it was not until five weeks later that he was confident that they were ready for operations. On 13th April they left to attack gun batteries along the Channel coast. From then on the crews became engaged in attacking V1 rocket sites, airfields and a variety of strategic targets in France, especially marshalling yards.

172

Operations appeared to progress reasonably smoothly, that is until one day in May.

On 27th May, as the aircraft were departing on a mission, one of the A-20s had just taken off when it collided violently with a low-flying P-51 from a nearby airfield. The Mustang disintegrated and the A-20 crashed into a field to the south of the airfield near Church End. A farmer's widow, Mrs Betty Everitt, who was walking her dog, witnessed the accident and rushed across to the crashed A-20. With little thought for her own safety she immediately dragged one airman out of the aircraft and, whilst she was attempting to save another crewman, part of the bomb load exploded, killing her and the airman. There is a memorial in Ashdon church to this courageous lady, as well as another plaque in her honour in the old control tower. Within days the USAAF set up a fund to help and support her orphaned son.

The target of this mission, which had started so tragically, was the marshalling yards at Amiens. Two boxes of aircraft, a total of 38 A-20s, had been despatched for this operation with the 640th squadron taking the lead. As the first formation was about 27 miles from the target and flying at an altitude of about 11,500 feet, it suddenly encountered an intense and accurate barrage of flak. Within minutes the leading aircraft were severely damaged. The first two exploded and fell to earth with no signs of any survivors. A third aircraft, piloted by Captain Leslie Huff, lost one engine, so the Captain decided to turn back for home. However, the aircraft quickly began to lose height and the crew were ordered to bale out. The two gunners managed to bale out but the bombardier was trapped. By the time the aircraft was over the English Channel the bombardier had managed to extricate himself and he and Captain Huff succeeded in escaping. Both officers were later picked up later by the RAF Air Sea Rescue services. Meanwhile the other A-20s in the leading formation had regrouped sufficiently to make their bombing run; only two survived without any flak damage, and one aircraft had to make a crash-landing on the nearest available airfield in England, but the crew escaped with just bruises. It had been a rather unhappy day for the Group.

The 409th flew two missions on D-Day, attacking a coastal battery, a bridge and a railway embankment to the rear of the Utah beach-head. On this day the A-20 Groups made a total of 269 sorties with 206 crews managing to bomb, dropping over 260 tons but five aircraft were lost. This loss rate (1.8%) was the heaviest sustained by the Ninth Air Force on the day. For the rest of the month the Group was engaged in continuing the 'interdiction campaign' – a massive air offensive against enemy troop movements, rail and road bridges. Towards the end of the month they were also involved in the battle for Cherbourg by attacking gun positions and troop positions. Throughout June the three Light Bomb Groups made over 3,300 sorties, dropping some 3,000 tons of bombs, and lost 14 A-20s in the process, which again was slightly higher than their B-26 colleagues, but nevertheless a valuable contribution to the Ninth's offensive.

In the early days of July Colonel Pender moved on and he was replaced by Colonel Thomas R. Ford, who remained in command for the rest of the war. Without doubt, July could well be called 'bridges' month, with the Ninth Bomb Groups being allocated 36 bridges as priority targets. It was ultimately discovered that at least 20 of these were effectively put out of action, of which three were accounted for by the A-20 Groups. From 7th to 31st the bridges across the Loire were attacked by the Ninth Bomb Groups and they ranged from Nantes to Tours; in all 16 missions were launched against these bridges, with at least six out of seven being severely damaged.

Besides bridges, the 409th was involved in air-ground support around St Lô, Caen and especially enemy troop concentrations (SS Panzer Corps) at Ussy, just to the north of Falaise, as well as attacking ammunition and fuel dumps. During the rest of their stay at Little Walden the A-20s ranged over the battleground and even went as far west as Brest, which was attacked on four occasions during the first week of September. However, their days in Essex were now numbered and on 18th September the Group up and left for an airfield at Bretigny, which was about 20 miles south of Paris. The Group had mounted 123 missions from Little Walden, in which ten aircraft were lost in action. The commemoration panel to the 409th, which is displayed in the old control tower, records that a total of 257 combat missions were flown during the war. It also states, 'The men of this Organization served to preserve the right of Nations to determine their own destiny.' Amen to those sentiments.

Within ten days the airfield came alive again with the 'sweet and dulcet' tones of the Packard Merlin engines of the P-51s of the 361st Fighter Group. The airfield had now been passed back to the Eighth Air Force and the reason given for the move of the 361st was because 'Little Walden offered better facilities than their old base' – Bottisham in Cambridgeshire, which had been its home since the end of November 1943. One further factor that might have influenced the decision to move

P-51s of 374th squadron of 361st Fighter Group. (USAF)

was that on 15th September the Eighth Fighter Command was reorganised with the various Fighter Groups being allocated to three Bombardment Divisions and placed under their control. As the 361st had been seconded to the Second Division, its move into Essex would at least bring it slightly closer to its 'big brothers' – the Division's B-24s – which were operating mainly from airfields in Norfolk.

The 361st had been the last P-47 Group to join the Eighth, and had been operational since the previous January, but since May the Group had converted to P-51s and its pilots were now well experienced with these splendid fighters. About a month before its arrival at Little Walden, the Group had lost Colonel Thomas Christian Jr., its orginal and popular Commanding Officer, he had been killed in action. The 361st was temporarily led by Lieutenant Colonel Roy Caviness, who had two spells as acting CO before commanding the Group at the end of the war. Within days Lieutenant Colonel Joseph J. 'Joe' Kruzel, who had been the Group's Executive Officer, took over the command. Kruzel had previously served with distinction in the Pacific, where he had shot down three Japanese aircraft, and now proceeded to add four Luftwaffe fighters to his total.

At this stage of the air war the P-51s had effectively gained the measure of the Luftwaffe day-fighters. They had the pace on the Me109Gs and FW190As and could certainly out-turn them. Also, the American pilots had some other advantages over the Luftwaffe pilots other than being far more numerous (about ten to one). They were now being supplied with the Berger pressure suits, known as 'G suits', which enabled the pilots to make swifter and sharper air manoeuvres without

175

blacking out because of the 'G factor'. Also the P-51s were beginning to be fitted with new gyroscopic gunsights. These were British designed sights mainly developed for use in the RAF's heavy bombers, but they had been successfully adapted for fighters and were soon dubbed 'No miss em' by the American pilots! These sights allowed for more successful and accurate firing at nearly twice the previous maximum range, as well offering deflection shooting. The USAAF later devised their own version – the K-14 – which later became a standard feature on all P-51s. These innovations, and the fact that the P-51 guns released 80 rounds per second against the 60 and 30 rounds by the FW190 and Me109 respectively, gave the American fighter pilots the upper hand over their opponents.

Almost as proof of this air superiority over the Luftwaffe, the Group returned from their first mission mounted from Little Walden, on 27th September, with the claims of 18 victories for the loss of just one pilot. However, bare statistics do not begin to reveal the true and tragic story of the day's operation. Actually this mission to the Henschel engine works at Kassel was a complete and tragic disaster for one B-24 Group, the 445th from Tibenham in Norfolk. The Group's aircraft had strayed about 20 miles to the east of the main bomber formations and paid dearly for the minor navigational error. In a matter of minutes the Group lost 25 B-24s to a strong force of armoured FW190s, which were escorted by Me109s. It was the 376th squadron from Little Walden that responded to the crews' desperate call for help. Led by First Lieutenant Victor Bocquin, the P-51s probably prevented the complete annihilation of the 445th's bombers. One fighter pilot alone, First Lieutenant William Beyer, shot down five FW190s with Lieutenant Bocquin weighing in with another three victories. The sudden arrival of the Group's yellow-nosed P-51s must have seemed 'heaven-sent' – a direct answer to the bomber crews' prayers! The scene was later described as '...fantastic...a sky full of blazing aircraft, parachutes, smoke and the debris of battle...It was indescribable. Hollywood couldn't think of anything to match it.' The Group still lost 30 B-24s, which was the highest loss ever sustained by any Group on a single mission. The 376th also created a record with its 18 victories, which was then the highest total for any fighter squadron engaged in a single day's mission.

The aerial superiority of the American fighters would be seriously tested with the appearance of the Luftwaffe's 'jet' fighters – the Me163 and Me262 – during late September. Despite this, October proved to be a very quiet month for large air combats; it was almost as if the Luftwaffe was a spent force. As if to dispel such optimistic thoughts, whilst on an escort mission to eastern Germany, on 7th October, at least 25 jet fighters were identified by the escorting fighters. When Lieutenant Urban L. Drew of the 361st sighted two Me262s taking off from Achmer airfield, he dived down to attack and managed to destroy them both. Although the 'jets' were very vulnerable at such times, it was still a notable achievement for the young pilot, and probably just retribution because a few days earlier Drew had chased a Me262 for a considerable distance to no avail because of its far superior speed. November proved to be a vastly different affair, with the Luftwaffe opposing the Eighth in considerable strength on a number of occasions and these air battles were very bitter and became quite critical in the European air war. On 26th of the month, when it was estimated that more than 400 Luftwaffe fighters were airborne over the Hanover area, the Group, under the leadership of Captain John Duncan, claimed 21 enemy aircraft without a single loss.

Christmas 1944 turned out to be a rather eventful time for the Group's pilots. On the 23rd they were engaged in escort duty for B-24s attacking targets at Junkerath, west of Koblenz, and three enemy aircraft were destroyed for the loss of a single P-51. Operations on Christmas Eve added another four victories to the Group's total. Then on Christmas Day it was decided, in order to give escort assistance to the Ninth's fighter/bombers that were heavily engaged in the Ardennes campaign, that two of the Eighth's Fighter Groups would be sent to operate from airfields on the Continent. One of these was the 361st. Most of the Group's pilots packed their bags and left for St Dizier airfield in Belgium, where they stayed until the middle of February operating under the control of the Ninth Air Force. When their spell of secondment with the Ninth came to an end, the pilots moved over to another Belgian airfield, Chièvres, and were now joined by the rest of the pilots and the ground crews from Little Walden.

However, the airfield did not stay silent for very long because, within two weeks, a Group of B-17s arrived. It was the 493rd, or the so-called 'Helton's Hellcats', a name they had adopted from their original Commanding Officer, Colonel Elbert Helton. The Group was now led by Colonel Robert Landry, who was the only Eighth Air Force officer to command both a Bomber and Fighter Group (56th), and the American crews had been forced to vacate their permanent base at Debach in Suffolk because its concrete runways were in need of urgent repair due to subsidence; it had been built by American engineers.

B-17G of 493rd Bomb Group. (USAF)

The 493rd was the most junior Bomb Group in the Eighth, and had entered the air war on D-Day. The crews' first operation from Little Walden was mounted on 1st March to the marshalling yards at Ulm in Germany, and on the next mission, two days later, two B-17s were lost over Brunswick. Other targets during their stay at the airfield included Dortmund, Berlin, Hanover, Ruhland, Hamburg and Brandenburg, during which another two aircraft were lost, before they moved back to Debach at the beginning of April.

By 9th April the 361st had returned 'home' and were quickly back in action, although by now the air battle was rapidly coming to a close, indeed the pilots would be active only on another seven days. On 16th over 900 USAAF fighters were airborne – a staggering demonstration of the Eighth's air power – and the 361st managed to add a single victory in the air to their total but in the large scale strafing of enemy airfields, when the fighters claimed over 720 enemy aircraft destroyed, two pilots failed to return to Little Walden – the Group's last casualties of the war. Their final and 441st mission was sent out from Little Walden on 25th April. The Group had lost 81 aircraft, missing in action, and claimed 226 enemy aircraft destroyed in the air and another 105 on the ground. Unlike some of the other Fighter Groups in the Eighth the 361st was not noted for the number of its fighter aces – 'just' ten. Captain Dale F. Spencer led the field with nine and a half victories, followed closely by Captain William R. Beyer (an ace in a day on 27th September) with nine aircraft destroyed, and Captain Urban L. Drew claiming six.

After VE day the Group stayed on longer than most other Fighter

The old control tower at Little Walden. (by kind permission of Roger Lynn Associates)

Groups. Little Walden had also become the headquarters of the Eighth's 65th Fighter Wing. Towards the end of September the Group was joined by the personnel of the 56th Fighter Group, who moved in from Boxted. They left for the United States in October, and were followed by the 361st at the beginning of November, sailing from Southampton on 4th November on the *Queen Mary* – returning home in style! The USAAF handed over the airfield to the RAF at the end of January 1946, although it was not until May 1958 that it was finally relinquished.

16

MATCHING

There is a plaque on the east wall of the delightful Norman church of St Mary the Virgin at Matching Green and it bears the badge of 391st Bomb Group (Medium), which occupied the nearby airfield for barely eight months. The plaque has been placed there by the surviving officers and men of the Group and the inscription neatly encapsulates not only the operational performance of the 391st whilst flying from Matching, but also the strong bonds of friendship that were established during 1944. That this amity has survived the test of time is evidenced by the brick memorial to the Group, which was unveiled in May 1992 by a party of 'veterans' of the 391st, who revisited their old airfield 48 years later.

Whilst operating from Matching during January to September 1944 the 391st, according to the inscription, '...flew 6,000 sorties and dropped 18 million pounds of high explosives on Hitler's European Fortress, suffering the loss of 197 airmen killed, wounded or missing... and in appreciation of your friendship, with the hope that Americans and Englishmen will continue to stand together in the great trials to come for free men.' It should also be noted that the Group lost 20 B-26s in the process.

The airfield, which was situated to the east of Matching Green, was built during 1943 by the 834th and 840th Engineer Aviation Battalions, and had been allocated to the USAAF in August 1942. It was scheduled to be completed by the spring of 1943 but was not ready for occupation until the following November. Some of the delay was caused by the need to clear part of Mann Wood in order to lay down the main runway. During the summer of 1943 it was recognised that at least twelve VHB

Multifoot paving machine in operation on concrete runways at Matching – 4th September 1943. (Smithsonian Institution)

(Very Heavy Bomber) airfields with 3,000 yard runways would be needed to cater for the B-29s and the Vickers Windsors when they came into service. The 'Windsor' never left the drawing board, and the B-29 (Superfortress) only operated against Japan. However, Matching was seriously considered as a site for one of these enhanced airfields but the idea was abandoned because of 'too many agricultural objections'. Ultimately Marham, Sculthorpe and Lakenheath were the only East Anglian airfields to be selected for further development.

The first American servicemen moved in during November and they belonged to the 13th Replacement Control Depot, which remained at Matching until the following June. It would be almost two months (30th January 1944) before the first B-26s of the 391st Group flew in after a long and protracted journey via the southern ferry route. The crews had left their base at Hunter Field in Georgia on 3rd January, and the last aircraft did not arrive until 24th February! By this time the Group's personnel had settled into their new homes – the Nissen huts – that were grouped in five sites to the east of the airfield. The 391st was commanded by Colonel Gerald E. Williams, one of only two Commanding Officers to lead a B-26 Group for the whole duration of the war. The Group took its allotted place in the 99th Bomb Wing, and like the other new Groups it received an infusion of experienced crews and pilots from the experienced B-26 Groups.

'Station 166', as it was known in USAAF official records, was not formally handed over by the RAF until 4th March, when the RAF Ensign was ceremoniously lowered and the Stars and Stripes raised in its place. The airfield then became 'an American Island in England' – at least according to the Group's official record of the occasion! RAF and American Guards of Honour stood to attention whilst Squadron Leader Nelson presented the deeds of the airfield to Major Dillenger of the Station's headquarters, with Wing Commander Martin and Lieutenant Colonel David S. Blackwell, the Group Executive Officer, in attendance. This short official ceremony was similar to those throughout the length and breadth of East Anglia as airfields were transferred to the USAAF. And, of course, a similar one took place in reverse when the Americans ended their brief tenures.

On 15th February the Group launched its first operation, in a little over two weeks after its arrival at Matching and before it was up to full complement, which was no mean achievement. The 391st was engaged in attacking enemy airfields and 'No Ball' targets, but almost straightaway the airmen were made aware of the vagaries of the British weather, which successfully intervened to curb the Ninth's operations for almost a week. As a result of these unfavourable conditions it was not until the 24th that the Ninth Bomber Command was able to launch a major operation (226 B-26s) against a group of airfields – Leeuwarden, Gilze-Riger and Deelen – situated in Friesland in northern Holland. It proved to be quite a successful mission, as well as being the deepest penetration raid so far by the B-26s.

During March the Ninth Bomber Command had now become a force to be reckoned with, having seven Medium and one Light Bomb Groups fully operational. As a result of the increased forces at its command, it managed to fly over 4,000 sorties with more than 25% of them being directed at 34 V1 rocket sites, although enemy airfields were still the preferred targets. Nevertheless it was during this month that the Ninth began its famous offensive against rail targets, and almost a half of the missions during the month were directed against marshalling yards, railway sheds and works as well as important rail junctions.

The first rail junction to suffer was Longueau, to the south of Amiens, followed four days later (6th) by Hirson, which was close to the border between France and Belgium. The Group, along with the 323rd at Earls Colne, attacked this important junction in quite perfect visual bombing conditions, and the photographic evidence suggested that the bombing was most effective. As has already been noted, the Creil marshalling yards came in for the heaviest treatment with 54 of the Group's aircraft active on 7th, and again on 20th when four Groups (including the 391st) dropped almost 200 tons of bombs. Then three days later the target was again bombed by the 391st and very heavy damage was caused. So impressive was this operation that the Command's chiefs sent out a congratulatory message to the six Groups taking part in this 'outstanding success'.

The unfavourable report on the Groups' performances during March and early April, which resulted in a substantial 're-training programme', would appear to have cast some reflection on the officers serving with the two Bomb Wings' staff. It was they who were responsible for the supervision of training with the operational control of the Bomb Groups resting with Bomber Command's headquarters staff at Marks Hall. On 8th April this all changed, with the two Wings taking over the operational control of their Bomb Groups. Under the new procedure Command headquarters issued the combat orders for each mission but the Bomb Wings would decide which Groups would participate and in what strength. This information was then passed to each Group's Operations Room; this was the nerve centre of the airfield and it was usually housed in a windowless concrete building reputed to be fire and blast proof and secure other than from a direct hit. At Matching the room was set about ½ mile to the east of the main technical sites. It was here that the CO and the Group Executive Officer, Lieutenant Colonel David Blackwell, would decide on the make-up of the Group's force and, most importantly, which officers would lead the mission.

During April other material changes were brought in. As has already been noted a Pathfinder squadron had been formed at Andrews Field, and now more operations were being led by a Pathfinder (PFF) aircraft. This had not passed unnoticed and the PFF aircraft began to receive special treatment by the enemy, who knew full well that if the lead aircraft could be destroyed it could seriously disrupt the bombing attack. On 18th April the Group's operation against coastal fortifications at Calais was led by a PFF aircraft, which was heavily hit by flak, and its pilot, First Lieutenant Charles G. Aldous, was wounded. He was the first Pathfinder casualty, although it would be some weeks before the first PFF aircraft was shot down. Also during the month 'Window' was used for the first time. This was a British invention, which had been in use by Bomber Command from July 1943 and by the Eighth Air Force since December. It involved thin metallic strips (each 27 cm long by 2 cm wide) of aluminium foil being released in bundles with the intention of nullifying the radar that controlled the enemy's gun and searchlight batteries. On 18th April when 277 B-26s attacked railroad targets and gun batteries at Dunkirk, 24 aircraft dispensed 'Window'. On subsequent selected missions at least two aircraft per Group would drop this rather simple but very effective screen.

Marshalling yards again came under attack during April and May and they ranged from Malines, Hasselt and Namur in Belgium to Béthune to the south-west of Lille, the latter target being bombed no less than eight times in just 20 days. On 23rd Namur was heavily bombed by four Groups, causing fires so intense and smoke so heavy that even on the following day the photographs could not reveal the damage that had been inflicted. The crews were continually briefed about their bombing techniques to ensure greater accuracy and thus reduce civilian casualties to the absolute minimum. The Allied Air Chiefs were concerned about the effect their heavy bombardment was having on the civilian population. It was now decided that the B-26 Groups would bomb in flights of six aircraft in a box of 18 aircraft flying on converging lines of attack, a tactic which seemed to improve the bombing results. Enemy airfields within a 130 mile radius of the Normandy beach-heads were attacked again and again, as were the gun batteries along the Channel coast. The B-26s were proving effective in these 'softening up' operations, which were conducted with very minimal losses compared with the Eighth Air Force casualties.

May was a hectic month for all B-26 Groups and some 15,000 tons of bombs were dropped, which was an increase of 76% on the previous month. This increased operational activity brought in its wake another problem for the Ninth Air Force – an acute shortage of bombs. The problem was never completely resolved, and in fact it became worse when the B-26 Groups went over to operate from French airfields later in the year. The other shortage that bedevilled the Ninth was an adequate supply of replacement crews. Although there was a massive influx of men into the USAAF the training programme was rather long. All of the new crews, on arrival from the States, were sent first to No 3 Combat

Lieutenant General Lewis H. Brereton, CO of the Ninth Air Force, with Colonel Gerald E. Williams, CO of 391st Bomb Group at Matching, and on the right Colonel Thomas Hall. Both Colonels received decorations. (via Bryan Jones)

Crew Replacement at Toome Bridge in Northern Ireland. It was here that the flying procedures used in England were inculcated, additional instrument and formation training was given, and an island in Lough Neagh was used as a bombing range. The young airmen were lectured on the techniques of escape and evasion, and they were even given a 'cram' course on French, which must have proved useful when they were serving from airfields in France!

Like all B-26 Groups the 391st flew two missions on D-Day, attacking coastal fortifications and gun emplacements. Throughout the day's operations the B-26 Groups only claimed two enemy aircraft destroyed; one of these – a FW190 – fell to the guns of 391st over the Point du Hoc. It seems that 20 FW190s had 'appeared from nowhere' to attack the Group's leading formation. The following days saw the Group attacking road and rail bridges and road blocks, some of the bridges were near to Paris and the others along the river Seine in what was called the 'Paris to Orléans Gap'. One of the problems in attacking bridges, besides the size

185

B-26s line up at Matching. (USAF)

of the target and the fact that they were heavily defended, was that they were invariably only partially damaged (despite using 2,000 pound bombs) and the Wehrmacht's engineers became rather adept and proficient at repairing them quickly, and so the crews were forced to return again to the same targets.

These missions were all part of the 'interdiction campaign' – the Allied Air Forces' attempt to seal off the battlefield and prevent the movement of troops, armour and supplies to the German front-lines. Field Marshal von Rundsteadt had to admit that '...The Allied Air Forces paralysed all movement by day and made it difficult by night. They had smashed the bridges over the Loire as well as the Seine, shutting off the whole area...' Without doubt the 391st made a valuable contribution to this 'overwhelming air victory' (Field Marshal Rommel's words) because during the month of June the Group had launched 29 missions – more than 1,000 individual sorties – with very low casualties.

On 27th July Brigadier General Samuel E. Anderson, the Ninth Bomb Commander, visited Matching to present awards to the various crewmen who had been honoured for their actions during the previous month. No doubt the General took the opportunity to praise the Group on its performance in 'Operation Cobra'. This was the now famous offensive of the American 1st and 3rd Armies, which started on 25th July and resulted in the successful break-out from St Lô two days later. Before the American ground offensive began at 11 am on 25th, a strip of enemy territory just 5 miles long and 1 mile wide suffered an intense aerial bombardment from the Ninth fighter/bombers as well as the Eighth's heavies. One German officer later recalled 'It was hell...the planes kept coming overhead like a conveyor belt...' The Ninth Bomb Groups – 580 aircraft in total – bombed enemy strong points and troop concentrations behind the enemy lines, and out of the range of artillery fire; their attack continued for almost an hour. Almost inevitably, some crews 'bombed short', causing over 480 American casualties on the ground, of which 102 were fatal. Nevertheless it was a shattering and awesome demonstration of the use of air power in support of ground forces.

The month of August proved to be another frantic period of operations for the Group and the Ninth Air Force as a whole. Over 9,100 bomber sorties were made, with well over 10,000 tons of bombs being dropped on a range of targets from bridges to road and rail junctions as well as specific strikes made in direct support of the ground forces. Early in September the Group was directed to set up a special leaflet dropping mission. Just eight B-26s left Matching to drop propaganda leaflets over Ostend, Dunkirk, Calais, Le Havre, Lorient and Arras – it sounds like a 'Cook's tour'! These leaflet missions were not too popular amongst the crews, who felt that if they were going to risk their lives over enemy territory, they would much prefer to drop something that exploded rather than 'a batch of fancy words'!

As the Allied Armies advanced out of the Normandy enclave during August, the American Engineer Aviation Battalions moved in swiftly to prepare landing grounds and to repair existing airfields for the arrival of the Ninth Air Force's fighters and bombers. By the end of August the 98th Bomb Wing had left their Essex bases for forward airfields in Hampshire, and it was now just a matter of time before the Groups of the 99th Wing would find themselves making the 'full leap' to operate from airfields in France.

Thus it was on 19th September that the men of the 391st finally bade farewell to all the friends they had made in Matching and set off for their new base – Amy airfield at Roye about 30 miles to the south-east of Amiens. It was from here that the 391st won its DUC for its operations in the 'Battle of the Bulge' – the heavy and bloody fighting in the Ardennes forest during the Christmas period.

After the departure of the B-26s the Ninth Air Force retained the airfield and some C-47s (Skytrains) of the Ninth Troop Carrier Command moved in briefly for training exercises with British airborne troops. Once they had left, the airfield passed back to the RAF and it was placed under the control of No 3 Group of Bomber Command, which had its headquarters at Exning near Newmarket. Their records show that at the end of 1944 the airfield had been placed under 'Care and Maintenance'.

In the New Year Matching became yet another airfield to pass over to No 38 Group and an Operational and Refresher Training Unit arrived with Stirling IVs and Horsa gliders. Like several other Essex airfields Matching became marginally involved in 'Operation Varsity' – when just 14 Stirlings and Horsas left for Holland. In the following month most of the Unit converted to Halifax IIIs, and it stayed for another six months before moving to Wethersfield.

Quite quickly the land was passed back to the original owners – the Rowe family at Rockwood Hall – and the airfield returned to agricultural use. Most of the runways were taken up, although part of one is now used as a public road. One of the hangars survived for over 30 years before being dismantled and re-erected at North Weald. Parts of the perimeter road have survived but the most abiding memory of the old wartime airfield is the control tower, which can easily be sighted from the road.

17

NORTH WEALD

Although North Weald Bassett has a long and ancient history, its chief claims to fame relate to the 20th century and reside in its radio station, the masts of which dominated the skyline from 1921, and its airfield, which was an important fighter station during the Second World War. The radio station finally closed in 1985 but the airfield is still very much alive and well, no longer in the Service but fully engaged in private flying, gliding and its popular 'Fighter Meets'. The village sign proudly acknowledges the strong and long links with the RAF as it portrays a Hurricane with an aircraft hangar in the background.

The association with Service flying dates from August 1916 when a small airfield to the west of the village was established by the Royal Flying Corps for their Home Defence Force. During the next two years the airfield was improved and enlarged but like other Essex wartime airfields North Weald Bassett was sadly neglected after 1919. In the mid-1920s its potential was recognised and with the moderate expansion of the RAF the airfield was resuscitated.

Reconstruction work began in 1926 and on 27th September 1927 the new station, RAF North Weald ('Bassett' had now been dropped), opened. During the 1930s North Weald was modernised to bring it up to the improved Service standards and to provide facilities for an increased establishment. By 1939 the airfield covered some 400 acres and was 'E' Sector station in No 11 Group. The original four grass runways had been replaced by two permanent runways, 933 and 923 yards long and each 50 feet wide. These were a 'luxury' and unique for a fighter station in those days, although Sir Hugh Dowding had maintained in 1938, 'We

Blenheim 1F of No 25 squadron at North Weald – February 1940. (RAF Museum)

must have these runways at almost all fighter stations if we are to be able to operate fighters by day and night during a wet winter.' There were two C type and eight blister hangars and it was provided with night landing facilities.

In the ten days before the outbreak of the Second World War there was intense activity at North Weald and on 23rd August all regular personnel were recalled from leave. On the following day the Station Defence Scheme was put into operation and the aircraft set around the airfield at the various dispersal points. The camouflaging of all buildings was started and then on 27th of the month the first pilots and airmen of the Volunteer Reserve began to arrive. By 1st September the Operations Room was being manned continuously, armed guards were mounted and full blackout regulations were sedulously enforced. On the following day there was the General Mobilisation of the RAF, including the Auxiliary Air Force and Reserves, and as a result No 604 'The County of Middlesex' squadron arrived with its Bristol Blenheim 1Fs at North Weald – its agreed war station – to join the two regular fighter squadrons, Nos 56 and 151, both of which were equipped with Hurricanes.

The 56th was an old and proud squadron dating from the days of World War I, numbering two celebrated 'aces', Majors Ball and McCudden, VCs, amongst its pilots. During the Second World War its

Hurricanes of No 56 squadron in April 1940.

pilots flew Hurricanes, Spitfires and Typhoons and the squadron survived all the post-war cutbacks, at least until 1992. The squadron had made North Weald its home for the last twelve years, and one of its flights had been taken, in August 1936, to re-form No 151 squadron, the badge including an Essex 'seaxe' to show its origin.

Sergeant C. F. 'Jimmy' Rawnsley, an air gunner with No 604, recalled his emotions on that fateful Sunday in September 1939: '...as we stood on the grass by our aircraft, that we heard the tired voice of the Prime Minister as it came from a portable radio set. Now there would be no more pieces of paper and the time for words passed. We knew that at last we were in for what we had been expecting...' Later Jimmy Rawnsley with John 'Cat's Eyes' Cunningham would become a very successful night-fighting duo.

Within three days No 56 squadron would suffer the RAF's first fatal casualty – Pilot Officer Montagu Hulton-Harrop – who was shot down in the so-called 'Battle of Barking Creek'. The repercussions of this sad incident went deeper at North Weald as the Station Commander, Group Captain David Lucking, was unceremoniously removed from his post and court-martialled; although in December 1941 he was acting Air Commodore so perhaps his career did not suffer too greatly. The tragic accident did however cause some ill-feeling between North Weald and Hornchurch and, as one senior officer at the former recalled, 'it was a bad start to the war'.

For most of the winter No 56 squadron was operating from Martlesham Heath engaged on east coast convoy patrols but still

Formation take-off of Huricanes of No 151 squadron; the radio masts are in the background. (Imperial War Museum)

retaining a detachment of aircraft at North Weald, and by November had claimed its first enemy aircraft – two flying boats. No 151's pilots spent more time at the home airfield, and it was said that their first task was shooting down stray barrage balloons! The squadron was commanded by a famous pre-war officer, Squadron Leader Edward Donaldson. He had made his name leading aerobatic displays at the air shows at Hendon, and would ultimately gain the world air speed record in 1946 flying a Meteor at 616 mph. He retired as Air Commodore and then became a well-respected air correspondent for the *Daily Telegraph*. Donaldson's fine leadership of the squadron over France and Dunkirk in May 1940 brought him the award of a DSO.

By October 1939 it had been decided that the Blenheim 1Fs were not fast enough to compete with the Luftwaffe fighters for day operations and consequently they then concentrated on a night-flying role. Early in the New Year No 604 exchanged stations (Northolt) with No 25 squadron and, when the weather conditions allowed, the crews were engaged on operational trials of RDF (Radar). During May the squadron had been supplied with just two of the newest fighter then being developed – Westland Whirlwind. This single-seater, twin-engined fighter was tested for a night-fighter role but the pilots were decidedly unimpressed. The aircraft would operate briefly from Southend in June 1943.

The 'Blitzkreig' on France and the Low Countries which started on 10th May brought the North Weald squadrons into the grim realities of modern air warfare. On 16th May 'B' Flight of 56 squadron was despatched to Vitry-en-Artois to support the battered and beleagured resident RAF squadrons. 'A' Flight operated from Lille airfield but returned to North Weald at night. In just two days 'B' Flight lost six pilots, including the unlucky Seargeant 'Tommie' Rose, who had survived the infamous 'Battle of Barking Creek'. At the end of the Dunkirk operation the squadron had accounted for 14 enemy aircraft and it had been admirably led by Squadron Leader E. V. Knowles, known to his pilots as 'The Führer'! The squadron had lost some experienced pilots but several had lucky escapes, none more so than Pilot Officer Bryan J. Wicks, who was shot down on 22nd May and made a forced landing near the Belgian border. For ten days he managed to evade capture and when he finally arrived at Dunkirk he was arrested by the French as a spy! Wicks was handed over to the British authorities, who rushed him over the Channel in a motor torpedo boat to be interrogated by the Air Ministry and the Admiralty. Finally he was able to convince the authorities of his identity and was allowed to rejoin his squadron. Wicks later commanded No 64 squadron at Hornchurch but was killed in action at Malta in October 1942 at the age of 22 years!

At the end of May No 56 was sent to Digby for a rest, to re-equip and to train new pilots. During May another famous fighter squadron appeared on the scene – No 111 – which was the first to receive Hurricanes in December 1937. Like 151, the squadron's badge incorporated three Essex 'seaxes' signifying its six years at Hornchurch during 1928-34. Its pilots had also operated from a French airfield, and in six days of fighting they had managed to account for 16 enemy aircraft, including seven Ju87s (Stuka dive-bombers) in one day. The squadrons were using Gravesend and Manston as advance bases and North Weald's own satellite, Stapleford Tawney, was also coming into greater use. Even the Blenheims of No 25 squadron became involved with 'Operation Dynamo'; they acted as escorts for the armada of little ships that crossed back and fro from Dunkirk, as well as making patrols of the Dutch and Belgian coasts.

On 7th June a new Station Commander arrived at North Weald – Wing Commander Francis Victor Beamish, DSO and bar, DFC, AFC. Although he was only to stay there for about ten months, he made a tremendous impact on the station. He was an exceptional leader, and a great inspiritation to the many young fighter pilots who flew from North Weald. According to Air Chief Marshal Sir Basil Embry, 'He flew with his squadrons nearly every time they took to the air and set an example unsurpassed in the history of the RAF.' By the time he left North Weald in March 1941 he had destroyed five enemy aircraft, with another twelve probables. Beamish went missing in action in March 1942 whilst leading the Kenley Wing.

During the early weeks of the Battle of Britain it was Nos 56 and 151 squadrons that bore the brunt of the fighting from North Weald, although they did, at times, operate from Rochford and Martlesham Heath. Towards the end of August 151 found itself based at Stapleford Tawney and during the middle of this critical month detachments of Hurricanes from Northolt and Martlesham Heath – No 1 and No 257 – came to North Weald to augment the two embattled squadrons. On some particular days the air combats proved to be particularly costly; for instance, on 12th and 13th July the two squadrons lost six aircraft, although three pilots survived, including 151's commander – Squadron Leader Donaldson.

August proved to be a very harsh month for both 'home' squadrons – over 30 enemy aircraft were destroyed or severely damaged and No 151 squadron lost two commanders. A 'Halton brat' (as the ex-apprentices were known), Sergeant Frederick W. Higginson (later Wing Commander with DFC, DFM and OBE), became No 56's leading pilot with eleven victories to his credit, though a 'local' pilot Flying Officer Innes Westmacott, who had joined the squadron on 3rd August, had achieved four victories by the time he was shot down on 31st August. Although badly burned Westmacott managed to land his burning Hurricane near Little Baddow, not far from his home at Heybridge. On 31st the squadron lost four aircraft, which made a total of eleven in five days of fighting; it was quite plain that both squadrons sorely needed a rest from combat. The following day No 56 went to Boscombe Down and No 151 to Digby, being replaced by Nos 249 and 46 squadrons respectively. During August, whilst the Battle was raging overhead, a rather 'hush-hush' unit was being formed at North Weald – No 419 Flight – but because it moved to Stapleford Tawney in early September, it will be noted under that airfield.

Like all fighter airfields North Weald suffered several bombing raids. In the afternoon of 24th August over 200 bombs rained down on the airfield, causing considerable damage to the married quarters. One shelter received a direct hit killing nine members of 7th Battalion of the Essex Regiment, which was stationed at North Weald for airfield defence. A week later, on 31st, the airfield was under attack again, but on this day it was Debden that attracted the majority of the Luftwaffe's bombers.

North Weald's heaviest raid came on the morning of 3rd September just as No 249 squadron had landed for refuelling, though fortunately only three Hurricanes were destroyed. A few Blenheims of No 25 squadron, which had only returned to North Weald two days earlier, managed to clear the airfield only to come under attack from Hurricanes from 46 squadron then operating from Stapleford, and two Blenheims were shot down. The Operations Room, which was located in a bunker beneath the airfield, suffered a direct hit but the roof remained intact, and it was after this raid the station HQ moved to a nearby gracious country house – Blake Hall at Bobbingworth, which was owned by the Capel-Cure family. Subsequently the Operations Room also moved to the Hall and remained there for the rest of the war. The Airscene Museum, which is housed in the old Operations Room, has vividly brought the room 'back to life', as well as showing wartime memorabilia of North Weald airfield.

No 249 squadron was commanded by Squadron Leader John Grandy, DFC, who was an immensely popular and highly respected CO, and he had a most distinguished Service career reaching the rank of Marshal of the RAF. The squadron had only been formed in May 1940, but one of its pilots – Flight Lieutenant J. B. Nicolson – was awarded the only Victoria Cross of the Battle of Britain. The pilots went straight into action and on the 7th the squadron lost six aircraft but only one pilot. By the following day the squadron was down to just eight serviceable aircraft. The last **major** day of the Battle took place on 27th September, and the squadron lost five Hurricanes but Pilot Officer A. G. Lewis, DFC and bar, managed to make six kills. The following day he was shot down and badly burned. Lewis later served at Debden. The squadron's top scoring pilot was Pilot Officer Thomas Neil, DFC and bar, with eleven victories; he even managed to survive a mid-air collision with his Station CO, Wing Commander Beamish, and both airmen escaped unharmed. Neil later acted as a Flying Liaison Officer with the Ninth Air Force.

The Blenheim squadron – No 25 – managed to gain their first night victory of the war during the month, but the pilots began to receive their first Beaufighters. This aircraft was originally intended as a long range fighter but with the heavy night raids on London, which started from 7th September, it was quickly rushed into service as the best night-fighter available to Fighter Command. Immensely strong and robust, it was able to take the heavy and cumbersome Airborne Interception (AI) radar set. The Beaufighter developed into a most effective and versatile night-fighter as well as later proving to be a rather deadly anti-shipping strike aircraft with Coastal Command. In early October No 25 left with their Beaufighters for Debden.

On 8th October yet another famous Hurricane squadron arrived at 'the Weald' – No 257 or the 'Burma' – so called in recognition of the financial support it had received from that country. Its pilots were known known as 'the Death or Glory boys' from the squadron's motto! According to one of the pilots, '[it] was a very demoralised squadron until Bob Stanford Tuck arrived. He vitalised us and we soon went to the top.' Squadron Leader R. R. Stanford Tuck, DSO, DFC, two bars, was one of the legendary figures of the war. When he was shot down in 1942 and taken prisoner whilst leading the Biggin Hill Wing, he had 29 victories (which since the war has been amended to 30) to his name.

Stanford Tuck had a rather fortunate escape on 29th October when the airfield was again bombed. He and two other pilots had just taken off when a bomb exploded below them, and two of the Hurricanes nearly collided; the other pilot, Sergeant A. G. Girdwood, was killed when his Hurricane crashed in flames. The airfield was left badly cratered and the guard room and some dispersal huts were destroyed, with 51 injured including 19 fatally. The squadron had another well-known pilot, the Canadian Howard 'Boy' Blatchford, who would later command the 257th. During November the pilots scored heavily when opposing the 'Regia Aeronautica', or the Italian Air Force in their ill-fated raids on Harwich and Ipswich; on 11th November the squadron claimed eight and a half aircraft destroyed with another four damaged, without a single loss.

Towards the end of the year 257 moved out and the 'old and familiar' 56 squadron made a welcome return 'home'. It was now commanded by Squadron Leader H. M. Pinford, although in the New Year he would be replaced by Norman Ryder, DFC, who had been a Flight Commander with 41 squadron at Hornchurch. The pilots of No 249 were still in

Spitfire VB of No 121 'Eagle' squadron.

residence and on 29th December just two of them were despatched to Boulogne on the squadron's first offensive sweep. From now on the Hurricane squadrons would be engaged in a variety of operations, ranging from Blenheim escorts and east coast convoy patrols to fighter sweeps. When No 56 was re-equipped with Hurricane IIBs, the pilots also flew some night patrols but with scant success. No 56 bade its final and sad farewell to North Weald in June 1941, and in 1942 would pioneer operations with Typhoons very effectively, especially under the leadership of Squadron Leader Hugh 'Cocky' Dundas, DFC.

North Weald's long association with the well-loved 'Hurries' was fast coming to a close, but not before another well-known Hurricane squadron – No 242 – made its appearance during the spring of 1941. Its fame was largely based on its associations with Squadron Leader Douglas Bader and the Duxford Wing during the Battle of Britain. Bader was no longer with the squadron as he was commanding the Tangmere Wing. The squadron first operated from Stapleford Tawney before coming to North Weald in May.

During the summer three new squadrons came to North Weald. The first was No 71, the 'Eagle' squadron, which was largely composed of American volunteer pilots although it had a British commander, Squadron Leader H. Woodhouse, AFC. The keen and enthusiastic American pilots soon became engaged in Rhubarbs, convoy patrols, sweeps and bomber escorts. On 21st July, Pilot Officer W. 'Wild Bill' Dunn achieved the Eagles' first confirmed victory – a Me109 over Lille. Dunn later became a Lieutenant Colonel with the USAAF. In August the

197

squadron began to convert to Spitfire IIs. But the first Spitfires to appear at the airfield (during July) belonged to No 111 squadron, which had been greatly involved in the Battle of Britain whilst operating from Croydon and Debden. 'Treble-One' would spend much of the war in North Africa and Malta but in the 1950s it was re-formed at North Weald and became the RAF's aerobatic display team, known as 'The Black Arrows'. They were followed into North Weald by the Spitfire IIs of No 222 squadron, which was destined to make the airfield its home for the next twelve months. It was probably best known for the fact that it was formed on the very same day as the Royal Air Force – 1st April 1918 – and, as has already been noted, served at Hornchurch during the Battle of Britain. A second 'Eagle' squadron, No 121, replaced its American colleagues at the end of 1941, and Pilot Officer Mooney managed to bag the squadron's first FW190 on 22nd March, but it would move to Southend before being transferred to the Eighth Air Force. From now onwards until late 1943, the North Weald Wing would be comprised of Spitfire squadrons.

Of all the Spitfire squadrons that operated from North Weald during the next two years, probably two stand out – Nos 331 and 332. They were the longest residents, and made an immense contribution to the station's operations over the period, as well as leaving a lasting impression on North Weald. Both squadrons were manned mainly by Norwegian airmen and commanded by Scandinavian officers at the rank of Major. These Norwegian pilots are fittingly remembered by the fine stone monolith sited near the old main entrance to the airfield, which was unveiled in June 1952 by Princess Astrid, then Crown Princess of Norway. This memorial is unique, as it is dedicated to 'the Royal Air Force Station North Weald and to the people of the District.' Also the old Officers' Mess has been renamed 'Norway House'.

The first Norwegian fighter squadron had been formed at Catterick in July 1941, followed by No 332 in January 1942. At the end of the war both squadrons became part of the re-formed Royal Norwegian Air Force. It was No 331 that first came to the airfield first, in May 1942, followed a month later by its sister squadron, and they both stayed until March 1944. During their long stay at North Weald the pilots were engaged in the whole range of Fighter Command's operations – Ramrods, Rhubarbs, Rodeos, Roadsteads and pure fighter sweeps. On 17th May 331 squadron went out on its first Ramrod or bomber escort, and two days later the pilots encountered their first FW190s with a probable victory. At the end of the month the squadron's pilots made their first confirmed victory – a Me109F. Their compatriots' first enemy kill occurred on 31st July when a FW190 and a Me109F fell to their guns, but unfortunately four pilots were lost in the combat. Both squadrons were involved in the Dieppe operation, although on detachment from Manston.

Several famous pilots commanded the Norwegian Wing, including the ebullient New Zealander, Pat Jameson, DFC and bar, and David Scott-Malden, DSO, DFC and bar, who later commanded RAF Hornchurch during 1944/5. Perhaps the most renowned Commander was Lieutenant Colonel Kaj Birksted, DSO, DFC, or 'Birk', as he was universally known. 'Birk' was a Danish pilot of exceptional skill; it was said that 'he flew like an angel and shot like William Tell'! He had commanded No 331 squadron from September 1942 to April 1943, and completed 400 operational sorties by the end of the war. Birksted later worked for NATO and died in February 1996, aged 80 years.

By the early months of 1944 both squadrons were equipped with Spitfire IXs, and the pilots became engaged on Army Co-operation exercises and later dive-bombing operations, which were really preparatory to being directly involved in the impending invasion of Europe. The two squadrons, along with No 66, which had operated from the airfield in March, left North Weald and moved off, on 31st March, to the advanced landing ground of Bognor, where they formed No 132 Wing of the Second Tactical Air Force and became engaged in attacking coastal targets, as well as flying beach-head patrols on D-Day.

Hornchurch Sector control had closed in February and the airfield's Operations Room became responsible for Andrews Field, Hornchurch, Southend, Castle Camps, Bradwell Bay and Stapleford Tawney; although with the centre of air operations concentrating on northern France it was clear that the airfield would become less and less involved in the European air war. In the last week of April 1944 three fighter squadrons (Nos 33, 74 and 127) arrived at the Weald from bases in the Middle East. They were in the process of exchanging their Mark Vs for Mark IXs, but by the middle of May all three had departed for Lympne in Kent.

There was a relative lull in proceedings until August when the next fighters appeared at North Weald. They were flown by other European airmen – Czechoslovakian. The two Czech squadrons, Nos 310 and 312, were equipped with Spitfire IXs. In the same month another Spitfire squadron settled in; it was No 234, which had mainly served in No 10 Group of Fighter Command. During the four months it spent at North

Left. The Norwegian Memorial at North Weald.
Right. The village sign at North Weald Bassett.

Weald, the pilots converted to Mustang IIIs, and thus became engaged in long-range bomber escorts over Germany before finally moving at the end of the year to Bentwaters in Suffolk. The two Czech squadrons were also engaged in escort duties as well as dive-bombing operations, particularly to the so-called 'Big Ben' targets (V2 rocket sites). When No 312 left for Bradwell Bay in October, its replacement was another Czech squadron – No 313. But by the end of the year the two Czech squadrons had also moved to Bradwell Bay to form the Czech Spitfire Wing.

There was no doubt now that the airfield's final days as an operational station were nigh. One Spitfire squadron – No 63 – was disbanded at North Weald at the end of January 1945, but there was still a Spitfire presence at North Weald in the form of No 26 squadron, which had originally been formed back in 1915 from South African pilots and as a result its badge reflected these origins with the head of a springbok. During the Second World War the re-formed squadron had been mainly engaged on Army Co-operation duties. When its Spitfires left in the early days of April, it was to be after VE Day before the last 'wartime' fighters arrived. No 130 squadron had recently been stationed at Fassberg in Germany and been actively engaged in the last but still fierce air combats with the dying Luftwaffe. They were just 'birds in passage', for after a very brief stay the pilots moved to the far north of Scotland before leaving to serve in Norway.

For the last six years North Weald had been the home of mainly Hurricanes and Spitfires, and fleetingly, in September 1945, those glorious days returned. Group Captain Douglas Bader, who had been released from Colditz Castle in April, was given command of the North Weald Sector briefly; he had been selected to organise and lead the Victory fly past over London on 15th September 1945, which coincidentally was the fifth anniversary of the Battle of Britain. The fly past comprised some 300 bombers and fighters – both British and American. Lord Dowding came to the airfield to talk about the arrangements and to meet some of 'The Few' such as Wing Commanders Dennis Crowley-Milling, Stanley Turner and Stanford Tuck, who would take part in the Victory flight. It was a fitting and splendid finale to the airfield's wartime existence.

In March 1949 the airfield returned once again to Fighter Command, and ultimately echoed to the thrilling sounds of jet fighters from No 111 squadron. In 1958 the airfield was put on a 'Care and Maintenance' status until it was finally closed in September 1964. Much of the history of this famous Fighter Command station is splendidly recalled in the North Weald Memorial Collection at Ad Astra House, which is open to the public on Sundays.

18
RIDGEWELL

Ridgewell was the only Essex airfield to be solely used as a heavy bomber station, both with the RAF and the USAAF; the only airfield in the county, in fact, to house an Eighth Air Force Bomb Group (Heavy) for any length of time. Almost 350 missions were mounted from Ridgewell, and the contribution its two combat units made to the bombardment of German targets was immense, but unfortunately rather costly in men and machines. The American memorial at Ridgewell bears a message that perhaps best captures the bravery and sacrifices of all these bomber crews, be they British or American: 'Let this memorial be an inspiration to the oppressed and a warning to would-be aggressors that peace is our ultimate goal. Further, let it remind all former members of their proud heritage and give them renewed strength to meet the challenges of the future'.

The airfield, sited to the east of the village of Ridgewell, was one of the earliest Class A bomber stations to be built in Essex. Ridgewell was ready for occupation towards the end of 1942, and although it had been allocated to the Eighth Air Force in the previous June, the Eighth did not have a Heavy Bomb Group ready for operations so it was 'loaned' back to the RAF. It was passed over to No 3 Group of Bomber Command, which at that time mainly comprised Short Stirling squadrons, so it was fairly certain that Stirlings would soon arrive at Ridgewell. The airfield was allocated as a satellite for RAF Stradishall, which was then greatly involved with operational conversion training for aircrews within the Group.

Stirling III of No 90 squadron.

It was just after Christmas 1942 when the first Stirlings landed at the airfield, the first one crash-landing on approach – not an auspicious start! The Short Stirling was one of the series of heavy bombers designed to the famous pre-war specification B12/36, which had such a major effect on the bombing offensive and in essence dictated the format of Bomber Command's strike force. It was the earliest of the RAF's great triumvirate of four-engined bombers, coming into service in August 1940 and flying its first operation in February 1941. Although the aircraft had certain operational limitations, notably its low ceiling height and cruising speed, the Stirling proved to be a most sturdy and versatile aircraft that could sustain considerable damage. At the time (1941) it was the first RAF bomber with the range and bomb capacity capable of delivering what Winston Churchill called 'the shattering strikes of retributive justice'.

It was No 90 squadron that brought its Stirlings to Ridgewell. For a First World War squadron the 90th had already experienced a rather irregular wartime existence. Re-formed in March 1937, it had been involved in the Service's early trials of the Bristol Blenheims, but soon after the outbreak of the war it had become a purely operational training unit. Then, in May 1941, it was re-formed as a bomber squadron and equipped with Flying Fortresses (B-17s), the only RAF unit to fly these aircraft operationally. It was a most unhappy and unsatisfactory period; of the 51 missions mounted over 50% were abandoned for a variety of reasons, and only 50 tons of bombs were ever dropped operationally.

The squadron was disbanded again in February 1942, only to be re-formed as a Stirling squadron nine months later at RAF Bottesford.

It was on the night of 8th/9th January 1943 that the squadron went out on its first operation – mine laying. Bomber Command was committed to a heavy programme of mine laying, at least 1,000 mines per month. It was later claimed that for every mine dropped by the RAF, on average 50 tons of enemy shipping was sunk. The crews called mine laying 'gardening', because each sea area around the European coasts was given a code-name of flowers or vegetables! For instance the Kiel Bay was known as 'Wallflowers', 'Quince' or 'Radishes' and the West Baltic as 'Sweet Peas'. During their short period at Ridgewell the crews undertook their fair share of 'gardening'! Though not quite as lethal as bombing operations over Germany, mine laying was not necessarily an 'easy' mission as the average loss rate of 3.3% testifies. Air Chief Marshal Sir Arthur Harris was never too enamoured with this type of operation but was forced to acquiesce with the dictates of the Air Ministry, with the proviso that they did not greatly interfere with his bombing offensive of Germany. At the end of April the squadrons dropped no less than 1,050 mines in just two nights – a record for Bomber Command.

On the night of 4th/5th February the squadron was part of a 188 strong force that attacked the Fiat and Lancia motor works at Turin in northern Italy. These Italian operations were usually mounted when the weather conditions over Germany precluded night-bombing. The crews regarded these long trips as vastly preferable to the shorter runs to Germany simply because the Italian flak defences were so much weaker, despite the fact that the Swiss Alps formed a formidable barrier especially for Stirlings. On this Turin operation only three aircraft (Lancasters) were lost – just 1.5%. This compared very favourably with a major Berlin operation mounted on 1st/2nd March when 300 aircraft attacked the Templehof railway works for the loss of 17 aircraft (5.6%). This was the heaviest RAF raid so far on the German capital and as will be seen later the American B-17s from Ridgewell would also suffer over the same target.

It was the 'Battle of the Ruhr' – the Command's first major offensive of the war – that greatly occupied the crews for most of their time at Ridgewell. From 5th March until 14th July 1943 concentrated attacks were launched against a variety of strategic targets in the Ruhr, and this proved to be the first major success for Bomber Command (the famous 'Dambusters raid' was part of the Battle), but it was achieved at no small cost. Since May 1940 the Ruhr had become a favourite RAF target, and amongst the crews it had acquired the names of 'The Happy Valley', 'The Land of No Return' or 'The Graveyard of the RAF'; certainly the British war cemeteries at Rheinberg and Reichswald Forest contain the graves of the many RAF airmen who were lost over Ruhr targets.

Essen, the largest town in the Ruhr, was the target for the first operation and in particular the massive Krupps munitions complex. Over 440 aircraft left at dusk and in the space of just 40 minutes the waves of Halifaxes, Stirlings, Wellingtons and lastly Lancasters left behind a scene of devastation, it was a most effective operation with the loss of 14 aircraft (3.2%). No 90 squadron lost one aircraft, which crashed at Mönchen-gladbach. The squadron's next casualty was on the night of 16th/17th April over Mannheim when one of its Stirlings crash-landed near Laon in France. Seven of the crew managed to escape, evading capture and subsequently arriving back in England via the French underground. Unfortunately the pilot, Pilot Officer White, who was badly injured in the chest, was taken prisoner; White was on his last trip before completing his first successful tour of operations! Two aircraft failed to return to Ridgewell on 12th May after the fourth attack on Duisberg – one had come down over Holland and the other had the bad luck to be shot down by a night-fighter whilst returning over the North Sea, none of the crew were rescued.

The last Ruhr operation from Ridgewell took place on 29th/30th May and was directed at Wuppertal, some 15 miles south-east of Essen. It proved to be a costly mission with 33 aircraft lost (4.6%), with just one from Ridgewell. The squadron was on the move once again – to West Wickham in Cambridgeshire. During their stay at Ridgewell 54 missions had been launched from the airfield and seven aircraft had been lost over Ruhr targets. Shortly after its move to West Wickham the squadron lost its commanding officer when Squadron Leader J. Dugdale, DFC, was killed when his Stirling crashed into the North Sea on return from an operation to Essen. The squadron later moved to Tuddenham in Suffolk and it was from there that it completed the war. There is a memorial to No 90 squadron on the village green at Tuddenham.

The first American airmen arrived at Ridgewell on 3rd June; the ground personnel of the 381st Bomb Group (Heavy), which had arrived from the United States on the *Queen Elizabeth*. The first aircraft – B-17Fs – began to fly in from Bovingdon in Hertfordshire on the 15th and by the following day there were 45 standing around the airfield. The Group had been activated in November 1942 but had not started training until 5th January at Pyote Air Base in Texas; and yet four months later the crews were flying their aircraft to the United Kindom via the northern ferry route from Gander in Newfoundland to Prestwick and then down to the Combat Crew Replacement Centre at Bovingdon.

The 381st, under the command of Colonel Joseph J. Nazzaro, was placed in the 1st Bomb Wing (later to be renamed 1st Bomb Division) joining the 'veteran' Bomb Groups that all operated from airfields to the west of Ridgewell. These Groups had borne the brunt of the Eighth's early operations and from June 1943 their aircraft carried Divisional identification codes, which were in the form of geometrical symbols on the vertical tails and upper right wings and within these symbols was the Group's identification letter; a triangle shape denoted the 1st Wing/Division and the letter 'L' for the 381st. In addition each squadron within the Group had a special code – VE, VP, GD and MS for 532 to 535 squadrons respectively.

The crews were not given long to settle into their new surroundings before their first mission. On 22nd June 22 aircraft left for the Ford and General Motors works at Antwerp. They had the luxury of a large escort of P-47s for this operation but nevertheless three B-17s failed to return to Ridgewell; two had been lost over Holland and the third crash-landed in Kent near North Foreland, injuring six of the crew. The next day when the aircraft were being prepared for a mission to Villacoublay, tragedy struck as one B-17 blew up, damaging another aircraft nearby and killing 22 airmen and one civilian. Sadly, the mission was recalled after the aircraft had formed due to the weather. The Group's apparent run of bad luck continued into the next month when on 14th July a B-17 exploded during assembly and crashed near Rattlesden killing six of the ten man crew. On the subsequent operation – to Glisy airfield near Amiens – one aircraft was lost in action and another collided with a FW190 but managed to return and crash-land at Manston.

On 24th July the Eighth Air Force launched its first attack on Norwegian targets – Bergen, Trondheim and Heroya. The 1st Wing's target was the large nitrate factory at Heroya and all of the aircraft arrived back safely from this long flight except one – *Georgia Rebel* from Ridgewell. This aircraft crash-landed at Vaannacka in neutral Sweden and the crew was interned. This was the first USAAF aircraft to make an emergency landing in neutral Sweden, and later in 1944 the whole question of landing in Sweden became a deep concern for the Eighth Air Force. Following a mission to Berlin 18 damaged aircraft landed there and by then quite an 'American colony' of interned crews had been established with a 'special American air-attaché' being appointed to

B-17s of 381st line up for a mission; 533rd squadron area in the foreground.
(Smithsonian Institution)

look after their interests! The Swedish government were loath to allow
any action that might be thought to impinge on their strict policy of
neutrality. However, towards the end of 1944 American ground
personnel were allowed into the country to repair the damaged aircraft,
and ultimately an agreement was reached whereby the aircraft and
crews were released providing neither took any further part in
operations over Europe.

The names of Schweinfurt and Regensburg became etched on the
collective memories of those crews unfortunate enough to take part in
what was reckoned to be 'the most intensive air battle of the Second
World War'. For the men of the 381st it was Schweinfurt that brought
out the cold sweat of fear; a vital ball-bearing target about 70 miles east
of Frankfurt and set deep in southern Germany. Years later many of the
survivors of this harrowing operation would vividly recall, on each
anniversary – 17th August – the horrors and anguish of the mission. The

B-17 of 381st Bomb Group coming in to land at Ridgewell. (Smithsonian Institution)

two B-17 Wings were intending to attack the targets in a two-pronged strike, a most ambitious operation, and possibly planned to demonstrate the effectiveness of the Eighth's daylight bombing.

The 4th Bomb Wing's target was Regensburg and its Messerschmitt factories about 100 miles further south, and the Wing's B-17s would continue due south after their attack to land in North Africa. The 1st Wing would tackle Schweinfurt and return back to their home airfields. All the formations were due to leave at the same time but the weather intervened and the departure of the Regensburg force was delayed as long as was possible considering their long flight to Africa. As a result the Schweinfurt mission followed 3½ hours later, and this time lapse proved to be fatal for so many crews of 1st Bomb Wing.

The 381st was positioned in the low group of the leading formation (a notoriously vulnerable spot) with one of its squadrons in the high composite group. The whole formation was reckoned to be about 50 miles long, The leaders crossed the Dutch coast at 13.40 hours and soon the escorting Spitfires and P-47s would reach the extent of their range, roughly the Belgian/German border. The Luftwaffe fighters waited for the escorts to turn back before they made their attacks. As one member of the 381st recalled, 'I watched a large number, an overwhelming number of enemy fighters steadily climbing on course... It was the greatest concept of massing of enemy fighters that I ever saw in my time...' The Luftwaffe had already taken quite a toll of the earlier force and because of the time delay they had been able to be reserviced and call up reinforcements to greet the earlier Regensburg force, which they assumed would be returning to the UK So they were ready and prepared in great numbers for the hapless 1st Bomb Wing, and what followed was a vicious, brutal and intense air battle, which one survivor described, 'Never before or after did I ever see such incessant action...it was the most terrible experience of my life...'

Some 4½ hours later the shattered remnants of the Schweinfurt force limped back over the North Sea. Of the 230 aircraft that had left, 36 had been shot down, this was in addition to the 24 lost on the earlier Regensburg force. The 381st suffered the heaviest loss in the whole of 1st Wing; of the 26 B-17s that had left Ridgewell eleven had been destroyed and twelve returned with battle damage. Over 100 airmen had been lost; most ended up as prisoners of war, although ten were rescued from the sea about 20 miles off Felixstowe. It was a disaster of high magnitude, not only for the Group but also for the Eighth Air Force, with its concept and belief in the self-defensive bomber formation being shattered.

During October crisis point for the Eighth was reached in what became known as 'The Black Week'. From 8th to 14th the 381st was engaged in four major operations – Bremen, Anklam, Munster and Schweinfurt (again). The mission to the Bremen shipyards on 8th proved to be a severe test of the crews' courage and determination. The Group lost seven of its 18 B-17s to a strong force of enemy fighters with another 72 airmen lost in action, and for its performance on this day it was awarded its first DUC. The next day the Group was still able to send out 16 aircraft on an operation to the Arado airframe factory at Anklam, north of Berlin near the Baltic coast. Well over 200 enemy fighters opposed the Eighth's 115 B-17s and 18 failed to make it back to England, of which three came from Ridgewell. It is perhaps not too surprising that only six aircraft were available for the Munster raid but all returned safely. Then on 14th the Eighth returned in strength to Schweinfurt – 291 aircraft – only to result in yet another 'blood bath' with 60 aircraft (20%!) being shot down. Colonel 'Joe' Nazzaro must have breathed a heavy sigh of relief when all but one of the 17 B-17s landed back at the airfield, although twelve of them had sustained heavy damage.

Just before Christmas 1943 (20th) the 381st, yet again, suffered the heaviest losses in the Division when the port area of Bremen was the target. The 1st Division lost 13 aircraft, of which four came from Ridgewell. On Christmas Eve the Eighth launched a massive operation (722 aircraft) against the V1 rocket sites in the Pas de Calais without a single casualty – 22 sites were attacked and some 1,700 tons of high explosives were dropped, with what the Command chiefs described as 'excellent results'. Soon the Pas de Calais would become known to the crews as 'the rocket coast' as rumours quickly circulated about Hitler's new secret weapon.

It was not far into the New Year (11th) before the Eighth Air Force suffered another sharp and severe setback when a total of 42 aircraft were shot down and another five 'written off' whilst attacking aircraft factories at Oschersleben and Halberstadt. On this fateful day the Group was part of a 177 strong force directed at the Focke Wulf plant in Oschersleben and the Luftwaffe mounted its strongest opposition since the Schweinfurt operation back in October, with the result that eight B-17s failed to return to Ridgewell. All of the Division's Groups were awarded a Distinguished Unit Citation for their part in the operation. Unfortunately Colonel Nazzaro had left Ridgewell just two days before the Group gained their second coveted DUC. His successor, Colonel Harry P. Leber Jr., led the 381st for the next thirteen months.

B-17s of 381st Bomb Group; 532 squadron to the front followed by 533rd squadron. (Smithsonian Institution)

The 381st again paid heavily for another strike at the German aircraft industry when on 22nd February six aircraft were lost over Oschersleben. It was yet another grim mission for the Eighth as 38 out of 289 B-17s were destroyed (13%). The first week of March saw the Eighth Air Force launch its offensive against Berlin. The first operation, on the 4th, was bedevilled by bad weather and the Group attacked Bonn as an optional target, losing one aircraft. The more successful mission occurred two days later when the 1st Division Groups battled their way to the Erkner ball-bearing plant about 16 miles south of Berlin. The fighter opposition was intense, the Luftwaffe grouped above Dummer lake to the west of the capital. It was estimated that more than 300 Luftwaffe fighters were in action. The 381st was in the leading formation and lost three aircraft, one of which was *Linda Mary*, which was the last of the original B-17s to have come over from the States with the 381st. During its time at Ridgewell the Group bombed the German capital on

212

16 occasions losing just 19 aircraft in the process, a rather excellent record considering the strength of Berlin flak defences. Their most costly mission was on 24th May when six aircraft were lost out of a total of 33 destroyed. Even at this stage of the war the Eighth were still suffering heavy casualties – nearly 490 airmen were missing on this single mission – but despite the fact that the loss rate was 5.3%, it was still considered 'acceptable'!

Most of the Eighth's Bomb Groups could boast of 'long-serving' aircraft and the 381st was no exception, having several rugged B-17s that had managed to complete over 100 combat missions despite the Eighth's heavy losses. One of the two most famous aircraft at Ridgewell was *Rotherhithe's Revenge*, which ultimately completed 122 missions. The aircraft had been purchased by contributions from the people of Bermondsey. The other B-17 was called *Stage Door Canteen*, which completed 105 missions. It had been formally named by Mary Churchill, the Prime Minister's daughter, who was accompanied by several famous British film stars, such as Vivien Leigh, Anna Neagle, Jean Kent and Phyllis Calvert. Indeed Ridgewell was a popular Eighth Air Force base for visiting celebrities, perhaps because it was relatively close to London.

When the Eighth Air Force returned to German targets after D-Day the 381st lost three aircraft over Berlin on 21st June but then proceeded to mount missions to oil targets and aircraft factories as well as air strikes in support of the Allied armies notably at Caen. All these missions were conducted with the minimum of losses, the crews achieving an amazingly low casualty rate and often returning intact or with just a single aircraft missing. What a change from the days of late 1943, and the chances of the crews now completing a tour of operations – 35 missions – were greatly enhanced.

During Christmas 1944 Ridgewell became rather crowded with almost 80 additional B-17s spread around the airfield. They had been unable to make it back to their home bases in the east Midlands because of fog. It was not until 3rd February that the Group lost its first aircraft in 1945. Berlin was again the crews' downfall and two aircraft were lost whilst attacking the Templehof railway works (where No 90 squadron had been active two years earlier). The last aircraft to be lost to enemy action fell on 8th April over oil targets at Derben. Sadly, just before the war ended a B-17 taking airmen for a leave break in Northern Ireland crashed on the Isle of Man, killing 30 airmen.

The Group's 296th and final mission went out from Ridgewell on 25th

April to the Skoda motor works at Pilsen in Czechoslovakia. It had been a long and costly war for the 381st – 131 aircraft missing in action. Within a month the majority of the aircraft had left the airfield, and they were followed by the ground personnel in mid-June.

In August 1982, a group of 381st veterans made an emotional return to Ridgewell for the dedication of the splendid memorial erected on the site of the station's sick quarters. They were led by Colonel Dexter Lishon of 535th squadron, one of the original members of the Group, who as a Captain had been shot down in October 1943 over Bremen. The veterans found that some of the old airfield had survived the passage of time; the hangars were still intact and were being used for storage by the USAF at Wethersfield, which was then still an active airfield.

19
RIVENHALL

One of the most elegant and attractive village signs in the county is to be found at Rivenhall. It proudly commemorates the Allied Air Forces that operated from the local airfield, and both RAF and USAAF rondels have been incorporated into the design. There is also a plaque listing the combat units that served at Rivenhall during the Second World War, which is housed in a GEC-Marconi building at Chelmsford.

The airfield is sited about two miles to the north of Rivenhall and situated far closer to the village of Silver End, indeed it was known locally and to the Americans as 'Silver End 'drome'. The construction work was started in the early months of 1943 by W. & C. French, who were responsible for several other Essex airfields. In this instance they were only contracted to lay the runways, perimeter roads and hard-standings. All the buildings were erected by Bovis Ltd and they were situated to the south-east of the airfield.

The urgency of the war situation during the winter of 1943/4 can be seen in the haste in which the airfield was brought into use. When the first American personnel arrived at Rivenhall in January, the accommodation and technical units were not completed. Furthermore the Ninth Fighter Group – the 363rd – which had been allocated to the airfield, was not only desperately short of aircraft but also trained pilots. Just one squadron (382nd) arrived on 22nd January from Keevil in Wiltshire, where the American airmen had been kicking their heels since before Christmas 1943. The reason for the lack of aircraft was that the 363rd had been selected as the third USAAF unit to have the new P-51Bs, then in short supply. The problem of the lack of trained pilots was

P-51 Maggie's Drawers *of 380th squadron of 363rd Fighter Group. (USAF)*

slightly easier to resolve, 27 experienced pilots were transferred from the Eighth's 356th Group stationed at Martlesham Heath, who had been flying operationally since the previous October.

The Group's Commanding Officer, Colonel John R. Ulricson, had only eleven P-51s to start a conversion programme, which was sorely needed as most American fighter pilots had completed their training on P-39s (Airacobras). Even the pilots that had been drafted in would also require some conversion time as they had been flying P-47s. In such frustrating circumstances it was really quite amazing that on 23rd February, 24 pilots set off in their new and sleek P-51s on their first mission, although because of heavy snow showers the pilots were forced to return early. The following day, Major James Howard – the hero of the 354th Group at Boxted – led the Group on its first operational mission, which proved to be withdrawal support for the Eighth Air Force heavies returning from Schweinfurt and Gotha. For most of its time at Rivenhall the 363rd would operate escort missions under the control of the Eighth Fighter Command.

It was not until 3rd March that the pilots were tested in combat with the Luftwaffe. The occasion was the first USAAF daylight raid on Berlin. The weather was really atrocious with heavy cloud formations up to 29,000 feet with the result that most of the bombers were recalled; one bomber formation did not receive the recall message and carried on regardless, so it was decided that some of the fighter escort should also carry on to provide some protection. Major Howard was leading the Group for the last time, and he did a fine job considering that only 25 of the original 36 P-51s remained, the rest having turned back for a variety of mechanical faults. The pilots survived the weather and the air battle very well, claiming a Me109 and a Me410 as well as damaging another three Me109s. There was considerable jubilation when all of the pilots returned safely to Rivenhall.

Unfortunately the mission on the following day turned out to be a vastly different affair. The Eighth had decided to launch another operation on Berlin despite quite severe weather. The Group was able to put 33 aircraft up but again a third were forced to return early to Rivenhall. The remainder, along with the 354th Group, were detailed to provide escort support in the area of Berlin, but heavy cloud conditions were again encountered. Not far from Hamburg the depleted 363rd was attacked by a force of Me109s of the elite Luftwaffe unit – II/JG1 – and in a relatively short time half of the Group's P-51s were shot down. Out of the 110 P-51s active on this mission 16 were shot down (15%), of which eleven belonged to the Group; it was probably the Luftwaffe's most successful combat with P-51s throughout the war, which was scant consolation for the Group, smarting under a very harsh defeat. Indeed on 5th March there was only a Lieutenant with sufficient experience to lead the Group on their escort mission to Bordeaux. On 8th and 9th March there were yet more missions to Berlin; the first being led by an experienced pilot from Boxted – Lieutenant O'Connors – and it proved to be moderately successful, with five enemy aircraft claimed destroyed for the loss of just one pilot. It is probably just as well that the poor weather prevented any operations for about ten days, giving the pilots time to reflect on the actions of the last few weeks.

On 13th April Brigadier General Elwood Quesada, the Commander of the Ninth Fighter Command, arrived at the airfield in his P-38 Lightning, and he presented decorations to some twelve pilots. He also must have taken the opportunity to explain the future role of the Ninth's fighters in the next two months. Soon the pilots were introduced into the techniques of using their P-51s as fighter/bombers. Each Fighter Group

B-26 of 599th squadron of 397th Bomb Group. (USAF)

in the Ninth was given at least two weeks to practise bombing attacks in preparation for their tactical support role. The training programme required that every pilot should complete at least five dive-bombing and five low-level attacks, and each squadron had to undertake at least three dive or glide-bombing exercises to gain experience working as units. Soon the Essex countryside resounded to the noise of low-flying aircraft buzzing along at almost tree-top height. The Ninth Air Force had also established a 'low-level attack unit' at RAF Milfield in Northumberland, which already housed the RAF's admirable Fighter Leaders' School. The American unit was under the command of Colonel Arthur Sanderson, and its intention was to inculcate the low-level techniques that had proved so successful in the Ninth's operations over North Africa and Italy.

On 5th April the Group went out on a ground-strafing mission of enemy airfields in northern France, and just a single P-51 was lost to ground flak. Five days later the pilots gained their first operational experience of dive-bombing when attacking marshalling yards at Hasselt in Belgium, and in the afternoon they provided an escort for a Ninth B-26 force engaged in attacking railway targets in France. The Group's last mission from Rivenhall took place on 13th – another escort

218

mission for the Eighth's Fighter Command and two Me109s were claimed for the loss of a single aircraft. The following day the Group's P-51s left for an Advanced Landing Ground at Staplehurst in Kent. Whilst serving at Rivenhall 20 missions had been completed for the loss of 16 P-51s in action whilst claiming 13 enemy aircraft destroyed.

It was on Saturday 15th April that Colonel Richard T. Coiner Jr. led his B-26s into Rivenhall after just 'a short hop' from nearby Gosfield, where the Group had been in residence for about a week whilst waiting for their airfield to be vacated. The 397th was the last Medium Bomb Group to be activated by the Ninth Air Force, but despite this Colonel Coiner was fortunate in having some experienced pilots as his senior commanders. Lieutenant Colonel Franklyn Allen (598th squadron) had served operationally in the 'Pacific theater', Major 'Casey' Dempster (597th) was a pre-war officer and Lieutenant Colonel Frank Wood had flown with Pan American Airways. Another Major, Rollin M. Winningham, a regular air officer since 1938, would later go on to command the 323rd Bomb Group.

For the Group's first mission 36 crews left to attack a V1 rocket site at Le Plouy Ferme in the Pas de Calais. This was followed on the next two days to other 'No Ball' sites (Bois de Coupelle and Vacquerille), and each of the missions were led by Colonel Coiner, as were the next two. The Colonel, a 33 year old Texan, often led the Group's missions in his appropriately named *Lucky Star*. He remained as Commanding Officer until after the war, one of just two Ninth commanders to do so. A Colonel in the USAAF was equivalent in rank to a RAF Group Captain, and the RAF were quite set against their senior officers flying in operations; of course there were several noted exceptions to this rule as will be seen later. The American commanders felt that flying with their pilots was the best way to check on the discipline of their formation flying and the accuracy of their bombing.

One of the Group's earliest successful operations (27th April) was led by Lieutenant Colonel Allen, and was directed at the coastal defences at Ouistreham, which would defend what later became known as the Normandy beach-head 'Sword'. Photographic evidence subsequently disclosed that 97% of the bombs had fallen within the target area – a high standard of bombing accuracy which was not always achieved either by the 386th or other Groups, or at least not until PFF (Pathfinder) techniques were brought into more general use during June and July.

The 397th, like their near neighbours at Boreham, ultimately acquired a reputation in the Ninth as 'bridge busters'. This may have been because Colonel Coiner was reported as saying, '...of the fourteen bridges behind the Invasion coast which were destroyed or damaged by all Bomb Groups in our 98th Bomb Wing from May 26th – June 1st, the airmen under my command accounted for nine – 64% of the total.' Whatever is the truth in this matter, during their short time at Rivenhall well over one third of their targets proved to be road or rail bridges. Their first attack on a bridge was mounted on 8th May – a railway bridge at Oissel just south of Rouen. One B-26 fell to flak but the crew survived and ended up as prisoners, and 26 aircraft returned with some form of battle damage, evidence of the intensity of the enemy's flak over such targets, as the crews would find to their cost in late June. On the following day whilst attacking a 'No Ball' site at Le Grismont (led by Majors Bronson and Winningham), although all the aircraft returned to Rivenhall one of the crew received fatal injuries.

The month of May proved to be a very hectic period, with 26 missions launched and the enemy's coastal defences at Etaples, Gravelines, Ste Marie au Bosc and Varengeville-sur-Mer attacked with some reasonable results, although both Etaples and Ste Marie au Bosc were bombed on three separate operations. Thereafter until the end of the month bridges at Liège, Le Manoir, Orival, Rouen, Conflans and Maisons Laffitte were bombed. Because the Group was relatively late in coming into the fray, marshalling yards and airfields did not greatly figure amongst their targets. However, on 20th May the airfield at Denain/Prouvy was attacked, but with little effect because of the 10/10 cloud cover, which proved to be a continual problem for the Ninth Bomber Command. A week later when the Group was sent to attack the defences at Ste Marie au Bosc, north of Le Havre, which covered the sea approaches to the invasion beaches, the expedition was for the first time led by Pathfinder aircraft.

For the first six days of June (including D-Day) the Group was again engaged on bombing coastal defences at Le Havre and Camiers. On the 'big day' itself the morning mission was over the Utah beach-head with the specific target being the beach defences at the Dunes de Varreville. The afternoon operation was directed at gun batteries at Trouville, some miles to the east of the Sword beach-head. This was the Group's 41st operation in just under 50 days, which was an impressive achievement. The bridge at Chartres was attacked three times during the month and on the last mission, on 17th June, one B-26 ditched in the English Channel with the only survivor – Captain 'Gus' Williams – being rescued after three hours in the water.

It was on their 58th mission on 24th June that the crews encountered their sternest test and the mission brought about their heaviest loss so far. The target was a rail bridge at Maisons Laffitte on the Seine about 15 miles north-west of Paris, which they had attacked previously (at the end of May). All of the crews agreed that it was the 'thickest flak yet seen', and they experienced a most torrid time, which unfortunately resulted in six B-26s being shot down; all the surviving 33 B-26s were damaged to some extent, and 25 crewmen were wounded. After this rather costly mission the weather intervened once again and the 397th was grounded until the 30th when two operations were launched against Thury Harcourt bridge across the Orne, south of Caen, and a road junction at Condé sur Noireau, slightly further south. Poor weather over the target areas reduced the effectiveness of the bombing.

In July, out of the 22 missions, half were directed at bridges and all offered stiff flak opposition. On 16th two bridges were attacked on two separate missions – to Boissey la Londe, south-west of Rouen, and to Nantes on the Loire, one of the most distant targets from Rivenhall. On this latter operation a B-26 named *By Golly* was severely damaged but nevertheless the pilot, Captain John Q. West, managed to make an emergency landing at a landing strip at Azeville, which had only been completed earlier in the month. All of the crew managed to make their escape before the aircraft burst into flames. The crew were back at Rivenhall after a couple of days, and later Captain John West was awarded the DSC. Earlier in the month the Group had lost one of its most experienced pilots and leaders when Major Bronson failed to return from attacking enemy transport targets at Ussy near Laval, well behind the enemy's front lines.

The final operation from Rivenhall took place on 4th August, when 36 B-26s led by Lieutenant Colonel Dempster bombed a rail bridge at Épernon, between Chartres and Paris. It was a rather unhappy mission, with two aircraft failing to return, this brought the total of aircraft lost to 16 in the 86 missions flown from Rivenhall. The Group left for Hurn in Hampshire, which was the first of five moves in the next ten months, wherein the 397th would be awarded a DUC for a brave and determined attack on an important railway bridge at Eller in Germany; during the mission seven aircraft were lost.

For the next two months the airfield was ominously quiet – it had been handed over to the RAF and came under the control of No 38 Group – but during the first week of October it reverberated to the sounds of Bristol Hercules engines of the Stirling IVs of Nos 295 and 570

Stirling IIIs: Nos 295 and 570 squadrons operated these aircraft from Rivenhall. (RAF Museum)

squadrons. They arrived with their Horsa gliders from RAF Harwell. Both squadrons had been busily regrouping after their D-Day operations and more recently over Arnhem, the famous airborne operation which proved so costly in aircraft and men. No 295 had lost five aircraft and No 570 had suffered heavier losses, with nine aircraft missing, 22 crew killed and another 16 made prisoners-of-war. By the end of the week there were almost 60 Stirlings and gliders and Rivenhall gave the appearance of a most active airfield once more.

Both squadrons were engaged in a training programme to enable the Stirling crews and the glider pilots to gain experience of the intricate air manoeuvres involved in airborne landings, with the glider pilots practising correct and safe landings. The squadrons were also engaged in the SOE (Special Operations Executive) missions that now were being mounted by the Group. The first such mission from Rivenhall took place on the night of 2nd/3rd November when eight Stirlings from No 295 were engaged in a drop over Norway, but the 10/10 cloud cover caused considerable problems and only a single Stirling managed to make a drop, but this was over an alternative dropping zone. One of the

(GEC Marconi)

Stirlings piloted by Group Captain W. E. Surplice, DSO, DFC, who was the Station Commander, failed to return. For the next two days an extensive air/sea search was made for the missing aircraft, which was thought to have ditched in the North Sea, but unfortunately without any success. Therefore, on 11th November, Group Captain Pope, DSO, took over the command of Rivenhall. The rather severe weather experienced during January resulted in all special operations being cancelled, and in February some of the crews found themselves back on straight bombing operations. However, on 24th February a Stirling of 295 squadron, piloted by Squadron Leader Stewart, achieved a notable first – dropping eleven containers of supplies inside Germany.

Like several other Essex aircrews the Rivenhall squadrons were actively involved in 'Operation Varsity'. A total of 60 Stirlings along with their gliders took off from the airfield early on the morning of 24th March. Almost 500 airborne troops, 50 jeeps and 36 trailers were carried by the two squadrons. The flight went reasonably well, although five crews had to return early to Rivenhall. Only one Stirling, from 295 squadron, was lost to ground flak; its pilot (Warrant Officer Symmons) remained at the controls long enough to allow his crew to bale out but the aircraft crashed before he could make his escape.

Both squadrons were engaged in drops over Denmark and Holland during April, and the last SOE mission from the airfield was mounted on the night of 26th/27th, rejoicing under the code-name 'Table Jam'! There were a number of dropping zones over Denmark but two aircraft from No 295 squadron failed to make it back to Rivenhall. But perhaps one of the most unfortunate incidents occurred after VE day, when 47 Stirlings from both squadrons were involved on 11th May, in 'Operation Doomsday', which was engaged in lifting British troops to Norway to form an occupation force. Sadly, three aircraft crashed due to the weather conditions and Air Vice Marshal J. R. Scarlett-Streatfield, the AOC of 38 Group, was a passenger in one of the Stirlings that crashed. The two Stirling squadrons stayed at Rivenhall until the beginning of 1946 when they were moved to Wethersfield.

The airfield then passed through a number of existences. It was initially used as a camp for released Polish prisoners-of-war. Then for a time Essex County Council used some of the camp buildings as a rest home for 'travellers of the road' – it was then known as 'The Wayfarers Hostel'. In June 1956 the Marconi Company, from nearby Chelmsford, took over the lease of the airfield and it was used for radar development work.

20

SOUTHEND (ROCHFORD)

In describing all these Essex airfields, we can only wonder how they might appear from the air during the war, but fortunately we are indebted to a young pilot for his vivid description of Rochford as he approached it for the first time:

> 'We circled Rochford in the late afternoon. The grass airfield looked small – only about a thousand yards long in the east-west direction and much less across. A railway line ran along an embankment at the eastern end – an obstacle which complicated an approach from that direction and constituted a dangerous trap for anyone mis-judging his landing and over-shooting from the west. It was clearly impossible to land a Spitfire other than in one of those two directions.
>
> There were two small hangers on the south side of the field, old fashioned buildings of the type which might have been put up during the First World War. There was a clubhouse in the south-east corner. There were no barrack blocks, parade grounds or other paraphernalia of a normal RAF station. This was a field which had been used as a centre for private flying enthusiasts, and was now pressed into war service.'

These were the first impressions of Pilot Officer Hugh Dundas of No 616 squadron as he and his fellow pilots flew into Rochford on 27th May 1940. The 19 year old pilot, who later gained the nickname 'Cocky', was destined to become one of the most celebrated RAF airmen of the war; a highly skilled Spitfire pilot, he ended as the youngest-ever Group Captain, commanding No 244 Wing. His recollections of Rochford are to be found in his memoir of the war *Flying Start*. Dundas was later knighted and died in 1995.

The small airfield had indeed been used in the latter years of the First World War when several squadrons were based there to counter the German Gotha bombers, which were threatening London and the eastern counties. During a daylight raid on Southend in December 1917, one of the attacking Gothas was shot down and it crashed quite close to the airfield. Like the majority of these wartime airfields, Rochford was relinquished and after a little private flying there during 1920, the airfield closed and passed over to agricultural use.

In the early 1930s many local authorities were keen to have their own airports; much of this enthusiasm had been fostered by Sir Alan Cobham, who did more than most to popularise flying during the inter-war years. Sir Alan, famed for his long-distance flights, had undertaken an extensive nationwide tour in an attempt to persuade local authorities to establish their own airports. Southend Corporation, realising the potential of the site at Rochford, duly purchased it and a clubhouse and two hangars were built.

In September 1935 it was officially opened as Southend Municipal Airport, although still known as Rochford. Two years later when the Royal Air Force Volunteer Reserve was formed, No 602 'City of Glasgow' squadron arrived for a summer camp. Like many other civil airfields, Rochford was used to train pilots for the RAF Volunteer Reserve, and they produced scores of fine pilots, who later made such a contribution to the RAF, especially during the early war years.

During August 1939 the Air Ministry requisitioned all such commercial airfields, which by now numbered almost 50, and this one now became known as RAF Rochford and was placed in No 11 Group of Fighter Command as a satellite field for RAF Hornchurch. Within a week of the outbreak of the war the first Spitfires from Hornchurch began to arrive; they belonged to No 54 squadron, and in the following month Blenheim 1Fs of No 600 'City of London' landed but only for a brief stay. It would be the Spitfires of Nos 54 and 74 squadrons that would be the most frequent visitors to Rochford over the next nine months. The pilots alternated between Hornchurch and Rochford, and they found the very basic facilities at the forward base a vast change to the comfortable and relatively luxurious quarters at Hornchurch. It was three Spitfires of No 74 that claimed the first enemy aircraft to be shot down over England when on 20th November 1939 a Heinkel 111, engaged in photo-reconnaissance over the Thames Estuary, was shot down into the sea near Southend. One of 74's pilots at the time was Pilot Officer the Hon Derek Dowding, the son of the AOC-in-C of Fighter

Command.

As in all fighter stations, be they large or small, the so-called 'Phoney War' and the harsh winter of 1939/40 severely curtailed operations, so the pilots of both squadrons saw very little action, but this just proved to be the lull before the storm. By early May this situation had drastically altered with the German invasion of France and the Low Countries. The last week of the month ended in 'Operation Dynamo' – the evacuation of Dunkirk – which lasted from May 26th to June 4th.

No 616, which was the last Auxiliary squadron to be formed, moved from Leconfield in Yorkshire to relieve the exhausted and battered No 74 squadron, which had experienced a torrid time over France. Earlier on their last day (27th) at Rochford the squadron had lost one of their most experienced pilots, Flight Lieutenant 'Paddy' or 'Treacle' Treacy, who had been with the squadron since 1936. He was shot down over France but evaded capture and finally returned in February 1941 via Spain and Eire. Sadly, he was killed later in the war, whilst operating from Stapleford Tawney. The pilots of No 616 had not been blooded in battle, but within hours of their arrival at Rochford they were ordered out on their first Dunkirk patrol. This proved to be uneventful but the young and inexperienced pilots would never forget the sight over Dunkirk, as Dundas recalls '...the black smoke rose from somewhere in the harbour area, thick, impenetrable, obscuring much of the town, rising to a height of about twelve and fifteen thousand feet, which stretched for many miles to the westward over Calais and beyond, down the Channel...'

During their short stay at the airfield the squadron opened their score with five enemy aircraft destroyed and another four probables, for the loss of two Spitfires. Their commander – Squadron Leader Marcus Robinson – was rather fortunate to survive one patrol, he was forced to crash-land his badly damaged aircraft at Manston. Only one pilot was killed – on the squadron's final sortie when he crashed on take-off from Rochford in thick ground fog.

With 616's departure 'back north', No 74 returned from their brief rest and were soon back in the fray. Their most famous pilot – Flight Lieutenant Adolph 'Sailor' Malan – the irrepressible and brilliant South African – claimed a notable first on the night of 18th/19th June when he became the first single-seater pilot of the war to destroy an enemy aircraft at night. The HeIII crashed in flames into the garden of the Bishop of Chelmsford. About an hour later he shot down a second Heinkel, which ended up in the sea just off Felixstowe. This was no mean achievement because the Spitfire was never noted for its night-

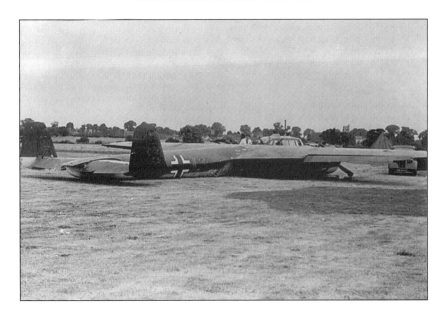

Dornier 17Z at the airfield – 26th August 1940. (Southend Museums Service)

fighting capabilities. It was on this night that Southend suffered its first civilian casualties of the war – 12 injured and 1 killed. The Luftwaffe had tried to destroy the Canewdon radar station, which was two miles to the north of the airfield.

Towards the end of June No 54 squadron returned once again, and for the next three weeks or so its pilots were in the thick of the fighting, although the Battle of Britain had not yet officially opened. By the time (25th July) its pilots had earned a well-deserved rest, five pilots had been killed in action; since the days of Dunkirk just five out of 15 pilots had survived. On its last two days at Rochford two of its most experienced pilots failed to return – Pilot Officers John Allen, DFC, and Basil Way, DFC – both had eight victories to their credit.

During August and September various squadrons from both Hornchurch and North Weald used Rochford as an advance base, as No 11 Group's chiefs tried to combat the seemingly endless Luftwaffe attacks, especially those directed at the fighter airfields. The first Hurricanes appeared in August when No 56 squadron from North Weald used the airfield. On 26th of the month a badly-damaged Dornier Do17Z made an emergency belly-landing on the airfield. It was part of a

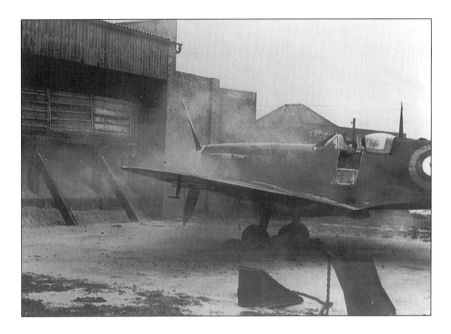

The cannons of a Spitfire being tested at the butts. (Southend Museums Service)

strong Luftwaffe force attempting to bomb Hornchurch and Debden airfields. The aircraft had been damaged by Spitfires of 65 squadron led by Flight Lieutenant Saunders. Two days later, in the early afternoon, the airfield was heavily bombed, leaving some 30 craters in the field, buildings damaged and the railway line blocked. Then, on 2nd September, another damaged Do17 made a crash-landing on the airfield. During this period Jeffrey Quill, the famous Spitfire test pilot, flew some sorties from Rochford with No 65 squadron mainly to test the aircraft under operational conditions; he was also credited with two kills!

The Spitfires of No 41 squadron were the most frequent visitors to Rochford during most of September. It was one of the highest scoring squadrons of the Battle of Britain, claiming over 90 aircraft destroyed. On the 5th of the month it had lost its CO, Squadron Leader H. R. L. 'Robin' Hood, in a collision with another Spitfire. The following day Flight Lieutenant Norman Ryder led eight Spitfires from Rochford and the pilots were engaged in a fierce combat with Me109s, in which they claimed six destroyed. In the last week of the month 12 aircraft were lost, although during the month its pilots had claimed 39 aircraft destroyed.

Foremost amongst its pilots were Pilot Officers E. S. Lock, DFC, and George Bennions, DFC. Lock became the top RAF 'ace' of the Battle of Britain with 18 victories; he went missing in action during February 1941. Bennions was seriously injured on 1st October, at the time he had 12 victories to his name. Besides its brave and valiant exploits in the Battle, the squadron's other claim to fame was that its new commanding officer was Donald Finlay, who had gained lasting renown as a high hurdler after winning a silver medal at the Berlin Olympics of 1936.

On October 26th 1940 Rochford became a station in its own right, and was known as RAF Southend, although the fighter control remained with Hornchurch. The first Station Commander was another legendary RAF airman – Wing Commander Basil Embry. He had not long returned to the country after some truly amazing escapades after being shot down whilst leading his Blenheim squadron (No 107) from Wattisham in Suffolk.

Embry found his new command to be in a rather sorry state, the airfield had been bombed several times, including the day he arrived and it still bore the heavy scars. He commented that officers, NCOs and men were all living in the clubhouse, which had become very overcrowded. Embry proceeded to requisition a number of local houses and made everybody, except those on duty, sleep outside the airfield. The neighbouring golf course was also brought into use, some aircraft were dispersed there and the clubhouse was converted into a sergeants' mess.

The squadron at Rochford at the time was No 264, which was equipped with Boulton Paul Defiants. This two-seater fighter had only come into service in December 1939 with the squadron, and had not become operational until the following March. It was the first fighter to have incorporated a power-driven gun turret instead of the conventional forward firing weapons. Sadly, the Battle of Britain cruelly exposed its major weakness – a vulnerability to attack from underneath. The squadron had arrived at Hornchurch on 21st August and some Defiants operated from both Rochford and Manston. In seven days of operations eleven aircraft, five pilots and nine gunners were lost with the result that, on 28th, the aircraft was withdrawn from daytime fighting with the intention of employing it solely as a night-fighter.

Southend, along with Gravesend, had been selected to house two night-fighting wings, although Embry was not convinced that the airfield was suitable for such a role. He was concerned that as the aircraft took off towards the river Thames, some two miles distant, the

Boulton Paul Defiant: No 264 squadron suffered heavily in the Battle of Britain.

pilots were required to make a quick turn almost as soon as they were airborne to avoid the barrage balloon at the mouth of the river, this had already caused two accidents. In addition to this hazard Embry pointed out that as there was no permanent lighting at the airfield further accidents might occur. In any case, he was most unhappy with the Defiants, in his view they were 'thoroughly bad night-fighters'! Embry expressed his grave misgivings and the proposed move of the second squadron – No 151 – from Digby was postponed. Before the year was out No 11 Group had abandoned the idea and Embry left to take over the command of RAF Wittering, on his way to a brilliant Service career, which culminated in the rank of Air Chief Marshal and a knighthood. As for the poor maligned Defiants, Fighter Command was able to remark, in May 1941, 'the Defiants have done well recently and they have become useful night-fighters.'

As Fighter Command moved forward to a more offensive role in early 1941 Southend became the forward base for a number of Spitfire squadrons that operated sweeps and Ramrods over France and Holland. For the next six months or so the old and familar squadrons – Nos 54 and 74 – along with two auxiliary squadrons – Nos 611 and 603 – used the airfield at various times. It was still in the front-line as was evinced on 11th May 1941 when it was dive-bombed and strafed by a force of Me109s, which caused considerable damage.

From August until early November a Canadian squadron – No 402 – was stationed there; as its number denotes it was the second Canadian

Czech pilots of No 313 squadron. (Southend Museums Service)

fighter squadron to be formed in Britain and had only been operational for five months. It had recently been supplied with Hurricane IIs, and besides the normal ration of fighter sweeps and escort duties, some of the pilots were experimenting with their Hurricanes operating as fighter/bombers. The aircraft were fitted with two 250 pound bombs and the first bombing mission was undertaken on 1st November when eight aircraft bombed Berck-sur-Mer airfield. Four days later the squadron moved to Warmwell in Dorset where it fully developed this role as a 'Hurribomber' unit.

As Southend was still linked to Hornchurch fighter control the airfield continued to play host to either Spitfire detachments or squadrons. But, on 1st May, the airfield was transferred to North Weald Sector, and the following day yet another Canadian squadron arrived – No 403. It had been formed in March 1941 and had lost three COs in less than a year of operations; now it was led by another illustrious pilot of the Battle of Britain – a New Zealander, Squadron Leader Alan 'Al' Deere. Deere was well used to Southend, having served with No 54 squadron during the Battle of Britain. He ultimately ended the war with 22 victories to his name, he retired from the Service in 1967 as an Air Commodore and died in September 1995, aged 77 years. During the Canadians' stay at Southend their Spitfire VBs were very active but the squadron had one tragic mission on 2nd June when it happened to be set upon by at least 30 FW190s with the result that six pilots were lost.

The following day the squadron left for Martlesham Heath and went later to Catterick for 'a rest and re-equip', and in their place came more North Americans, the United States pilots of No 121, the second 'Eagle' squadron. Their days in 'RAF blue' were now numbered because by the end of September the pilots would be serving in No 335 squadron of the 4th Fighter Group of the Eighth Air Force. Before they finally left RAF Fighter Command they had one notable success on 31st July. Whilst on a bomber escort mission, the pilots managed to claim seven enemy aircraft destroyed, which proved to be their biggest total on a single expedition. The mission was tinged with sadness as their British Commander, Squadron Leader Hugh Kennard, DFC, was severely wounded.

When the American pilots left for Debden in September, their place was taken by a Belgian squadron – No 350 – which had been originally formed in November 1941 from a nucleus of Belgian pilots that had managed to escape the invasion of their country. Prior to their arrival at Southend the pilots had been engaged in the Dieppe operation on 19th August, when they claimed seven enemy aircraft destroyed and another twelve damaged. Commanded by Squadron Leader D. A. Guillame, DFC, their Spitfire VBs were engaged on a variety of operations but mainly 'Rhubarbs'. On October 26th a Do17, which had been shot down by anti-aircraft fire crashed onto the squadron's dispersal area causing some damage and one fatality. The squadron left for Hornchurch towards the end of the year, although it would make a brief return almost a year later.

At the beginning of June 1943 the airfield was transferred back into the Hornchurch Sector and remained there until the Operations Room closed down in February 1944. During June fairly rare RAF fighters made a brief appearance at Southend, the Westland Whirlwinds of No 137 squadron. This twin-engined aircraft had first come into service in the summer of 1940 but was not ready for operations, with just two squadrons, until the end of the year. Only some 110 of these unusual aircraft were produced largely because of continual problems with its Rolls-Royce Peregrine engines, which made maintenance rather difficult. Compared with contemporary fighters, the Whirlwind had a good turn of speed (maximum 360 mph), at least at low altitudes, and with a superior range it should have become a useful addition to Fighter Command. The aircraft proved not to be really suitable for escort duties and was ultimately used as a ground strike aircraft. After mounting a few Whirlwind missions from Southend the squadron began to convert to Hurricane IVs, which could be armed with up to eight 60 pound rocket projectiles.

Since the early months of 1942 the airfield had housed a Target Towing Flight (No 1488), which had originally been equipped with the doughty 'Lizzies' – Westland Lysanders. Now the airfield bowed out of the Second World War with the establishment of No 17 Armament Practice Camp for the use of the many fighter squadrons of No 11 Group. The Camp's small Miles Masters and Martinets mingled with the Spitfire IXs and Mustang IIIs of various squadrons that arrived for about a week or so to prepare their pilots for their ground strike role after the D-Day invasion.

In 1946 the airfield was de-requisitioned and on 1st January 1947 civil flying was resumed once again. Known once again as Southend Municipal Airport it is now a flourishing civil airfield with many regular passenger services. During 1995 a new terminal building was opened, in which there is a montage of photographs and facts tracing the history of the airfield from its early days. Also in the building is a small memorial plaque for all the RAF personnel who served at the airfield during the Second World War.

21

STANSTED
MOUNTFICHET

In the spacious award-winning passenger terminal at London Stansted, which was opened by HM the Queen in March 1991, there is a small display cabinet containing some wartime mementoes and a brief record of the airfield's American connections during the Second World War when it was a base for thousands of USAAF airmen. These days Stansted has established itself as London's third international airport, and is now capable of handling eight million passengers a year. I think that it is rather doubtful whether many of the passengers who use the airport are aware of its wartime existence, especially as virtually all vestiges of the old airfield have disappeared under the massive development that has taken place in order to make London Stansted a 'World Class Airport'.

The site, close to the large and old village of Stansted Mountfichet, was selected for an airfield in the spring of 1942, and it took its name from the nearby village; but all too soon the name was shortened to just plain 'Stansted' and sometimes corrupted, both in speech and word, to 'Stanstead'. It was during July 1942 that the US Engineers of 817th Battalion arrived and in the following month they cut the first sod with a certain amount of ceremony, because along with Andrews Field and Gosfield it was amongst the first American built airfields in East Anglia. This Battalion stayed on the project for several months before being moved out pending a posting to North Africa. Two other US Engineer Aviation Battalions – 825th and 850th – arrived to complete the construction work.

Nissen or 'Quonset' huts at wartime Stansted. (Stansted Airport Ltd)

Early in its existence it was earmarked for an 'Advanced Air Depot', which involved even more building work, with the need for additional aircraft hard-standings, hangars and workshops. The depot was placed to the east of the main runway towards the village of Takeley. Ultimately the whole site covered almost 3,000 acres, which made it the largest Ninth Air Force base in East Anglia. The airfield was ready for occupation in July 1943 though it was not formally opened until 7th August. Just a few miles down the A120 road there was another USAAF airfield (Great Dunmow) taking shape, which opened almost at the same time.

By October 1943 Stansted was transferred from the Eighth to the Ninth Air Force Service Command, which was based at Sunninghill Park near Ascot, under the command of Major General J. Miller. Stansted then became known as No 2 Tactical Air Depot (just one of six) with the 30th and 91st Air Depot Groups setting up their establishments. These units provided comprehensive aircraft maintenance, assembly, servicing, modification, supply, reclamation and repair services for the Ninth Air Force Groups in Essex, and as such were almost exclusively concerned with B-26s.

Stansted airfield soon became a bustling American 'township' with a myriad of ancillary units, besides the two Depot Groups, also being based there, as well as a range of medical and veterinary sections, signals companies, firefighter platoons, truck companies and several Military Police companies. But it was not until the beginning of February 1944 that the first operational combat Group arrived at Stansted. It was the 344th (Medium) Bomb Group commanded by Colonel Reginald F. C. Vance. This Group became known as 'The Silver Streaks', not necessarily from from the fact that their B-26 aircraft remained in their natural aluminium finish, but mainly, I suspect, from their badge, which depicted four silver arrows or 'streaks' and carried the defiant motto 'We Win or Die'!

Some 60 or so bare-metal aircraft (15 to each squadron, later increased to 21) arrived during the next few days. Many crews were convinced that their aircraft were slightly faster than the normal drab olive-green coloured B-26s. Soon the aircraft would be given the Group's markings – a 36" high white triangle on both sides of the tailplane. They were also marked with the squadrons' identification codes – K9, Y5, N3 and 7I for the 494th to the 497th respectively – in large grey block letters to the forward of the national insignia. It is interesting to note that earlier in April (4th) the 1,585th and last B-26 rolled off the production lines at Martin's factory in Nebraska; although the crews would not yet be aware of the fact that the B-26 was drawing close to the end of its operational life. However, the final B-26s would leave the main Baltimore factory towards the end of March 1945.

The 344th was relatively late coming onto the scene because it had been largely used as a replacement training unit in the United States before moving to England. The four squadrons became part of the 99th Bomb Wing, which had its headquarters at Great Dunmow. Within a month of their arrival at Stansted the crews were ready for their first operation. On 6th March 1944, 37 crews left to bomb Conches, some miles to the west of Evreux. Thus began the Group's operations from Essex, which were to continue until the end of September.

Soon the crews found out all the various problems and frustrations of operating in the weather conditions prevailing over northern Europe; frequently missions were cancelled, and often the crews found themselves attacking targets which were obscured by heavy clouds. On one of their early missions, to Soesterberg in Holland, two B-26s collided in mid-air when emerging from heavy clouds and the twelve crewmen were all killed; mid-air collision was an inherent risk in both the Eighth

Wartime propaganda photograph: four pilots posing as aircrew of a B-26. (Stansted Airport Ltd)

and Ninth Air Forces, dedicated as they were to tight formation flying. At least one third of the aircraft on the Soesterberg mission returned to the airfield with quite severe flak damage. As with all B-26 Groups, the 344th found themselves bombing Creil marshalling yards and especially on 20th March when they were part of a 126 strong force, which dropped almost 200 tons of bombs; the bombing results of this mission were considered quite spectacular and it resulted in a congratulatory message being sent from the Ninth Bomber chiefs to each of the four Bomb Groups engaged in this operation.

Throughout April and May the crews were engaged in a wide variety of tactical targets – communication lines, roads, canals and railways, coastal defences, airfields and V1 rocket sites. For example, on 23rd April, the 344th attacked the marshalling yards at Namur in Belgium and over a month later (30th May) a bridge at Rouen – indeed the road and rail bridges along river Seine from Paris to the coast became the special preserve of the B-26 Groups. In the immediate days before D-Day the 344th bombed gun positions at Quend Plage, north of the

Somme estuary. Two days later (4th) the crews were in action over Courcelles-sur-Seine, where a bridge was the specific target. On this mission one aircraft crashed shortly after take-off and the explosions from the two 2,000 pound bombs killed two members of the crew with the other four being seriously injured. Despite this very unfortunate and distressing accident, the next day the crews were back to routine and directed to attack what was called a 'Headquarters Shelter' at Wissant on the Channel coast, just to the west of Calais. Perhaps, even at this late stage, the Allied Command chiefs were still trying to confound the enemy as to the actual location of the imminent invasion?

On D-Day itself the 344th was given the honour to lead all of the Ninth's B-26 Groups on their first bombing mission of the day, perhaps this was in recognition of the Group's growing reputation for the accuracy of its bombing. A 'maximum effort' was the order of the day; 56 aircraft in three formations, all painted in their invasion stripes, left Stansted at four o'clock in the morning, led by Colonel Vance. The Group's specific targets were the gun fortifications of Beau Guillot, just south of the Utah beach-head, La Madelaine opposite the Green beach-head, and St-Martin-de-Varreville at the rear of the landing areas – all on the Cherbourg peninsula. The crews had been carefully briefed to make their attack from 5,000 feet, or even lower should the cloud conditions over the target areas so dictate.

The main objects of these attacks were the immediate beach defences and, according to the Group's records, 'the demoralisation of the enemy front line defences and the disruption of communication lines for reserve forces.' For this operation the B-26s were loaded with 250 pound bombs rather than their normal 1,000 or 2,000 pounders, largely to prevent creating too many large craters, which would have created obstacles for the American invading forces and their armoured vehicles. Furthermore, the crews were briefed to clear out of the area by making a wide detour across the peninsula, as soon as their bombing runs (which lasted just about 15 seconds) had been completed, because the Eighth Air Force heavies were planned to arrive just five minutes later! The timing of all these bombing operations on D-Day was most critical and had to be completed before the first troops landed on the various beach-heads,

The Group's records for this D-Day mission read, ' There is good reason to believe that our bombing caused the enemy much distress...' All the B-26 Bomb Groups mounted two missions on D-Day and in the afternoon the 344th was directed to attack marshalling yards at Amiens, well behind the enemy lines. On 8th June Major General Lewis Brereton, the Commanding General of the Ninth Air Force, sent a message of commendation to all the B-26 Bomb Groups:

'I feel it a distinct privilege to be your Commander and to congratulate each officer and every man of this air force on magnificent, individual and collective efforts in preparation for this battle.

Your past operations have been marked by relentless destruction of enemy installations and equipment bringing once again brilliant achievement to this command. I am more than gratified by the results.

Today the 9th Air Force is participating in the greatest campaign of them all.

With our gallant Allies we take the offensive to exterminate this ruthless foe.

I am confident that you will give your utmost and with resolute courage and firm determination pay any human price in the destruction of this common enemy.

Go to it. God speed and good luck. I am proud to be one of you and your Commander.'

Most B-26 crews felt that they would be lucky to survive the D-Day missions, especially when they realised that they would be attacking at low-level, their experiences of the enemy flak at medium height had been traumatic enough. However, of the 736 B-26s despatched only six aircraft were lost in total, which was an amazingly low casualty rate (0.8%) considering the number of aircraft taking part; but one of the missing B-26s came from the 344th. The D-Day operations gave a clear demonstration of the effectiveness and durability of the B-26 – and also a testimony to the excellent performances of the B-26 crews.

Immediately after D-Day the B-26 Groups concentrated their efforts on fuel and ammunition dumps – Domfront, Forêt d'Andaine, Forêt de Grimbosq and Valognes – both close to the enemy lines and further afield. Radar installations also came in for some selective bombing, especially at Cap Frehel and St Pierre Eglise. After the first V1 rockets landed on south-east England on the night of 12th/13th June the B-26 Groups returned to 'No Ball' targets on the 18th of the month. The following couple of days saw stormy weather over Normandy which precluded much operational flying but by the 22nd the Group was providing tactical support for the American forces in the Cotentin peninsula and this continued until Cherbourg was captured by the Allied forces towards the end of the month.

B-26 Sad Sack of 344th Bomb Group at Stansted. (Stansted Airport Ltd)

The month of July proved to be the Group's most successful period whilst operating from Stansted. The American offensive at St Lô commenced on 25th July, but two days previously a number of bridges and a fuel dump in Normandy were very effectively attacked by the 344th along with ten other Groups – all using Pathfinder techniques. On 24th 39 B-26s from Stansted bombed an important bridge on the river Loire near Tours. As in all attacks against bridges, the crews encountered heavy and severe flak and the lead formation was scattered, but nevertheless the rest of the crews carried out the attack with great determination and courage, with the result that vital parts of the bridge were destroyed. All but eight of the aircraft returned to Stansted with considerable flak damage. The following day troop concentrations behind the enemy lines at St Lô were bombed, then on the 26th an important supply depot was heavily damaged. For the operations on these three days the 344th was awarded a DUC – a just recognition of the Group's excellence.

For the next two months the Group's B-26s ranged over a wide variety of targets, which included the port of Brest but by the end of September the Group had flown its last mission from Stansted, moving to 'A-59' airfield at Cormeilles, about 10 miles north-east of Lisieux. In almost

Fine aerial view of Stansted, with the award-winning passenger terminal in foreground. (Stansted Airport Ltd)

seven months of operations from Stansted over 100 missions had been mounted with 26 aircraft being lost in action, which must be admitted was an above average loss rate for B-26 Groups. The Group's records neatly sum up their service at Stansted 'We have occupied station 169 at Stansted for seven months during which period the 344th had engaged the enemy in a total of 146 missions and had dropped a total of 7,739 tons of explosives on his installations from Holland and Brest.'

The USAAF continued to use the airfield although most of the Ninth Air Force units were now operating from the Continent. The Eighth Air Force used it as a Base Air Depot, and it became mainly a storage area for B-17s and P-47s. Later in 1945 the base was also used as a 'Rest and Rehabilitation Centre' for returning US servicemen, and it was not until 12th August that the airfield was handed over to the RAF, who brought in a Maintenance Unit (No 263). During 1946 and 1947 the airfield also housed German prisoners-of-war.

It was on 14th December 1946 that the airfield was opened for civilian use and a company set up a charter cargo service with six surplus Halifax bombers. However, the airfield's American connections were not quite over, as early in 1954 the USAF Engineers (815th Battalion) moved in again to extend the main runway for the use of jet aircraft. It was ultimately lengthened to 3,048 metres, which made it then the longest runway in the country, and ultimately had a great bearing on its subsequent development as the third London airport. After the Americans finally left Stansted in April 1957, the airfield saw many different activities – trooping flights, civil pilot training, aircraft production, charter passenger and cargo flights.

The various Government White Papers and the subsequent long public inquiries are now past history. Since June 1985 when the final go-ahead was given to develop Stansted into a major international airport, the airfield has been transformed into London's third airport with its splendid passenger terminal and new control tower, catering for both internal UK flights and regular services to Europe and America, as well as a considerable number of freight movements.

22

STAPLEFORD TAWNEY

In the immediate pre-war years small private airfields like Stapleford Tawney proved to be heaven-sent for the Air Ministry, faced as it was by a surge of willing recruits for the RAF Volunteer Reserve, all of whom were desperately keen to learn to fly. The facilities provided by these airfields were ideal for basic flying training for these 'weekend' airmen. The number of Battle of Britain pilots that passed through these flying schools was a lasting testimony to the contribution such airfields played in the rapid build-up of the RAF Reserve during the last two years of peace.

In 1938 No 21 Elementary and Reserve Flying Training School was established at Stapleford Tawney with the flying training being conducted by Reid and Signist Ltd under contract from the Ministry. Without doubt, the school's most famous pupil was J. E. 'Johnnie' Johnson, who became the RAF's top-scoring pilot with 38 victories to his credit, and he retired from the Service in 1966 as a highly decorated Air Vice Marshal. Johnson, who was a civil engineer at Loughton, went to Stapleford Tawney at the weekends for his flying training on Tiger Moths, and he later recalled the instructor's warning about Hurricanes from nearby North Weald, 'Keep a sharp look-out for those brutes. They come at you at a terrific speed and, head on, look no bigger than a razor blade.'

Shortly after the outbreak of the war the airfield was requisitioned, and some improvement work was commenced. A long perimeter track and dispersal points were laid down and a few extra buildings were erected to provide accommodation. The airfield was grass surfaced and according to some pilots it was 'extremely rough...with several ridges running across the field...'; by the end of March 1940 the airfield was considered ready and it became a satellite field for North Weald.

The first squadron to use the airfield on a regular basis was No 151, which began making patrols from Stapleford towards the end of August. During its short stay, the squadron lost six aircraft and two pilots, one of which was the commander – Squadron Leader Eric King – who was killed in action on 30th of the month. King had previously been a supernumary Commander with No 249, and only nine days earlier his Hurricane had been shot down by a Me110 near North Weald. The squadron's move to Digby in Lincolnshire provided a much-needed respite but sadly the squadron's ill-luck continued to dog it because on 4th September Pilot Officer Richard Ambrose, who had only joined the squadron on 26th August, was killed when his Hurricane struck a crane and burst into flames when taking off for Digby. Ambrose is buried in Epping cemetery.

The replacement squadron was No 46, which had already experienced a rather eventful war. In April it had been sent out to Norway and after some rather bitter air-fighting, it was ordered back to England in early June. Rather than leave its valuable Hurricanes behind, they were flown on board the aircraft carrier HMS *Glorious*, despite the pilots having had no previous deck landing practice. Sadly the carrier was sunk by German cruisers on the way back, all the aircraft were lost and only two pilots (Squadron Leader Richard Cross, DFC, and Flight Lieutenant P. Jameson) survived the sinking, being rescued after three days afloat in a Carley float. Pat Jameson would later serve at North Weald as the Wing Commander (Flying). Other members of the squadron returned safely by another vessel. Most of their time at Digby had been spent on replacing the aircraft and pilots and then working up to operational readiness under a new Commander, Squadron Leader J. R. Maclachlan, who was a permanent RAF officer, but he only stayed until October.

The pilots went straight into action, claiming their first victory on 2nd September when a Me109 was destroyed for the loss of one pilot. On the following day when North Weald suffered its heavy Luftwaffe attack, the squadron lost five aircraft whilst accounting for two enemy bombers. The next day three more Hurricanes were lost and, by a quirk of fate, one of the pilots, Pilot Officer Charles Ambrose, was shot down near Rochford almost at the same time as Richard Ambrose was killed at Stapleford. Ambrose had to bale out again in November, but he survived the war and stayed in the RAF until 1972, retiring as a Group

A Heinkel 111 shot down near Chelmsford in the early years of the war. (Essex Chronicle)

Captain with a CBE, DFC and AFC.

During their first month of operations the squadron claimed 19 victories for the loss of 20 aircraft with eight pilots killed in action. The first two weeks of October proved to be much quieter, mainly because of several days of unfavourable weather, but yet by the end of the month the squadron had lost another nine Hurricanes and four experienced pilots. One of them, Pilot Officer William Pattulo, who had previously served with 151 and 249 squadrons, crashed into a house at Romford on 25th October. Pattulo, who was only 21 years old, died the following day from his injuries. The squadron's top-scoring pilot was Flight Lieutenant Alexander Rabagliati, DFC, a South African airman, who had joined the RAF in the pre-war days. He had been given a special Hurricane – one equipped with four cannons instead of the normal eight machine guns. By the end of the year Rabagliati was given command of the squadron. This talented and brave airman did not survive the war, being killed in July 1943 when commanding a Wing at Ludham in Norfolk. By November 8th the wet autumn weather had taken its toll of the airfield. It was declared unserviceable and No 46 moved back to North Weald; flying ceased at Stapleford until the following spring.

During August a highly secret unit moved into North Weald and its personnel kept themselves well apart from the rest of station. The unit was numbered 419 Flight and was under the command of Flight Lieutenant Walter Farley, a pre-war officer, who had considerable

A few Whitleys of No 419 Flight could be seen at the airfield during September 1940. (RAF Museum)

experience with Army Co-operation squadrons and thus was admirably suited to the clandestine and dangerous work of this Flight. It had been officially formed on 21st August as the operational air-arm of the Special Operations Executive (SOE), which was largely the brainchild of Dr Hugh Dalton, the Minister of Economic Warfare, who intended that the SOE should be used as a 'Fourth Arm' or 'Secret Army' – under which name its exploits were made into a very successful television series. The Executive's brief was to undertake 'irregular warfare in all its forms, which included industrial and military sabotage, propaganda, riots and strikes.' Winston Churchill thought that the SOE would 'set Europe ablaze'.

The Flight would use Armstrong Whitworth Whitleys to drop agents, supplies, radios and arms into occupied territory, and Westland Lysanders to pick up agents and other important people. Two Lysanders and two brand-new Whitley Vs arrived at North Weald during late August and two Whitley operations to drop a couple of agents into Holland and the Paris area were mounted from North Weald. The Luftwaffe raids on the airfield resulted in the Flight moving to

Stapleford on 4th September. According to one of the pilots there, they 'lived in bell tents and washed in the little stream near the airfield', and when they were bombed out of their tents they moved into nearby farm buildings!

The Whitley was certainly a large aircraft to use the airfield. It was the first twin-engined heavy bomber to be produced in quantity for the RAF, and it came into service in March 1937. The aircraft was sturdy, spacious and very reliable, but it was also known to its crews as 'the slab-sided lumbering giant'! The first specially adapted Mark Vs appeared early in 1940 with the first live parachute jumps by airborne troops being made in July; the aircraft seemed particularly suited to the clandestine missions undertaken by the Flight. Only two operations were conducted from Stapleford, one to Brest and the other to Fontainebleau, before the Flight moved to more permanent quarters at Stradishall in Suffolk on 9th October.

The airfield did not become operational again until 9th April when the Hurricanes of No 242 squadron flew in from Martlesham Heath. The squadron was now in the hands of Squadron Leader W. 'Paddy' Treacy, who had been a Flight Commander with 65 squadron at Hornchurch and had only recently returned to England after being shot down in May 1940. On the squadron's first operation from Stapleford (20th April), three Hurricanes collided in heavy cloud over the Channel and all three pilots (including Squadron Leader Treacy) were killed. Three days later the squadron's new CO arrived – Willard Whitney-Straight, MC – who was a scion of the wealthy American Whitney family. Whitney-Straight was one of the many colourful characters of Fighter Command. He was a well-known pre-war racing driver, an excellent pilot and fine leader, who had also owned his own airline! When he retired from the RAF he had reached the rank of Air Commodore.

Whilst at Stapleford the squadron was largely engaged in flying offensive sweeps over northern France and Holland, but it moved to North Weald towards the end of May. There was an interval of about three weeks before the next Hurricanes came on the scene – the Mark IIs of No 3 squadron. Its motto 'The third shall be the first' commemorated the fact that it was the oldest squadron in the RAF, having been formed on 13th May 1912. Whilst at Stapleford the pilots were engaged on night-flying practice from the nearby airfield at Hunsdon. The Hurricanes shared the airfield with Airspeed Oxfords and Tiger Moths (just like old times!) of a rather unusual flying unit – No 2 Camouflage Unit. The unit's crews were responsible for the aerial examination of all the

Austers of No 656 squadron arrived in March 1943. (RAF Museum)

camouflaged sites and installations in East Anglia.

Towards the end of 1941 a new Air Sea Rescue squadron was formed at the airfield – No 277. This was really bringing together a number of flights that were operating separately from several fighter airfields in No 11 Group. Stapleford became the squadron's headquarters for the next twelve months without any operational flying taking place from the airfield. The squadron's headquarters were sited at Dudbrook Hall, about five miles to the east of the airfield near Kelvedon Hatch; this building now houses a private nursing home.

In March 1943 Stapleford Tawney was taken out of Fighter Command and placed under the control of No 34 Wing of the Army Co-operation Command, and it became a satellite of Sawbridgeworth. The only Army Co-operation squadron to use the airfield was No 656, which arrived from Westley, near Bury St Edmunds, on 14th March. These squadrons were known as AOPs or Air Observation Posts, and were equipped with Austers.

Austers were of an American design and produced by Taylorcraft Aeroplanes (England) Ltd under licence. They were a direct military version of a very successful and popular pre-war civilian sports aircraft, which in 1938 could be bought for £450! The aircraft was designed to land and take off from small airfields, being very light in construction, indeed the manufacturer claimed that the tail section 'can be easily lifted by a young lady'! The aircraft certainly appeared rather fragile but it was, in fact, quite rugged and proved indispensable for Army Support duties. The USAAF had more than a few Austers around their East Anglian bases – normally reserved 'for the sole use of the CO'!

The Army Co-operation Command was disbanded on 1st June and by August the Auster squadron had departed for Liverpool for ultimate service in India. The airfield was now used in the build-up for the invasion of Europe and saw the arrival of various units – signals, repair and salvage companies. On 20th November a V2 rocket landed in the middle of the airfield, leaving a crater 60 feet in diameter. A more serious incident occurred on 23rd February 1945 when another rocket fell on the main camp site, killing 17 personnel and injuring another 50. Stapleford was close to the end of its wartime operational life with the final ground units leaving before VE Day.

Today the airfield is a scene of urgent activity with a flourishing flying club and an ample number of private aircraft buzzing in and out. A few of the old wartime buildings have survived, most notably the old NAAFI hut! Stapleford Tawney is continuing a proud tradition of flight which goes back to a time when the airfield was known simply as 'the Essex aerodrome'.

23

WETHERSFIELD

Without doubt Wethersfield is the best known American airfield in Essex, although most, if not all, this fame dates from the days of the Cold War when the airfield was developed into a major USAF front-line base. During this period it regularly hosted air displays, which attracted thousands of spectators. It also became the mecca for girls from near and far, who were 'bussed' in to share the social activities at the base – Wethersfield was for them 'a touch of Hollywood' right on their doorsteps! Considering that the airfield had a rather spasmodic and chequered wartime existence, it is perhaps surprising to discover that it was the last military airfield in the county surviving into the 1990s – even if only just.

The airfield, about six miles north of Braintree, was sited in a rather secluded area of countryside close to the villages of Finchingfield, Toppesfield and its namesake. The site had been first recognised as suitable for airfield development in 1941, and by December the main contractors, McDonald and Gibb, had moved in with their target completion date as the end of 1942. However, the construction work soon fell behind schedule because of a shortage of labour, equipment and materials, and by December 1942 only the concrete runways had been completed. By then the situation had materially altered and the airfield site had been allocated to the Eighth Air Force. The USAAF reserved it for a Heavy Bomb Group of the proposed 5th Bomb Division, which never came to fruition.

The partially completed airfield was 'loaned' back to the RAF and placed in No 3 Group of Bomber Command as a satellite airfield for RAF

Ridgewell, which itself was a satellite of RAF Stradishall. Whilst the construction work continued, Wethersfield appeared to act as nothing more than a reserve landing field, though it was hardly ever used in this role. In October 1943 'ownership' of the airfield was passed over to the Ninth Air Force but it would be yet another four months before the first combat unit moved in. This gave Wethersfield the dubious honour of having the longest period of gestation for any airfield in Essex – some 2¼ years!

The Ninth Air Force unit that finally moved in on 1st February 1944 was the 416th Bomb Group (Light), which was scheduled to be equipped with A-20s and to become part of the 97th Combat Bomb Wing, which would ultimately comprise three A-20 Bomb Groups. The Group's Commanding Officer, Colonel Harold L. Mace, had many problems on his hands, not least of which was a sad lack of aircraft! The A-20s were shipped over from the United States and required to be reassembled in this country. When the first aircraft did eventually arrive there were no tools, an insufficient number of spare parts and no extra plexiglass noses and side windows. When it was disclosed that these items would not be available from the United States until June or July at the earliest, a British company was prevailed upon to manufacture the missing items, and thus the crisis was averted. Even then Colonel Mace had to quickly organise a retraining programme for his crews to familiarise them with the formation flying at medium altitudes that was used by the Ninth Bomber Command. Also as the 416th was the first A-20 Group to arrive in England, it was temporarily attached to the 99th (B-26) Bomb Wing, which caused a few operational problems for the Wing's planning staff as the A-20s were about 50-60 mph faster than the B-26s.

By the beginning of March Colonel Mace had a sufficient number of aircraft and retrained crews to start operations and on 3rd March the first A-20 mission mounted by the Ninth Bomber Command left Wethersfield, but it was nothing more taxing or exciting than a diversionary operation over northern France. The Ninth's priorities during the month were airfields, marshalling yards, E boat yards and pens, railway sheds and repair shops, and V1 rocket sites, in that order, and the 416th slotted into this bombing programme. The Group's first 'live' operation was directed at a V1 rocket site and in the next three weeks nine attacks were made by the Ninth's bombers; by the end of month no less than 65 sites had been taken off the bombing schedule because they were considered 'sufficiently destroyed'. Mainly because

The formal hand-over of the airfield to 416th Bomb Group – 15th April 1944. (USAF)

of the heavy bombardment these sites had sustained and the vast number of bomb craters around the sites it became almost impossible to establish the true extent of the damage from aerial photographs. The Ninth Air Force alone had dropped over 4,200 tons without the combined and concentrated efforts of the heavy bombers of the Eighth and the RAF!

At the beginning of April the Group was almost up to its full complement of aircraft – 58 A-20s were now available for operations, so obviously the delivery problems had been resolved. During the middle of the month (15th) the airfield was formally handed over by the RAF to the USAAF, just two and half months late – everything concerned with Wethersfield appeared to suffer from some delay or other! The Group's crews were now engaged against 'invasion' targets – marshalling yards, airfields and coastal batteries, although some new V1 sites had been Identified. Some 24 coastal batteries had been listed by the end of April and the Group was engaged in attacking these targets during the run up to D-Day. It was thought that they would require a continual bombardment to cause appreciable damage, this was due to the strength and depth of their defences – the famed 'Atlantic Wall'. Indeed, the fortifications at Etaples were attacked on six separate occasions during the month of May.

On the big day – 6th June – the A-20 Groups were not in action until the early afternoon, the 416th sending out 54 aircraft on the first mission. They left Wethersfield at 1300 hours but by then the weather conditions had deteriorated, with the cloud ceiling so low that the crews were forced to bomb from about 1,700 feet. The target was a crossroads junction at Argentan – fairly deep behind the Normandy beach-heads. The effect was quite devastating; the junction was utterly destroyed and the town itself was blasted, though it must be admitted that the Eighth's heavies had attacked it earlier in the day. All the Group's A-20s arrived back at Wethersfield intact.

Just after eight o'clock in the evening the second mission left the airfield in worsening weather conditions (it was said that 'even the birds were grounded'!), which would mean a bombing attack from below 1,500 feet. After the crews had crossed the French coast near the mouth of the river Somme at about 3,000 feet they came under steady and constant flak. The three boxes of A-20s were led by Major Meng and their target was an important marshalling yard to the south-east of Dieppe. The crews were greeted by a most concentrated barrage of anti-aircraft fire over the target area in which two aircraft went down in flames, but one crew was seen to bale out. After the bombing run the CO of 669th squadron, Major Campbell, was shot down. Major Meng then proceeded to lead the battle-scarred aircraft back to Wethersfield, although two damaged aircraft were forced to crash-land as soon as they reached the English coast. Only five A-20s were lost on D-Day by the Ninth Air Force and three of these unfortunately came from the 416th.

The weather conditions over Normandy during the middle of June were not particularly favourable for air operations and this unsettled period culminated in the so-called 'Great Storm' of 20th, which made the taking of the port at Cherbourg most essential to maintain the supplies to the Allied forces. The Group was greatly involved in attacking enemy strongholds and troop concentrations in the Cotentin peninsula, and often these missions were conducted in the face of heavy and concentrated flak opposition. None more so than on 29th June when the crews attacked enemy entrenched troops at St Hilaire Vitre in the north-west of the peninsula. First Lieutenant Wayne Downing, who was leading one box of A-20s, felt it was 'the harshest and most accurate anti-aircraft fire' he had experienced. The crews were forced to attack at under 1,500 feet, and Downing saw an aircraft on his wing go down in

A-20s of 416th Bomb Group over the French coast. (USAF)

flames whilst making its bomb run. Although Downing's aircraft was severely damaged he managed to nurse it across the English Channel to make an emergency landing at Bognor Regis. The bravery and determination of the Ninth's bomb crews as they daily attacked targets in support of the ground troops should not be forgotten, and they played a vital role in the Battle of Normandy.

It was well known that Air Chief Marshal Sir Trafford Leigh-Mallory, the AOC of the Allied Expeditionary Air Forces, considered that the Ninth's bombers were the most effective force at destroying bridges – be they road or rail. On 6th August the 416th was given as a target the last remaining bridge still standing over the Seine – Oissel near Rouen. A number of B-26 Groups had already made several attempts to destroy

A-20 landing at Wethersfield, whilst harvesting continues – August 1944. (Imperial War Museum)

this particular bridge. The first mission, launched in the morning, was forced to abort because of the heavy cloud conditions. However, by late afternoon the weather had improved sufficiently for the Group to make another attempt. The bridge and the river banks were strongly defended for a number of miles, and on their run-in to the target the A-20 crews encountered almost a solid wall of fire. Nevertheless with extreme bravery and determination they succeeded in completing their attack and the bridge was utterly destroyed. The cost was three aircraft, which were shot down in the target area, and they included the lead A-20 piloted by Lieutenant Colonel Farmer, who was the Group's Deputy Commander. Despite the ferocious barrage Farmer had completed two runs over the target to ensure the accuracy of the bombing attack. Over 20 aircraft limped back to Wethersfield with heavy flak damage and another five had to make emergency landings at other English airfields. It had been a harsh and traumatic mission for all the crews. On 8th and 9th August the Group was active attacking targets in what became known as 'the Falaise Gap'. As a result of the operations on these three days the 416th was awarded a DUC, which was a recognition of the high operational standard the Group had achieved under Colonel Mace. Just a few days earlier Colonel Mace had left the Group to take up the command of the 98th Bomb Wing, and he was replaced by Colonel Theodore R. Aylesworth, who led the 416th for the rest of the war.

Nearly a third of the USAAF's total losses of aircraft whilst serving in

England were due to accidental causes. During August the 416th lost three aircraft in accidents quite close to the airfield. On 13th two A-20s came down near Sible Hedingham with two fatal casualities, and then twelve days later another aircraft crashed at Southey Green, when returning from a mission, and another two crewmen were killed. Earlier in the month a B-17 from the 381st Group at Ridgewell had crashed near to the airfield, killing all ten crew members. Any losses were hard to bear but to crash within sight of the airfield and safety seemed even more so.

Along with the two other A-20 Groups, the 416th were scheduled to leave Essex in September, and on 21st of the month the Group flew away to their new base – Villaroche airfield at Melun, to the south of Paris. Over 140 missions had been flown from Wethersfield with the loss of 21 aircraft, which was the heaviest of the A-20 Groups. It had proved to be a hectic six months of operations, during which time the 416th had served the Ninth Bomb Command with distinction, and at no small cost to crews and aircraft. The Group were later engaged in various support attacks, especially during the Allied armies' offensive against the Siegfried Line, the Ardennes campaign and the crossing of the Rhine; by then they were operating with A-26s.

The airfield was again transferred back to the RAF and like several others in Essex it came under the control of No 38 Group. During October two Stirling IV squadrons – Nos 196 and 299 – arrived from RAF Keevil, the troop carrier base in Wiltshire. The first squadron had started out as a pure bomber squadron with No 3 Group but was transferred to troop-carrying in November 1943. Both squadrons had been active during D-Day, and had more recently become involved in the ill-fated 'Operation Market Garden' – the Allied airborne landings in Holland. During this operation they had flown a total of 220 sorties – glider towing and resupplying the airborne forces – and had lost 15 aircraft. The squadrons were still licking their wounds and regrouping after the costly Arnhem operation.

Whilst at Wethersfield the squadrons were, amongst other activities, engaged in training exercises with new glider pilots and practice drops of airborne troops, where the nearby airfield of Great Sampford was used. As has already been noted, the Stirling squadrons of No 38 Group were dropping supplies to resistance forces in enemy occupied territories. On 4th November some of the Stirling crews were out on an air sea rescue operation looking for a trace of Group Captain Surplice's aircraft, which had failed to return to Rivenhall after a SOE drop over

Norway. Over Christmas 1944 Wethersfield resembled the heavy bomber base it had been designed, when 15 Lancasters from RAF Middleton St George in Durham used it as an emergency landing field after returning from an operation over Dusseldorf, because fog had closed down many of Bomber Command's bases in northern England.

The fickle hand of fate struck the airfield again in January 1945 when some sections of the runways began to break up and the two Stirling squadrons were transferred out to Gosfield, for a short period, before moving to Shepherd's Grove in Suffolk, where they remained for the duration of the war. It would have seemed that Wethersfield's operational days were over, but this was not to be so, because for a few brief days in March the USAAF reappeared on the scene.

The newcomers were members of the 316th Troop Carrier Group, which had come down from Cottesmore, then in the county of Rutland. The 316th was part of the Ninth Troop Carrier Command, and was commanded by Lieutenant Colonel Harvey Berger, who unfortunately was killed in an air accident in Germany on 3rd April. The Group was the only combat unit which served in the Ninth Air Force whilst it was operating in the Middle East. It had a proud service history, dating from the airborne landings in Sicily, Italy, and Holland and on D-Day. Some 80 C-47s (Skytrains) landed at Wethersfield on 21st March, to use the airfield as a forward base for 'Operation Varsity'. The Group uplifted British troops of the 6th Airborne Division and dropped them just to the north of the Wesel. The aircraft left Wethersfield on 24th and in the operation three C-47s were shot down, and four more were so badly damaged by flak that they had to make emergency landings near Eindhoven. The remaining aircraft made their way back direct to Cottesmore, and Wethersfield had seen its last wartime mission.

By October 1945 the runways had been repaired and a RAF Operational Training Unit arrived with a mixture of Stirlings and Halifaxes. The RAF station finally closed down at the end of August 1946 and the airfield was placed under 'Care and Maintenance' until the summer of 1952. Then, once again, Wethersfield assumed the role of 'Little America', as the 20th Fighter Wing moved in with its F-84G Thunderjets, which became an essential part of the NATO air forces. Subsequently the main runway was extended and the airfield was considerably developed for its new role. In 1970, largely because of the increase of commercial traffic at Stansted, it was decided, for safety reasons, to move the Fighter Wing, now equipped with F-100 Super Sabres, to Upper Heyford in Oxfordshire. Nevertheless the USAF retained personnel at the airfield until 1990 when, as a result of the major reduction of the USAF's commitment in Europe, the American airmen finally left Wethersfield after a tenure of almost 40 years. This decision effectively closed the chapter of American aviation in Essex, which had dated back to 1942. The airfield site is now in the hands of the Ministry of Defence police, who have established their training unit there, and as such is decidedly inaccessible to the public!

24

WORMINGFORD

Up until the summer of 1943 Essex could rightly be considered as 'fighter country' with the fighter squadrons operating from Debden, Hornchurch, North Weald and Southend reigning supreme in the county's skies. Therefore it seems appropriate that Wormingford should complete this study of the county's wartime airfields because by the end of 1943 it had become an active American fighter base of some importance; indeed it became the only American airfield that saw the operational use of all three major American fighters.

The airfield, which is situated to the south-west of Wormingford and some six miles north of Colchester, was built during that intense period of airfield construction (1942-3) by Richard Costain Ltd, helped by a number of sub-contractors. Earmarked for an Eighth Heavy Bomb Group, it never fulfilled this plan, and at the end of November 1943, although not yet completely finished, it was 'loaned' to the Ninth Air Force to accommodate one of its Fighter Groups that was on its way over from the United States.

On the last day of November, the 362nd arrived at Wormingford, commanded by Colonel Morton D. Magoffin, a fighter pilot for over five years and one of the most experienced Group commanders in the Ninth. The Group was assigned to the 70th Fighter Wing, but the pilots took rather a long time working up their P-47s to a state of operational readiness and did not venture out on their first mission until 8th February, when they escorted B-24s of the Eighth's 2nd Division bombing V1 rocket sites; all of the 41 fighters returned safely.

Two days later the Group joined a large force of fighters (over 450) to escort B-17s attacking Brunswick. This target had become particularly notorious for the Eighth's bomber crews; they had found to their cost that the Luftwaffe fighter units defending this important city were most experienced and very determined – hence their nickname 'The Battling Bastards of Brunswick'. Despite the presence of so many American fighters 29 B-17s were destroyed (17%) although 56 enemy fighters were claimed, and the pilots returned to Wormingford with their first victory but at the cost of one pilot. It was the Group's first taste of air combat.

From now onwards the Group's pilots were almost exclusively engaged on escort duties. On some days the Group mounted two missions – supporting the outward flight and then meeting the bombers as they withdrew. In the Berlin operations during the first week of March the Group was active on each mission. One pilot was lost on both 4th and 8th of the month, although on the latter mission one aircraft crash-landed on return to the airfield and another at Manston; both pilots survived but the aircraft were 'write-offs'.

On 26th March five of the Ninth's Fighter Groups were sent out on their first dive-bombing mission against marshalling yards and V1 rocket sites. This was in preparation for the Group's proper role in the Ninth as ground support fighter/bombers. However, before the 362nd left Wormingford to operate fully under the Ninth Air Support Command, there were further escort duties with the Eighth. On 8th April the Group was assigned another harsh Brunswick operation when 30 B-24s were lost. The Group managed to claim two enemy fighters without a loss. A week later the Group was on the move to an Advanced Landing Ground at Headcorn in Kent. During its stay the 362nd had mounted over 30 missions, losing five aircraft in action whilst claiming an equal number of victories. Subsequently the Group was awarded two DUCs for its brave and costly low-level missions when operating from airfields in France and Germany. A small and neat memorial dedicated to the 362nd was placed alongside a road near to the old airfield in 1992.

As the P-47s moved out on 15th April, the P-38s of the 55th Fighter Group moved in the following day from Nuthampstead in Hertfordshire. The Lockheed P-38 (Lightning) was quite a 'rara avis', as there were only three Groups equipped with them in the Eighth Air Force and ultimately only four in total. Without doubt it was a brilliant aircraft in concept and advanced for its time. The idea of a large twin-boom and twin-engined fighter was very revolutionary for 1937, when it was first designed as a high-altitude pursuit fighter. The P-38 was Lockheed's first military aircraft and when it was trialled in 1939 the

An aerial view of the airfield – January 1944. (Smithsonian Institution)

Army Air Corps were so impressed that they placed an order. Unfortunately the subsequent development by Lockheed became rather protracted and the initial P-38s did not come into service until 1941. It had first been named 'Atlanta' but soon 'Lightning' was thought a more appropriate name for a pursuit fighter! Perhaps its major attraction for the USAAF was its operational range; the first P-38s to come to Britain, in July 1942, were actually flown across the Atlantic – a quite amazing performance for fighters and, I am sure, a rather frightening experience for their pilots!

The RAF were somewhat dismissive of the aircraft after it had been trialled and tested, '...not likely to be of any use for anything except convoy escort and against the occasional unescorted bomber...' Nevertheless the first P-38s went to North Africa to serve with the 12th Air Force, and they showed up well against both FW190s and Me109s. It was in these air combats that the Luftwaffe pilots dubbed the aircraft 'Der Gabelschwanz Teufel' or 'the fork-tailed Devil'!

The 55th Group, which had launched the first P-38 operation on 15th October 1943, soon discovered some of the disadvantages of the aircraft. The twin Allison engines, provided with turbo-superchargers, proved to be a little unreliable especially at high altitudes and the cockpit heating was unsatisfactory, with its pilots suffering in very cold conditions. The air frame was not very substantial and the aircraft had a relatively low diving speed. Nevertheless it was certainly swift – about 410 mph at 25,000 feet and with extra fuel tanks it had a range in excess of 600 miles.

With its armament of four .50 machine guns and two 20 mm cannons grouped together in the nose, it was a formidable fighter. The P-38s, also, had the honour of being the first American aircraft to fly over the German capital – this was despite severe weather conditions on the day of the operation (3rd March 1944).

During the winter of 1943/4 the Eighth Fighter Command conducted experiments with some P-38s to develop their fighter/bomber capabilities. This resulted in some of the aircraft being modified with the installation of a plexiglass nose section to provide a cabin for a bombardier and space for a Norden bomb-sight. These modified P-38s became known as 'Droop Snoots' and it was planned to use them as the sighting aircraft for formations of fighter/bombers. On 10th April 38 of the Group's P-38s went out on their first 'Droop Snoot' operation, dropping 17 tons of bombs on Coulommiers airfield. The Group's CO, Colonel Jack Jenkins, decided to lead his pilots on a ground strafing of the airfield as well. Unfortunately two aircraft were shot down, including that of the CO, who managed to survive the crash-landing to end up as a prisoner.

When the Group arrived at Wormingford its pilots were very experienced in combat flying but had not been too successful in scoring victories. During the rest of the month several more 'Droop Snoot' bombing operations were flown, mainly directed at airfields in France. Perhaps the most successful mission was mounted on 27th to Roye/Amy airfield when 53 P-38s dropped 51 tons of bombs, and all the aircraft returned. It was during this month that a most experienced fighter pilot joined the Group – Major John Landers. He had already completed a combat tour in the Pacific and had six Japanese aircraft to his credit, which were proudly displayed on his aircraft. Landers took over command of the 38th squadron and added four German 'swastikas' before being promoted, in October, to command the 357th Fighter Group at Leiston.

The days of the P-38s in the Eighth Fighter Command were numbered as the decision had been made to re-equip all Groups (except the 56th) with P-51s; although the Ninth Air Force ultimately retained a few P-38 Groups. On May 21st the Eighth launched its first 'Chattanooga' operation – ground strafing of railways, canals and river traffic in Germany. Over 600 fighters took part and some 220 engines were attacked with 91 considered as destroyed. The 55th, which would later particularly become renowned for its ground strafing ended the day with 23 engines wrecked and damage done to another 15, as well as to

P-38s of 338th squadron of 55th Fighter Group. (Smithsonian Institution)

several canal and river barges. However, it did prove quite a costly operation with six pilots lost, but the crews had clearly demonstrated just how effective the P-38 was when operating at low altitudes as a fighter/bomber.

On D-Day the P-38 Groups were given the task of acting as convoy escorts for the armada of ships moving to and from the Normandy beaches. A rota system was set up to ensure that at least two P-38 squadrons would be on patrol from dawn to dusk. For the next ten days the Group's pilots flew regular patrols over the Normandy beaches before returning to fighter/bomber missions. On 7th July the Eighth launched a major offensive against oil, ball-bearing and aircraft plants in Germany, and the Group was part of the escort for B-24s attacking Lutzhendorf oil refineries – a hard and vicious air battle with 28 B-24s shot down. The 55th claimed 19½ victories with Captain Orville Goodman and Major Landers well to the fore in this battle and all P-38s got back to Wormingford. It was to be their most successful day's operation so far. A week later the Group mounted their last P-38 mission, which was a dive-bombing operation on rail targets around Paris. Despite its unfortunate record for unreliability there was (at least) one 'veteran' P-38 which had completed 96 sorties or 454 combat hours. Lieutenant Robert Riemensnider had flown 64 sorties in this aircraft, which he had named *Bobby*.

In the meanwhile the pilots had been busy training on 'war-weary' P-

An aerial shot of P-38s at Wormingford. (Smithsonian Institution)

51s and on 19th July they went out on their first mission with their new aircraft. However, during the next six weeks the pilots were not particularly successful with their P-51s, and during August more aircraft were lost in action than the number of victories claimed. Then suddenly, in September, matters changed quite dramatically and in the ten days from 3rd to 13th the Group's pilots destroyed 106 enemy aircraft for the loss of nine pilots. Their best day was the 11th when Lieutenant Colonel John McGinn was leading the Group and 28 enemy aircraft were destroyed. For their excellent performance over this 'purple period' the Group was awarded its first DUC.

Towards the end of October the Group's most famous fighter pilot and commander was drafted into Wormingford. He was Lieutenant Colonel Elwyn G. Righetti, who would soon earn the nickname of 'Eager El'. Righetti had enlisted in November 1939 and had received rapid promotion but had spent most of his time in training. Before this posting he had been in charge of the Advanced Instructors Training Unit in Texas. Considering that he was 29 years old – well advanced for a fighter pilot – and had no combat experience, the impact he made on the Group was amazing. In a very short time he demonstrated that he was an excellent pilot and a born leader, soon becoming a great inspiration to the young pilots. His special forte was attacking the German railway system and he ended up as the Eighth's top ground strafing pilot with 27 victories to his credit and another seven and a half in the air.

The Group's pilots had much to celebrate over Christmas 1944 when in two days (24th/25th) they scored 20 victories for the loss of four pilots, one of whom was killed in a collision with another P-51 over enemy territory. During January 1945 the 55th developed into one of the most successful Groups in the 66th Fighter Wing. On two days in February, 19th and 20th, whilst being led by Righetti, the Group destroyed 170 locomotives and ended the month with over 350. For its ground strafing exploits the Group received its second DUC. On 25th February whilst over Gielbelstadt airfield the pilots sighted some Me262s in the process of taking-off and they proceeded to destroy six of them, with Captain Donald Cummings claiming another Me262 later on in the mission. Considering that the Eighth Air Force destroyed a total of 20 Me262s in the whole of the month – this was quite an remarkable day for the 55th.

For about seven months some of the P-51s from 338 squadron had acted as a 'scouting force'. The Eighth Air Force realised back in May 1944 that it required very current weather information, as it had been found that the forecasted conditions could change quite dramatically during the course of an operation. The idea of the scouting force was for aircraft to go out ahead of the bomber formations seeking out high cloud formations and then finding a clearer route. The information would be transmitted back to the bomber leaders on a special bomber-fighter frequency. The pilots of these scouting forces were experienced bomber pilots who had completed a tour and been retrained to fly fighters. They knew all about the problems that adverse weather could cause to bomber formations! In February the Wormingford scouting force was formally designated the 3rd Scouting Force.

By the middle of April the Luftwaffe had been virtually cleared from the German skies. On 17th Lieutenant Colonel Righetti was leading the Group on an escort mission to Dresden and when he had handed over his charges to another Fighter Group, he decided to seek some ground strafing targets at an airfield north of Dresden. In the low-level attack his P-51 *Katydid* was struck by ground fire but he was seen to make a safe crash-landing not far from the airfield. The Group's pilots returned to

Wormingford with at least the consolation of knowing that their CO had landed safely, although it was still quite a blow especially as four days later the Group completed its final mission. After the war it became clear that Righetti was not a prisoner of war, nor was any grave located so it was assumed that he had been killed by German civilians angered by the Allied Air Forces' bombardment of Dresden. This fear of retribution at the hands of German civilians was quite strong amongst the bomber crews and pilots, especially in the later stages of the war, and it was said that Righetti always flew with a loaded revolver.

Ill-luck still seemed to dog the Group because Righetti's replacement, Colonel Ben Rimmerman, a famous fighter ace with the 353rd at nearby Raydon, was tragically killed in a night-flying accident on 20th May. The 55th had the unenviable record of having the second highest loss of fighters in the Eighth Fighter Command – 181. This figure was only exceeded by the 4th Group at Debden, which, of course, had been operational for over twelve months longer.

The 55th was selected to serve with the occupation forces in Germany and in July they left Wormingford for Gielbelstadt airfield in Bavaria, which by a strange coincidence was the very airfield where they had destroyed the six Me262s back in February. It does seem a great pity that no memorial exists in England to this famous American Fighter Group, which made such a contribution to the European air war and at such high cost. The old airfield is now used for more peaceful and quiet activities – by the gliders of the Essex and Suffolk Gliding Club.

25

CIVILIANS AT WAR

The people of Essex had more reason than most to fear the coming war. Of the 116 air raids on England during the First World War, almost one third were directed at Essex. Twenty-one years later there were still many people who had first-hand experiences of these raids when 'death rained from the skies'. Vivid memories of those days came flooding back when the Government made dire predictions of how the coming war would be waged from the air. It was clear that Essex would be thrust, once again, into the front line and it was envisaged that thousands upon thousands of homes would be destroyed, families killed and the sky would be 'black with bombers and the air poisoned by gas...'

The presence of three major fighter airfields, as well as the radar stations at Great Bromley, Walton-on-the-Naze and Canewdon, ensured that the county would receive attention from the Luftwaffe's bombers. The important factories, Ford's, Marconi's, Hoffmann's and Paxman's at Dagenham, Chelmsford and Colchester, along with the oil installations at Canvey Island and Thames Haven, all became strategic targets as did the port of Harwich. But what could not have been foreseen were the terrifying V1 and V2 rocket attacks of 1944/5, which landed quite indiscriminately, causing heavy civilian casualties.

In 1938 the major towns in Essex recruited their first civilian volunteers under the Air Raid Precautions Act, which had been passed in the previous year. By March Colchester had 800 volunteers on its books and later, during the Munich crisis, a whole phalanx of volunteer workers – wardens, firemen, special constables, first aid helpers, ambulance drivers, demolition and rescue workers, messengers and staff for mobile canteens – were recruited. A plethora of advisory and instructional publications on Civil Defence became available, including a Government endorsed range of instructional ARP cigarette cards, issued by the Imperial Tobacco Company. In retrospect these cards seemed to have frightened the public about the nature of the coming war rather more than having an instructional value!

Early in the following year the situation in Europe had drastically deteriorated and the country was put on a war footing. Air raid sirens were erected in the larger towns, millions of sandbags were filled – over 100,000 in Chelmsford in one month – and they suddenly appeared around the important public buildings. The construction of public shelters was rushed ahead, trenches were dug and buildings were requisitioned for Civil Defence buildings. Emergency water tanks and brick air raid warden posts were built in suburban streets, although some local authorities were slower than others in responding to the 'war mania' – as one writer to *The Times* described all the preparations.

The Government was particularly concerned about the threat of poison gas attacks, and ultimately over 38 million gas masks were distributed to the civilian population with instructions that in the event of war, they should be carried at all times – although it was reckoned that less than one in five people obeyed this order! Posters regarding their use were prominently displayed and the tops of GPO post boxes were coated with yellow gas detector paint. With typical sang-froid many cartoons appeared ridiculing these ugly and monstrous contraptions, but no one who was compelled to wear a gas mask, if only during the regular practice drills, has ever forgotten the chilling experience, or indeed the very distinctive smell of the rubber and disinfectant!

The provision of air-raid shelters to all households caused endless debate in the Government despite the fact that it knew full well that the public shelters would only accommodate about 10% of the total population. Ultimately air raid shelters were offered to all households at a cost of £7, but free to those households where the annual income was less than £250 per year. These shelters were of a corrugated sheet design, intended to be sunk several feet into the ground and then covered with earth or sandbags. They became known as 'Anderson' shelters from Sir John Anderson, who in 1938 had taken charge of the nation's Civil Defence. The Andersons had an inherent design fault; water continually seeped into the shelters and in many parts of the county they quickly became flooded. The Auxiliary Fire Services spent most of their time pumping out waterlogged shelters! In October 1939 mothers and children from Collier Row marched on Romford Town Hall demanding better shelters, with placards proclaiming 'Is Pneumonia better than Bombs?' When the Government discovered that many people would not use these shelters and preferred to stay in their houses, it introduced, in the autumn of 1941, an indoor shelter – the Morrison – which was named after Herbert Morrison, who had taken over Civil Defence responsibilities. Nevertheless the Anderson shelter became a poignant symbol of the wartime days.

At the beginning of September the mass evacuation of children was commenced. Essex was first classified as a 'reception area', appointed to take families and children from London, but it was subsequently designated as a 'neutral area' – one which would not receive nor send evacuees; although parts of the county and the coastal areas did become 'evacuation areas'. On 4th of the month a welter of Government instructions were issued concerning the procedure to be followed during air raids, and gas attacks, and the special arrangements for schools. Although places of entertainment were first closed, within a week cinemas were allowed to reopen in certain areas, much to the delight of the public, and throughout the war they brought a welcome release from the rigours and stresses of wartime life. By the 18th petrol was rationed, the first ominous sign of things to come. The establishment of the National Register, which enabled the issue of a National Identity Card to every person, brought the imposition of national rationing that much closer. The identity card and ration book became the two most important documents of the war. The Government vainly tried to persuade the country that food rationing might actually be beneficial to the nation's health – 'when, and if, it is introduced it could prove to be a blessing in disguise as a restricted dietary intake would be what the wise men of Harley Street would dictate for patients afflicted with dyspepsia'!

The first month of the war ended with a sharp rise in Income Tax – 7s 6d in the pound – which was the highest figure yet reached. There were also increased taxes on alcohol and tobacco. However, the black-out restrictions, the daily wail of air raid sirens and the sight of barrage balloons in the skies were the most immediate signs of war. It was the black-out regulations that the majority of people found most irksome and inconvenient. Heavy, dark material had to be placed at all windows, car headlights were hooded, traffic lights were deflected downwards and, of course, street lighting became a thing of the past. In the early

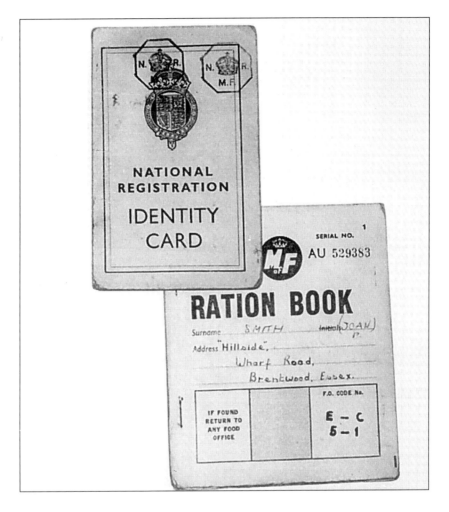

The two most important documents of the 'Home Front' during the war.

days of black-out there were twice as many road and other accidents and the ARP wardens became most unpopular with their over-zealous attempts to enforce the regulations, especially as the months passed with hardly a sign of enemy aircraft let alone any bombs. The black-out restrictions remained in force until September 1944 when partial, or 'half-lighting', was introduced, although in coastal areas the restrictions remained in force longer.

271

Victoria Avenue, Clacton-on-Sea: the scene of the first fatal civilian casualities of the war – April 30, 1940.

The winter of 1939/40 proved to be a most difficult time. The first rationing of foodstuffs had been introduced in November – bacon and butter – followed in the New Year by sugar, cheese, meat, eggs and tea (2 oz per person per week). The severe weather certainly did not make life any easier. In January East Anglia suffered its coldest winter since 1881; on several days many of the roads in the county were blocked with snow and on 20th of the month there were 20 degrees of frost! Coal supplies were desperately short, not necessarily because of the war, but mainly due to delivery problems caused by the weather. Most people who lived through that first winter readily agreed it was probably the worst period of the war – their first experiences of rationing, the winter black-outs and more especially, perhaps, all the uncertainty of what the future held for them and their families.

The so-called 'Phoney War' lasted until April 1940, although at the time it was universally known as 'The Bore War' or 'funny war'. It came to an abrupt end as far as the civilians were concerned on 30th April, and at a most unlikely place – the popular seaside resort of Clacton-on-Sea. About midnight a Heinkel 111, which was engaged on a mine-laying operation off the coast, was forced down below heavy fog and was badly damaged by anti-aircraft fire. The aircraft crashed onto a house at Victoria Avenue and its two sea-mines exploded creating a scene of utter devastation; over 50 houses were damaged and there were 162 civilian casualities, with two deaths. These were the first civilians to be killed in

England due to enemy action. The war had come to Essex with a vengeance. That summer the first 'London' civilian fatality occurred in Essex. A 76 year old Auxiliary fireman was killed at Loughton. This was considered a 'London' fatality because Loughton then came within the London Civil Defence Area.

With the fall of France and the Low Countries Britain was faced with a serious threat of invasion. The formation of an all-party coalition government headed by Winston Churchill only seemed to emphasise the perilous state of the country and most people were convinced that invasion was imminent. *Rules for Civilians in case of Invasion* were issued to all households, instructing people to stay indoors, hide maps, food, petrol and bicycles and 'to await further instructions'! Posters, especially addressed to 'the Country People of Britain', appeared which ordered everybody 'to keep the roads clear for our troops, no matter what happens...Remember, you will be far safer from bombing and machine gunning in your own home than you would be on the open roads. Remember, too, the Home Guard will be defending your village...'

The Treachery Act was passed on 23 May 1940, designed to deal with foreign agents or 'Fifth Columnists' – a term that first appeared in the Spanish Civil War. Aliens were rounded up and taken into custody, and slogans such as 'Careless talk costs lives', 'Be like Dad. Keep Mum' came into common parlance and were treated very seriously. Ed Murrow, the famous American broadcaster, recalled the time when he was arrested as a foreign spy in an Essex country public house because '...I asked too many questions about wartime life in the country at a time when everybody in the country was looking for spies...'! The gravity of the situation was vividly illustrated by the Prime Minister's famous speech at the end of May, which promised the country '...nothing but blood, toil, tears, and sweat... if you ask me what is our aim, I can answer in one word – it is victory.'

A coastal belt of the county, 20 miles wide, became a Defence Area, and virtually a 'no-go' area for civilians, with visitors needing permits. The fortifications included minefields, barbed wire barriers, anti-tank obstacles and pill boxes. Most of the coastal towns became almost deserted. At Clacton, out of a pre-war population of 25,000 perhaps only 3,000 to 4,000 remained and of these hardly any were children. Matters were worse in Southend where it was reported that '70% of the population have moved away and almost half of the houses are unoccupied.'

The Commander of the Home Forces, General Sir Edmund Ironside,

One of the many pill boxes to have survived in Essex – at Great Sampford.

had been given the task of establishing a defensive system in eastern England. In Essex these defences comprised three separate lines – the Colchester Stop-Line, the General Headquarters (GHQ) Line and the Outer London Defence Ring. They comprised literally hundreds of pill boxes, anti-tank traps, concrete and steel barriers and gun positions. Most of these strongpoints were sited alongside the natural barriers such as rivers, marshes and woods; although from the south of Chelmsford to Canvey Island a 12 foot deep and 20 foot wide ditch was dug to form a defence barrier. Many pill boxes have survived to the present, lonely and silent reminders of those days of 1940 that were so fraught with danger. There have been several serious proposals that they should become listed buildings.

On 14th May Anthony Eden, the Secretary of State for War, made a radio appeal for men between the ages of 17 and 65 years to enlist for a new force, to be known as the Local Defence Volunteers. The response was remarkable. Within 24 hours a quarter of a million men had come forward, and by the end of June there were one and a half million on the register. Prior to the LDV scheme a group of patriotic Essex men had formed a 'Legion of Frontiersmen', as well as another volunteer band

Recruits for LDV receiving rifle drill instruction – Buckhurst Hill, July 1940. (via T. Bracken)

known as 'County of Essex Volunteer Corps' – both organisations died a natural death with the advent of 'the Home Guard', as the LDVs became known, in July, at the insistence of Winston Churchill.

Almost every town and village in the county had its own platoon, and ultimately there were 20 battalions in Essex, all commanded by retired senior Army officers – the 'Colonel Blimps' – and 75% of the Home Guard were ex-servicemen. Their original and primary function was to deal with parachute invaders, but they also manned road blocks, made regular patrols of their territory and inspected the identity cards of persons moving around in the hours of darkness – hence their other name 'the Army of the Night'. In the early days they tended to be over-zealous in their activities and there were many examples of 'trigger happy' volunteers shooting first and asking questions afterwards, which resulted in some unfortunate accidents. At Romford a car did not stop on being challenged and the two Home Guardsmen fired at it, killing one of the passengers and injuring the other four. One senior

Army officer said in July 1940, with typical British humour, 'If the night is a little misty, the first big battle on English soil will probably be fought between the British Army and the LDV'!

Later, when the threat of invasion had receded, many of the Home Guard manned anti-aircraft batteries and took over a number of similar tasks, thus enabling regular Army units to be released for other military duties. The bumbling and comic images created by *Dad's Army* were a little unfair on what ultimately became a well-trained force. Although one recollection of the Home Guard in north-east Essex does smack a little of this popular BBC comedy: '... one or two old sweats who could be trusted to keep the enemy in the sights and to press the trigger steadily and effectively; there were younger ones of obvious merit and toughness; and there were the rest, the willing ones...'

Throughout the war bombs fell on almost every corner of Essex but usually in small numbers and often in open country, causing little damage and few injuries. Not suprisingly, the boroughs of Havering, Redbridge, Barking and Newham (now London boroughs) all suffered from heavy raids during the winter of 1940/1 with hundreds of people making a nightly 'trek' to the comparative safety of Epping Forest, where camps were set up for them. During the war Romford received 72 separate attacks, mostly at night, followed by Southend with 67 raids. Braintree, Brentwood, Chelmsford, Colchester and Harwich all suffered air raids but perhaps the most frightening and destructive weapons to be used (until the arrival of the rockets) were the so-called 'parachute' mines.

They were about 8 feet long and 2½ inches in diameter, and floated down suspended from a silk parachute. These mines created massive craters and produced extensive blast damage up to a radius of two miles; the Government called them 'indiscriminate form of aerial attack against the morale of the people.' On the night of 19th April 1941 ten mines fell on Romford, causing terrible devastation to properties and resulting in 54 fatalities, which was nearly one fifth of the total number of civilians killed during the war in Havering.

By the end of November 1940 there had been over 700 bombing incidents recorded in the county. During one of these, on 13th October, a solitary intruder dropped a few bombs on Chelmsford, one of which directly hit a house in New London Road and tragically killed the Mayor and his entire family. The county town had its most concentrated air raids during April and May 1943, when over 100 tons of bombs were dropped and considerable damage was sustained. In February 1941 the

THE ILLUSTRATED LONDON NEWS

SATURDAY, JUNE 29, 1940

"THE BATTLE OF BRITAIN" BEGINS WITH LITTLE BUT LOSS TO THE GERMANS: ONE OF THE SEVEN ENEMY BOMBERS BROUGHT DOWN IN THE FIRST MASS RAID CRASHES IN ESSEX.

(The Illustrated London News Picture Library)

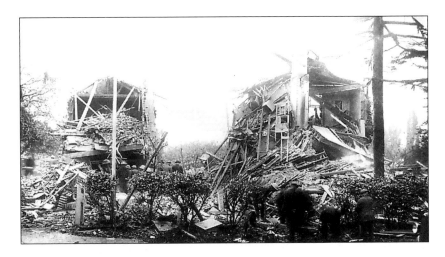

Brierley Place, New London Road, Chelmsford in October 1940, after a lone raider had dropped his bomb load on this residential area. The Mayor of Chelmsford and 5 members of his family were killed. (Essex Chronicle)

centre of Braintree was badly damaged by bombs with three people killed and another 23 injured. Colchester was attacked on numerous occasions, perhaps the most tragic being in August 1942 when 38 patients at Severalls hospital were killed. The town suffered a heavy raid in February 1944, 130 fires were reported and 14 properties completely destroyed, but amazingly only one life was lost. The Brittania works, which made engines for landing craft, was badly damaged but it was re-equipped and back in production within a few weeks, at the direct order of the Cabinet. The coastal towns of Clacton, Walton, Harwich and Southend became quite inured to air attacks and intruder raids.

Another potent threat from the air, besides enemy bombs, came in the form of crashing aircraft – both friendly and enemy; many of them landed on property and caused a number of casualties, some fatal. Such incidents probably reached a height during the Battle of Britain. At least 15 'accidents' of this kind were recorded in Havering up to the end of 1940, one of which was a Heinkel 111 that crashed in Hornchurch in October, killing three civilians when the burning petrol engulfed their Anderson shelter. These crashed aircraft created considerable public interest and were heaven sent for trophy hunters looking for souvenir items, at least if they were able to arrive on the scene before the Home Guard or the local police! Many of the sites have since been excavated by the Essex Historical Aircraft Society, and items they recovered are displayed at their musem at Canvey Island.

For those on the 'Home Front', 1941 could be considered as the nadir of the wartime years. The incessant night raids had taken their toll. Rationing had become more stringent and foodstuffs were in short supply due to the effective U-boat blockade of the Atlantic. Lord Woolton, the Minister of Food, offered a variety of recipes in *The Week's Food Facts* – most were only notable for their lack of meat! The first 'British Restaurants' opened in cities and large towns, run by the local authorities. The surroundings were rather spartan and the meals on offer were 'plain and wholesome'. Queues for even the basic necessities became part of everyday life, and from June clothing required 'coupons'. The war news was anything but cheering, the euphoria created by the Battle of Britain having long since dissipated. The general austerity of the times was reflected in the exhortation to save everything from rags and bones to old pots and pans and waste paper – 'Waste Not Want Not' was the guiding principle. But perhaps the major watchwords of the war were 'Dig for Victory', and all available land was turned over to food production. There seemed little hope or comfort, that is until the end of the year, when the United States entered the war. No longer was the country all alone in its fight for freedom.

One of the features of the early war years was the number of women taking on voluntary war-work. The Women's Voluntary Service (WVS) had been formed in 1938 to assist the ARP but its one million or so members became involved in a wide variety of duties – from operating reception and rest centres and mobile canteens, to dealing with evacuated children, distributing clothes to bombed-out families and manning telephones during air raids and emergencies. The conscription of women aged 19 to 24 (later extended to 31) was introduced in 1941. They were allowed to choose between service in the Women's Auxiliary Forces, the Civil Defence, the Land Army or certain factory work. Members of the Women's Auxiliary Air Force, which had been formed in June 1939, served at most of the RAF airfields in the county as well as operating many of the barrage balloons sites throughout Essex. Many women, of course, worked in the various wartime industries, especially the munitions factories.

Essex had one of the largest forces of Land Army girls in Britain by the end of 1943 there were 3,777 serving in the county – third only to Yorkshire and Kent. The Land Army girls in their distinctive 'uniform' – green jumper, khaki corduroy breeches and wide-brimmed hats –

V1 rocket or 'Doodlebug'. (Imperial War Museum)

became an integral part of the Essex countryside. All volunteers, the girls came from every walk of life and were first required to pass an interview and to provide evidence of good health by means of a medical certificate. Successful applicants were then either posted to a training centre or, more likely, to a farm. It was certainly a hard life – ploughing, harvesting, threshing, milking, fruit and potato picking, ditch-digging and so on. As their anthem suggested, 'Back to the land, we must all lend a hand, to the farms and the fields we must go...Though we can't fire a gun, We can still do our bit with the hoe...' There was often a concern for their moral welfare and it was suggested that 'it was unwise for land girls to be out after nine o'clock in the black-out'!

During the summer of 1942 the first Americans arrived in Essex and from then on parts of the county appeared to be 'another American state'. The village inns filled with US servicemen, the country roads were choked with their heavy lorries and jeeps, and the towns of Braintree, Chipping Ongar, Chelmsford, and Colchester echoed to the sounds of American accents. There was a certain amount of resentment at first, but soon the friendly and generous nature of the newcomers thawed most of the reserve of the locals. Unlike in Suffolk and Norfolk, the majority of Americans left Essex at the end of the summer of 1944, and their departure was regretted, not least by the female members of the community! In the short time that they had lived in the county, strong and firm bonds had been established which have lasted throughout the years.

The elation of the successful D-Day landings was all too brief, when ten days later the first V1 rocket to fall on Essex landed at Moor Hall, Rainham, followed by six more in the Romford area and one at Cold Norton. By the end of the day there were 14 fatalities, including six killed at Rush Green hospital in Romford. The rocket or 'Vergeltungswaffe' (reprisal weapon) soon became known as the 'doodlebug' or 'buzz-bomb' from the distinctive note of its engine. But what most people remembered was the period of silence, perhaps no more than ten seconds or so, before the sound of the explosion as the bomb hit. That brief interval was variously described as 'ominous', 'terrifying' and even 'deafening'. Until March 1945 a total of over 600 V1 rockets fell in Essex, including that part of the county that came within the London Defence Area – this was about 10% of the total number.

On 8th September the people of Epping heard a tremendous explosion and on investigation a 40 foot crater was discovered just outside the town – the first V2 rocket had landed in Essex. This was just the start of an assault that continued almost to the end of March. Many of the rockets dropped in open countryside and mostly in the south of the county, though Chelmsford, Ilford, Hornchurch, Romford, Rainham, Brentwood, Rayleigh, Southend and Canvey Island suffered particularly during the winter of 1944/5.

The A-4 (V2) rocket was 46 feet long, flew faster than the speed of sound and carried one ton of explosives. Unlike the V1 rockets these gave no warning of their approach and brought in their wake several human tragedies. On 27th September four people were killed at Ardleigh, then on 11th November one rocket that fell in Collier Row, Romford, resulted in 21 houses being damaged and 43 casualties, including 13 fatal. This was the same day that the Government first officially acknowledged that the rockets had been landing 'for the last few weeks'! The Hoffmann's ball-bearing works at Chelmsford was struck on 19th December and 40 people were killed, with another 152 injured. Rural Essex received its last rockets on 21st March, when Boreham, Bardfield Saling and Stansted suffered slight damage, but with no injuries. Five days later (26th) the last rockets fell in the district of Romford with five fatalities.

Now that enemy's last desperate bid had failed, the 'People's War', as it had become known, was rapidly coming to an end. The Home Guard had been disbanded in December 1944, many of the annoying restrictions had been lifted, and although rationing remained there was certainly a bright light at the end of the tunnel. By the end of April both Hitler and Mussolini were dead. The news of Germany's unconditional surrender came at lunchtime on 7th May, but even before the national holiday (VE Day) was announced, the victory celebrations had begun.

For the first time since September 1939, the country was treated to a weather forecast for the Big Day; they had been censored 'to prevent valuable information being provided to the enemy'. VE Day was predicted to start warm and sunny but rain was expected later. It was stressed that 'the recent warm snap will not continue'. In the event the forecast turned out to be wrong! There was a heavy thunderstorm in the night when ½ inch of rain fell, but the morning dawned clear and bright, and by the afternoon the temperature reached 75°, well above the average for early May. The people basked in the unseasonal warm weather and celebrated the hard-won victory, following Winston Churchill's advice that 'we may allow ourselves a brief period of rejoicing.' Every town and village in the county organised its own celebrations – grand parades, street parties and firework displays.

On 27th July a letter appeared in *The Times* in which the writer enquired, 'Is it now time that we received some directions as what to do with our gas masks?' – the 'People's War' had really come to an end! The cost in human terms was high, over 60,000 civilians had been killed due to enemy action. In several churches in Essex there are memorial plaques to those civilians who were killed during the long and harrowing conflict. The survivors have not forgotten their experiences – the wail of the sirens, the shelters, the falling bombs and rockets, the black-out, the rationing, the queues, the lack of sleep... and 'ITMA'. In 1995 there were spectacular nationwide celebrations to mark the fiftieth anniversary of the famous victory, so it is perhaps appropriate to recall the adage 'Those who cannot remember the past are condemned to repeat it'.

BIBLIOGRAPHY

During my research I consulted various books. I list them below with my grateful thanks to the authors.

Air Ministry, *The Battle of Britain*, HMSO 1941.
Armitage, Michael, *The Royal Air Force: An Illustrated History*, Cassell, 1993.
Bates, H. E., *Flying Bombs over England*, Froglets, 1994.
Bowyer, Chas, *Fighter Command: 1936-1968*, Dent, 1980.
Bowyer, Michael J.F., *Action Stations: 1. Military Airfields of East Anglia*, Patrick Stephens, 1990.
Braybrooks, K., *Wingspan: A History of RAF Debden*, RAF Debden, 1946.
Calder, Angus, *The People's War: Britain 1939–1945*, Pimlico, 1992.
Croall, Jonathan, *Don't You Know There's a War On?: the People's Voice*, Hutchinson, 1989.
Deighton, Len, *Fighter: The True Story of the Battle of Britain*, J. Cape, 1977.
Delve, Ken, *D-Day: The Air Battle*, Arms & Armour, 1994.
Dundas, Hugh, *Flying Start*, S. Paul, 1988.
Embry, Sir Basil, *Mission Completed*, Methuen, 1957.
Fox, George H., *8th Air Force Remembered*, ISO Publications, 1991.
Freeman, Roger A., *U.K. Airfields of the Ninth Air Force: Then and Now*, Battle of Britain Prints, 1994
Freeman, Roger A., *The Mighty Eighth*, Arms & Armour, 1989.
Freeman, Roger A., *The Mighty Eighth War Manual*, Jane's Publishing Co., 1984.
Halpenny, Bruce B., *Military Airfields of Greater London*, Patrick Stephens, 1980.

Hamlin, John F., *Support and Strike! A Concise History of the US Ninth Air, Force in Europe*, GMS Enterprises, 1991.

Hockley-Farrar, Anthony, *The Army in the Air: The History of the Army Air Corps*, Alan Sutton, 1994.

Hough, Richard & Richards, Denis, *The Battle of Britain: The Jubilee History*, Hodder & Stoughton, 1989.

Jackson, Robert, *Guinness Book of Air Warfare*, Guinness Publishing, 1993.

Johnson, 'Johnnie', *Wing Leader*, Chatto & Windus, 1956.

Jones, Bryan, *Wings and Wheels: The History of Boreham Airfield*, Ford Motorsport.

Kee, Robert, *1945: The World We Fought For*, Penguin, 1995.

Kinsey, Gordon, *Aviation: Flight over Eastern Counties*, T. Dalton, 1977.

Merrick, K.A., *Flights of the Forgotten: Special Duties Ops in WWII*, Arms & Armour, 1989.

Middlebrook, Martin, *The Schweinfurt – Regensburg Mission: American Raids on 17 August 1943*, Allen Lane, 1983.

Moench, John O., *Marauder Men: An account of the B-26 Marauder*, Malin Enterprises Inc, USA, 1989.

Moyes, Philip J.R., *Bomber Squadrons of the RAF*, Hutchinson, 1981.

Pope, Rodney, J., *Andrews Field*, Ian Henry Pubs, 1990.

Price, Alfred, *The Spitfire Story*, Arms & Armour, 1982.

Ramsey, W. G. (Ed), *The Battle of Britain: Then and Now*, Battle of Britain Prints, 1980.

Rawlings, John, *Fighter Squadrons of the RAF*, Crecy Books, 1993.

Richards, Denis, *The Royal Air Force, 1939-45*, HMSO, 1953.

Robinson, Anthony, *RAF Fighter Squadrons in the Battle of Britain*, Arms & Armour, 1987.

Rust, Kenn C., *The 9th Air Force in World War II*, Aero Publishers, USA, 1970.

Scutts, Terry, *Lions in the Sky*, Patrick Stephens, 1987.

Smith, David J., *Britain's Military Airfields, 1939-45*, PSL, 1989.

Stait, B.A., *Rivenhall: The Story of an Essex Airfield*, Alan Sutton, 1984.

Sutton, S/Ldr. H.T., *Raiders Approach: the Fighting Tradition of RAF Hornchurch*, Gale & Polden, 1956.

Webb, Edwin & Duncan John, *Blitz over Britain*, Spearmount Ltd, 1990.

Wynn, Kenneth G., *Men of the Battle of Britain*, Gliddon Books, 1989.

Zeigler, J. Gay, *Bridge Busters: The Story of the 394th Bomb Group*, Bradley Printers, USA, 1993.

ACKNOWLEDGEMENTS

I am deeply indebted to the following people for assisting me during the preparation of this book: Derek Aspinell, Gordon Curtis, Bryan Jones, Roy Rodwell of GEC-Marconi, Judith Slater of Stansted Airport Ltd, the staff at Chelmsford and Galleywood libraries. My thanks are also extended to Roger Lynn Associates for their permission to use photographs of their building at Little Walden, and to Random House UK Ltd for giving permission to reproduce an extract from *Flying Start* by Hugh Dundas, published by Stanley Paul.

For his patient and unstinting research into all my enquiries I would like to thank Norman G. Richards of the Archives Division of the National Air & Space Museum in Washington. I am grateful, too, to my wife, Joan, for her enthusiasm, tolerance, editing and photography, without which this book would have taken longer to produce, and, finally, to the various people I have met during my research around the County, who gave their time to share their local knowledge with me.

Graham Smith
Chelmsford, 1996

INDEX